Laravel 5.x Cookbook

A recipe-based book to help you efficiently create amazing
PHP-based applications with Laravel 5.x

Alfred Nutile

[PACKT] open source*
PUBLISHING   community experience distilled

BIRMINGHAM - MUMBAI

Laravel 5.x Cookbook

Copyright © 2016 Packt Publishing

First published: August 2016

Production reference: 1290816

Published by Packt Publishing Ltd.
Livery Place
35 Livery Street
Birmingham B3 2PB, UK.

ISBN 978-1-78646-208-4

www.packtpub.com

Credits

Author
Alfred Nutile

Reviewer
Andrew Cavanagh

Commissioning Editor
Amarabha Banerjee

Acquisition Editor
Reshma Raman

Content Development Editor
Parshva Sheth

Technical Editor
Gebin George
Prajakta Mhatre

Copy Editor
Safis Editing

Project Coordinator
Sheejal Shah

Proofreader
Safis Editing

Indexer
Tejal Daruwale Soni

Graphics
Abhinash Sahu

Production Coordinator
Aparna Bhagat

Cover Work
Aparna Bhagat

About the Author

Alfred Nutile is an Enterprise Architect and Laravel lead based in Western Massachusetts. He's been working in the industry since the mid 90's. He started in PHP and MySQL back around that time and has worked with Ruby on Rails, Drupal, and Angular along the way. He introduced Laravel into an enterprise web stack, where he is currently contracted at, as Laravel proved itself as an amazing framework to build API's and Angular heavy application.

You can read more about him and checkout his blog at `http://www.alfrednutile.info/` or follow him on Twitter at `https://twitter.com/alnutile`

Make sure to checkout the discount LaraCasts is offering those who buy the book!

Get a coupon for 50% on your first bill. Make it a yearly subscription and save $43!

Coupon Code: LaracastsLovesPackt

`https://laracasts.com/signup?plan=yearly&coupon=LaracastsLovesPackt.`

First let me say thanks to Taylor Otwell, I moved away from PHP to Rails and really was missing PHP only to be pointed to Laravel and have not looked back since. The framework makes my day to day work a pleasure and sometimes I feel guilty how easy it has made getting work done.

And Jeffrey Way for offering an amazing service that helped me to grow in understanding practical programming skills, keeping things simple, best practices and Laravel.

Of course I would like to thank Andrew Cavanagh for taking time to tediously edit this book. We have worked in the industry together for a number of years and currently both working on Laravel daily. And then there is my family who keeps me from getting too out of balanced since it is so easy to lose myself in the joy of building things on the computer!

About the Reviewer

Andrew Cavanagh is an experienced PHP developer whose background includes Drupal, Laravel, AngularJS, managing *nix servers (Apache and Nginx), project/budget/team management, and general haberdashy. He's currently focused on building enterprise web applications and tools. Andrew also enjoy cooking, amateur mycology, brewing, and long walks in imaginary places.

www.PacktPub.com

eBooks, discount offers, and more

Did you know that Packt offers eBook versions of every book published, with PDF and ePub files available? You can upgrade to the eBook version at www.PacktPub.com and as a print book customer, you are entitled to a discount on the eBook copy. Get in touch with us at customercare@packtpub.com for more details.

At www.PacktPub.com, you can also read a collection of free technical articles, sign up for a range of free newsletters and receive exclusive discounts and offers on Packt books and eBooks.

https://www2.packtpub.com/books/subscription/packtlib

Do you need instant solutions to your IT questions? PacktLib is Packt's online digital book library. Here, you can search, access, and read Packt's entire library of books.

Why Subscribe?

- ▸ Fully searchable across every book published by Packt
- ▸ Copy and paste, print, and bookmark content
- ▸ On demand and accessible via a web browser

Table of Contents

Preface

Laravel is a prominent member of a new generation of web frameworks. It is one of the most popular PHP frameworks and is also free and an open source. Laravel 5 is a substantial upgrade with a lot of new and more efficient workflows, at the same time retaining the features that made Laravel wildly successful. It comes with plenty of architectural as well as design-based changes.

The book is a blend of numerous recipes that will give you all the necessary tips you need to build an application. It starts with basic installation and configuration tasks and will get you up-and-running in no time. You will learn to create and customize your PHP app and tweak and re-design your existing apps for better performance. You will learn to implement practical recipes to utilize Laravel's modular structure, the latest method injection, route caching, and interfacing techniques to create responsive modern-day PHP apps that stand on their own against other apps. Efficient testing and deploying techniques will make you more confident with your Laravel skills as you move ahead with this book.

Towards the end of the book, you will understand a number of add-ons and new features essential to finalize your application to make it ready for subscriptions. You will be empowered to get your application out to the world.

What this book covers

Chapter 1, *Setting Up and Installing Laravel*, helps you setup Laravel on your local machine.

Chapter 2, *Using Composer Packages*, this will cover some key concepts to getting comfortable with this amazing tool.

Chapter 3, *Routing*, the heart of any web framework, this will dig into some use cases of Laravel routing.

Chapter 4, *Building Views and Adding Style*, digging into Blade, Bootstrap and other key areas to building an app.

Chapter 5, Working with Data, covers factories, seeding and a look at a scaffolding library to save you work.

Chapter 6, Adding Angular to Your App, all the key concepts to getting going with Angular in your application.

Chapter 7, Authentication, Security, and Subscriptions, covers protecting your application, building a subscription service, and an admin interface.

Chapter 8, Testing and Debugging Your Application, shows you how to think about your code using tests, having TravisCI run your tests on every push to Github, and more.

Chapter 9, Adding Advanced Features to Your App, teaches you about building Artisan commands, Scheduler, Clean URLs and more.

Chapter 10, Deploying Your App, this chapter will dig into CodeDeploy, Forge, TravisCI and other recipes to deploy your application.

What you need for this book

The entire list of this and the installation process has been explained in Chapter 1 of the Book.

Who this book is for

The ideal target audience for this book is PHP developers who have some basic PHP programming knowledge. No previous experience with Laravel is required for this book.

Sections

In this book, you will find several headings that appear frequently (Getting ready, How to do it, How it works, There's more, and See also).

To give clear instructions on how to complete a recipe, we use these sections as follows:

Getting ready

This section tells you what to expect in the recipe, and describes how to set up any software or any preliminary settings required for the recipe.

How to do it...

This section contains the steps required to follow the recipe.

How it works...

This section usually consists of a detailed explanation of what happened in the previous section.

There's more...

This section consists of additional information about the recipe in order to make the reader more knowledgeable about the recipe.

See also

This section provides helpful links to other useful information for the recipe.

Conventions

In this book, you will find a number of text styles that distinguish between different kinds of information. Here are some examples of these styles and an explanation of their meaning.

Code words in text, database table names, folder names, filenames, file extensions, pathnames, dummy URLs, user input, and Twitter handles are shown as follows: "You will need a terminal application, access to the `Git` command"

A block of code is set as follows:

```
public function __construct(ClientInterface $client)
{
/////
```

Any command-line input or output is written as follows:

```
>rm -rf composer.lock vendor
>composer install
```

New terms and **important words** are shown in bold. Words that you see on the screen, for example, in menus or dialog boxes, appear in the text like this: "First navigate to GitHub, **Settings**, and **Personal access tokens**."

Warnings or important notes appear in a box like this.

Tips and tricks appear like this.

Reader feedback

Feedback from our readers is always welcome. Let us know what you think about this book—what you liked or disliked. Reader feedback is important for us as it helps us develop titles that you will really get the most out of.

To send us general feedback, simply e-mail feedback@packtpub.com, and mention the book's title in the subject of your message.

If there is a topic that you have expertise in and you are interested in either writing or contributing to a book, see our author guide at www.packtpub.com/authors.

Customer support

Now that you are the proud owner of a Packt book, we have a number of things to help you to get the most from your purchase.

Downloading the example code

You can download the example code files for this book from your account at http://www.packtpub.com. If you purchased this book elsewhere, you can visit http://www.packtpub.com/support and register to have the files e-mailed directly to you.

You can download the code files by following these steps:

1. Log in or register to our website using your e-mail address and password.
2. Hover the mouse pointer on the **SUPPORT** tab at the top.
3. Click on **Code Downloads & Errata**.
4. Enter the name of the book in the **Search** box.
5. Select the book for which you're looking to download the code files.
6. Choose from the drop-down menu where you purchased this book from.
7. Click on **Code Download**.

You can also download the code files by clicking on the **Code Files** button on the book's webpage at the Packt Publishing website. This page can be accessed by entering the book's name in the **Search** box. Please note that you need to be logged in to your Packt account.

Once the file is downloaded, please make sure that you unzip or extract the folder using the latest version of:

- ▸ WinRAR / 7-Zip for Windows
- ▸ Zipeg / iZip / UnRarX for Mac
- ▸ 7-Zip / PeaZip for Linux

The code bundle for the book is also hosted on GitHub at `https://github.com/PacktPublishing/Laravel-5x-Cookbook/`. We also have other code bundles from our rich catalog of books and videos available at `https://github.com/PacktPublishing/`. Check them out!

Errata

Although we have taken every care to ensure the accuracy of our content, mistakes do happen. If you find a mistake in one of our books—maybe a mistake in the text or the code—we would be grateful if you could report this to us. By doing so, you can save other readers from frustration and help us improve subsequent versions of this book. If you find any errata, please report them by visiting `http://www.packtpub.com/submit-errata`, selecting your book, clicking on the **Errata Submission Form** link, and entering the details of your errata. Once your errata are verified, your submission will be accepted and the errata will be uploaded to our website or added to any list of existing errata under the Errata section of that title.

To view the previously submitted errata, go to `https://www.packtpub.com/books/content/support` and enter the name of the book in the search field. The required information will appear under the **Errata** section.

Piracy

Piracy of copyrighted material on the Internet is an ongoing problem across all media. At Packt, we take the protection of our copyright and licenses very seriously. If you come across any illegal copies of our works in any form on the Internet, please provide us with the location address or website name immediately so that we can pursue a remedy.

Please contact us at `copyright@packtpub.com` with a link to the suspected pirated material.

We appreciate your help in protecting our authors and our ability to bring you valuable content.

Questions

If you have a problem with any aspect of this book, you can contact us at `questions@packtpub.com`, and we will do our best to address the problem.

1
Setting Up and Installing Laravel

In this chapter, we will cover the following topics:

- ▸ Setting up Homestead
- ▸ Setting up composer and PHP on your local machine for faster Workflows
- ▸ Using `.env` for your local build
- ▸ Using sequel pro and connecting to local and remote databases
- ▸ Setting up your first application in Homestead
- ▸ Setting up Gulp and Elixir

Introduction

In this chapter, we will cover installing and setting up Laravel and Homestead. As I have often said in this book, the online Laravel docs are great, and I will refer to them as needed. This book should be regarded as a complement to the official documentation, expanding on the explanations found there and adding some tips and tricks for everyday use. Also, I will show a number of shortcuts to help speed up your workflow. Finally, I will touch on Gulp and Elixir.

Setting up Homestead

This section will work off the existing Laravel docs to make sure your Homestead is set up correctly, as well as give you some background as to what is going on.

Getting ready

You will need a terminal application, access to the `Git` command, and decent Internet. As for the terminal on Mac, I suggest iTerm, available at `https://www.iterm2.com/`; it really is a nice tool for something you are going to use quite often. For Windows, *git for Windows* `https://git-for-windows.github.io/` got me going quickly both for git and a Bash such as terminal. Linux has a nice terminal to begin with, and installing git is easy. As far as Vagrant and VirtualBox are concerned, I will link you to the related sites since they do a good job at explaining how to install each of them on your system.

How to do it...

The following are the steps to set up Homestead:

1. First, install VirtualBox as noted on their site at `https://www.virtualbox.org/wiki/Downloads`.

2. Once this is in place, install Vagrant from `https://www.vagrantup.com/`.

   At this point, Vagrant will be ready to use at the command line:

```
>vagrant
Usage: vagrant [options] <command> [<args>]

    -v, --version                 Print the version and exit.
    -h, --help                    Print this help.

Common commands:
    box              manages boxes: installation, removal, etc.
    connect          connect to a remotely shared Vagrant environment
    destroy          stops and deletes all traces of the vagrant machine
    global-status    outputs status Vagrant environments for this user
    halt             stops the vagrant machine
    help             shows the help for a subcommand
    init             initializes a new Vagrant environment by creating a Vagrantfile
    login            log in to HashiCorp's Atlas
    package          packages a running vagrant environment into a box
    plugin           manages plugins: install, uninstall, update, etc.
    port             displays information about guest port mappings
    powershell       connects to machine via powershell remoting
    provision        provisions the vagrant machine
    push             deploys code in this environment to a configured destination
    rdp              connects to machine via RDP
    reload           restarts vagrant machine, loads new Vagrantfile configuration
    resume           resume a suspended vagrant machine
    share            share your Vagrant environment with anyone in the world
```

   You will not really need to open VirtualBox.

For Windows users, this link helped me a lot to get started with Homestead: `http://blog.teamtreehouse.com/laravel-homestead-on-windows`.

3. Make a folder in your home directory called `Code` with a capital C.

   On a Mac, this will look like—`/Users/alfrednutile/Code`.

4. From here, the online docs do a great job of getting you going on the final Homestead installation and setup—`https://laravel.com/docs/5.2/homestead`.

How it works...

When done, you will have the `Homestead.yml` configuration information in the `~/.homestead` folder to modify as needed. On Mac, this would be `/Users/alfrednutile/.homestead/Homestead.yml`.

 Laravel Docs talk about shortcuts in the Daily Usage section at `https://laravel.com/docs/5.2/homestead#daily-usage`.

Also, you should have made a new folder called `~/Code` to be the base folder for all your projects. For example, my folder looks like this:

- `/Users/alfrednutile/Code/app1`
- `/Users/alfrednutile/Code/app2`

You can have multiple applications within your `code` folder. In this example, `app1` is the root folder for the `app1` application, and `app2` is the root folder for the `app2` code. Keep in mind that the Vagrant box will later on *mount* this `Code` folder into the `/home/vagrant/Code` folder inside the Vagrant client.

 I do my migration and PHPUnit work inside Homestead using the `ssh` shortcut that the online documents show you. But I do a lot of work outside Homestead inside the `Code/app1` directory, such as all the `Git` commands and much of composer. This creates a much faster workflow for the file intense commands.

There's more...

You can, of course, manually set up your own machine for Nginx, PHP, MySQL, and all the rest, but there are a lot of reasons why the preceding one is best. On a team or alone, having your environment contained like this makes upgrading your machine, going from desktop to laptop, pushing code to production, having up-to-date libraries for new apps and older libraries for legacy apps, and more so much easier.

See also

- ▸ **Laravel**: https://laravel.com/docs/5.1/homestead.
- ▸ **Vagrant**: https://www.vagrantup.com/
- ▸ **VirtualBox**: https://www.virtualbox.org/wiki/Downloads

Setting composer and PHP on your local machine for faster Workflows

In this section, we will cover some tips on using PHP and composer outside of the Homestead box to help with your workflow.

Getting ready

As with the preceding sections, you will need to have a terminal and decent internet. I will cover this using a Mac, but Windows and Linux have their systems to install the software. By default, you can install Xcode on a Mac and get pretty far with PHP, but it tends to be an older version of PHP. Here, we will use Homebrew to install PHP 5.6. We will also use Homebrew later on in this book as well.

How to do it...

1. Visit the `http://brew.sh/` site, and run the command they show there to install Homebrew on your Mac.

2. Follow the instructions at `https://github.com/Homebrew/homebrew-php` to get the PHP5.6 setup.

3. After you are done with step 2, add to your `~/.bash_profile` so that we can use this version of PHP:

   ```
   export PATH="$(brew --prefix php56)/bin:$PATH"
   ```

4. Then, update your current session:

   ```
   >source ~/.bash_profile
   ```

5. Then, we will make sure our PHP is set up properly:

```
>which php
```

You will see the `/usr/local/opt/php56/bin/php` output and type:

```
>php -v
```

This will show that you are running 5.6.19 or a higher version.

6. Set up `mycrypt` as follows:

```
>brew install php56-mcrypt
```

7. Then, we will install composer as seen at `https://getcomposer.org/download/`:

```
>php -r "readfile('https://getcomposer.org/installer');" >
composer-setup.php
>php -r "if (hash('SHA384', file_get_contents('composer-setup.
php')) ===

625196afcca95a5abf44391188c695c6c1456e16154c75a211d238cc3bc5cb47')
{ echo 'Installer verified'; } else { echo 'Installer corrupt';
unlink('composer-setup.php'); } echo PHP_EOL;"
>php composer-setup.php
>php -r "unlink('composer-setup.php');"
>sudo mv composer.phar /usr/local/composer
```

What is ~/? That is shorthand for your Home directory. When I use this, for example, `>source ~/.bash_profile`, your operating system will know it is in your home folder, for example, `/Users/alfrednutile/.bash_profile`.

How it works...

That was a lot of steps! Let's cover what we did and why. We began by installing Homebrew to make installing packages *easier*. We will periodically need to install packages such as `wget`, `Webdriver`, and more as we progress through this book. Using the `brew` command supplied by Homebrew makes installing these packages a snap.

Then, we used Brew to make sure we have a current version of PHP on our Mac. But considering we already have Homestead, why do this? There is some work you do outside of Homestead, for example, getting and installing Laravel using composer, running envoy, and more. And some of these you can run in Homestead, but you will see some speed difference outside of it. So, you still need it on your machine, but in this case, we are not so worried about it being the *wrong* version for one of our many applications.

The `mcrypt` part of the installation took care of the extension that we need to run common commands such as `php artisan key:generate` and other commands in Laravel.

We finalized the PHP setup with Bash shortcuts, so when we open the terminal, we are ready to use PHP and not the version that comes with Xcode on Mac.

We then use PHP to download and install composer, the biggest advancement in PHP since I started 15 years ago in my opinion, and you will see more of composer shortly.

Finally, we are ready to download Laravel!

There's more...

You could, of course, use Brew to install MySQL and more. But for now, we are going to leave all of this inside the Homestead box that we set up earlier.

See also

- ▶ **Composer Install**: `https://getcomposer.org/download/`
- ▶ **Composer Docs** : `https://getcomposer.org/doc/`
- ▶ **Brew**: `http://brew.sh/`

Setting up your first application in Homestead

In this section, we will download Laravel and set up our local site to use for the rest of our recipes taking advantage of Homestead.

Getting ready

We have Homestead installed. My home folder called `~/Code` is where we will be working.

How to do it...

1. Type the following in the terminal:
   ```
   >cd ~/Code
   ```

2. Then, download Laravel to a new folder:
   ```
   >composer create-project --prefer-dist laravel/laravel recipes
   ```

3. Move into the directory for your new application:

   ```
   >cd recipes
   ```

4. Now we need to tell Homestead about our new application:

   ```
   >cd ~/.homestead && subl Homestead.yml
   ```

5. Once the editor pops open, you can add your new site:

   ```
   15
   16   sites:
   17
   18       - map: recipes.dev
   19           to: /home/vagrant/Code/recipes/public
   20
   ```

6. Under database:

   ```
   93
   94
   95   databases:
   96       - recipes_local
   ```

7. Click on **Save** and close the editor.

8. Then, start up Homestead or just provision it:

   ```
   >homestead provision
   ```

   You may be asked for a password, which is your system admin password and not the Homestead password.

9. Then, we need to edit our system Host file (in this case, our local computer and not Vagrant and Homestead); this will again ask for our system password:

   ```
   >sudo subl /etc/hosts
   ```

    I will show a shortcut command in the *How it works...* section.

10. Next, edit the host file to set your `recipes.dev` domain right next to the default Homestead IP of `192.168.10.10`; then, save and close the editor:

    ```
    100   192.168.10.10   recipes.dev
    ```

11. Then, visit your site at `https://recipes.dev`! You may get an SSL warning but click on **Advanced** and **Proceed**:

How it works...

The composer command that we ran gets Laravel from its database of applications and libraries at `https://packagist.org/` then download it. We began by installing Homebrew to make installing packages *easier*. We will periodically need to install packages such as `Wget`, `Webdriver`, and more as we progress through this book. Using the `brew` command supplied by Homebrew makes installing these packages a snap.

I also used some shortcuts. One shortcut was `subl`, which was what you get when you install `http://www.sublimetext.com/`. But you can use whatever editor you want.

Using some of the preceding tips will make a shortcut called `hedit` adding to my `~/.bash_ profile`:

```
alias homesteadedit='cd ~/.homestead && subl Homestead.yml'
```

So, we are editing the main file that Laravel uses for all its Homestead settings. You will be here a lot, so shortcuts really pay off.

The same is applicable with the `hostedit` command that I used:

```
alias hostedit='sudo subl /etc/hosts'
```

Here, we are adding to our `.bash_profile` a quick way to edit the file and add the needed domain `recipes.dev` and save and exit. Now, when you visit `https://recipes.dev`, your operating system will know that it is really for Homestead.

See also

- ▶ **Laravel Docs for Homestead**: `https://laravel.com/docs/5.2/homestead`
- ▶ **Some tips there on Windows and the host file**: `http://sherriflemings.blogspot.ca/2015/03/laravel-homestead-on-windows-8.html`
- ▶ **Laracasts (overall a great place for getting started)**: `https://laracasts.com/lessons/say-hello-to-laravel-homestead-two`

Using .env for your local build

This was one of the best changes to Laravel from version 4 and 5 in my opinion. When I was doing Ruby on Rails work, it also had this feature, and this is the key to help create an application that falls in the *Twelve Factor App workflow*. You will learn how to use this file for setting keys to some recipes later on in the book. In this example, we will start using it to set up our database.

For the rest of this book, I will use PHPStorm for my editor, which helped me a ton to explore Laravel and PHP code when I first started. Make sure your editor has plugins to easily click and explore classes.

Getting ready

When you installed Laravel, it copied the `.env` file into place. So, just open your editor of choice and open the application directory.

How to do it...

1. Open .env in your editor.

2. Alter the file as follows, so the database name and the URL match what we would put in our Homestead setup file:

```
.env - recipes - [~/Code/recipes]
APP_ENV=local
APP_DEBUG=true
APP_KEY=Xidkr59zYNuPVKWqHLiWwppEgK3EfYrJ
APP_URL=https://recipes.dev

DB_HOST=127.0.0.1
DB_PORT=3306
DB_DATABASE=recipes_local
DB_USERNAME=homestead
DB_PASSWORD=secret

CACHE_DRIVER=file
SESSION_DRIVER=file
QUEUE_DRIVER=sync

REDIS_HOST=127.0.0.1
REDIS_PASSWORD=null
REDIS_PORT=6379

MAIL_DRIVER=smtp
MAIL_HOST=mailtrap.io
MAIL_PORT=2525
MAIL_USERNAME=null
MAIL_PASSWORD=null
MAIL_ENCRYPTION=null
```

How it works...

First of all, this is a *hidden* file. The . in front of it makes it hard to see in File Managers and even the command line. When at the command line, ls -a * is how to show this hidden file. Most code editors or IDEs will show you these.

Also note that Laravel comes with a `.gitignore` file that includes this file:

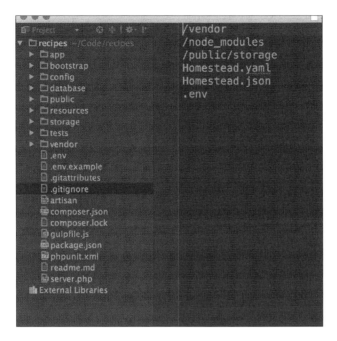

We will have to consider the addition or changes of any settings in `env`, as we push this application to Production for everyone to see when we are done. I will cover this more in *Chapter 10, Deploying Your App*.

So, what did we change in this file? Most of what you see was already there; we just set two things:

- `DB_DATABASE=recipes_local`
- `APP_URL=https://recipes.dev`

This is it, really! If you look back, this is what we set in the `Homestead.yml` file. You can see what we called the database and domain name. So now we need to tell our application what database table to use and which Homestead is made for us. Yeah, for Homestead!

See also

- **The 12 Factor App**: `http://12factor.net/`
- **PHPStorm**: `https://www.jetbrains.com/`
- **DotEnv (library that handles the .env file)**: `https://packagist.org/packages/vlucas/phpdotenv`

Using sequel pro and connecting to local and remote databases

Soon, we will be doing migrations, saving data to the database, and other day-to-day workflows, but sometimes, it is nice to look into the database. For example, you may want to export Production and the environment that has your *live* data down to local to review some bug. This section will show how to use Sequel Pro to do secure, over SSH, connections to your database. This allows you to get to your database with almost zero risk other than SSH.

How to do it...

The following are the steps to connect sequel pro to local and remote databases:

1. Download and install Sequel Pro from `http://www.sequelpro.com/`.

2. Add a new connection to Homestead:

3. Add *new connection* to a remote Host:

How it works...

In the past, I have used `phpMyAdmin`, and it was better than just the command line. But Sequel Pro really was a game changer. For one, I did not have to install `phpMyAdmin` on my servers and risk issues related to security. Second, it is a good interface and makes it really easy to check out data, tables, do queries, and so on when needed.

So, what you saw previously was simply a setup for Homestead using the *Standard* tab and Port 33060, which is what Homestead forwards its MySQL port to.

When we deploy our first server, it will have SSH port 22 open, but never will I have MySQL open only on `127.0.0.1`.

 For the most part, you only want three ports open on your server: 22 for SSH, 80 to redirect web requests to SSL/HTTPS, and 443 to serve your website.

So, to connect to this we select the **SSH** tab, and enter the information for the database on the server, since we will be on the server after the SSH step. Then, we enter the information for SSH; in this case, I had to go into my home folder to use my SSH public key. If you did not set up a key on your server, then most likely, you are using a password, so enter that instead.

 If you do not have the `a.ssh` folder in your Home directory (~/), then take a moment to create it. From the command line, run `ssh-keygen -t rsa` and just answer yes to all the questions. Do not add a password. You now have a public key.

It is really this simple. Now, you have this great UI to look into your database once in a while; though after using Laravel with *php artisan migrate* and eloquent, I am not in the database often.

See also

- ▶ **SequelPro**: `http://www.sequelpro.com/`.
- ▶ **Generating Public Keys Mac and Windows**: `https://help.github.com/articles/generating-an-ssh-key/`.

Setting up Gulp and Elixir

Elixir is new in Laravel 5.x and is a wrapper around Gulp, which is a well-known JavaScript build system. We will use it to manage assets later on in the book. For now, we just want to get it installed.

How to do it...

1. SSH into Homestead:

   ```
   >homestead ssh
   >cd ~/Code/recipes
   ```

2. Install Gulp using the following:

   ```
   >npm install
   ```

3. When it is done, try the following:

   ```
   > node_modules/gulp/bin/gulp.js -v
   ```

How it works...

Once again, Homestead is making our work easier; NPM is already installed! So, we can use this to not only install Gulp but also other JavaScript libraries that we need. How to do this? If you look into the Laravel application that we downloaded, you will now see the =package. json file:

This is the file that NPM uses, just as PHP uses composer.json, to know what to install. Here, it is getting Elixir, Gulp, and Sass for us. Elixir is new in Laravel 5.x and is a wrapper around Gulp, which is a well-known JavaScript build system.

Notice too that if you type *which gulp*, it is installed globally, thanks to Homestead again!

Elixir will come in later, but for now, note gulpfile.js that is right above the package. json file; this is where we will set up our asset workflow later on.

See also

- ► **NPM**: https://www.npmjs.com/
- ► **Gulp**: http://gulpjs.com/
- ► **Elixir**: https://laravel.com/docs/5.2/elixir

2
Using Composer Packages

In this chapter, we will cover the following topics:

- ► Working with the composer install command and avoiding the Composer update
- ► Downloading and installing Guzzle using Composer
- ► Making a provider
- ► Using the Facade pattern
- ► Using private packages

Introduction

We will cover some of the day-to-day workflows of setting up Laravel to use composer and many of the packages that exist out there for us to easily use in our PHP applications.

Working with Composer install command and avoiding Composer update

Composer is an amazing tool in PHP which allows us to pull in libraries from `https://packagist.org/` and even our own private repositories. We will cover how to install a library and note some steps to save time.

Getting ready

We covered installing Composer on your Mac in *Chapter 1, Setting Up and Installing Laravel*, though you can use it inside Homestead if you need to.

How to do it...

Perform the following steps to install Guzzle using Composer:

1. In this example, we will use Composer to install Guzzle (a powerful PHP HTTP client). Make sure you are in your App directory, and in this example, I will be on my local computer and not in Homestead just to make the file processing go faster:

   ```
   >composer require "guzzlehttp/guzzle":"^6.1"
   ```

   This will take a minute or less to run.

2. And that is it!

How it works...

First, let me say this is a good example of a short tip, which is better than a long one. Maybe other instructions will tell you to put this into your composer.json file and then run composer update, but stay away from composer update unless you really like waiting around, and you really need to update everything you have installed!

What else happened here is really good to understand, since this is a big part of Laravel and modern PHP. Composer added the library to your vendor folder:

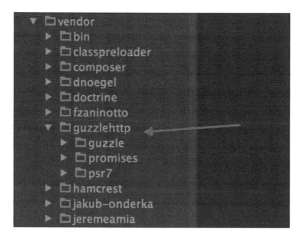

It made a folder for the libraries called `Vendor Name` and `Projects Name`. Then, it updated `composer.json` to load this new library!

```
▼  recipes ~/Code/recipes            "keywords": ["framework", "laravel"],
  ▶  app                             "license": "MIT",
  ▶  bootstrap                       "type": "project",
  ▶  config                          "require": {
  ▶  database                            "php": ">=5.5.9",
  ▶  public                              "laravel/framework": "5.2.*",
  ▶  resources                           "guzzlehttp/guzzle": "^6.1"
  ▶  storage                         },
  ▶  tests                           "require-dev": {
  ▶  vendor                              "fzaninotto/faker": "~1.4",
      .env                              "mockery/mockery": "0.9.*",
      .env.example                      "phpunit/phpunit": "~4.0",
      .gitattributes                    "symfony/css-selector": "2.8.*|3.0.*",
      .gitignore                        "symfony/dom-crawler": "2.8.*|3.0.*"
      artisan                         },
      composer.json                   "autoload": {
      composer.lock
      gulpfile.js
      package.json
```

This means we did not even have to edit the file.

Also note that there is a `composer.lock` file now in the root of your application, which you never edited. It shows what Composer pulled in to satisfy the dependencies of all the libraries that you have installed, as well as the file called `vendor/autoload.php` to build up all the PHP namespaces.

We will use Composer a number of times in this book. It really has changed the way we build apps in PHP for the better.

There's more...

If we look inside the `Composer.json` file, we will also notice some default namespaces and hooks that we can add to as needed:

```json
{
    "name": "laravel/laravel",
    "description": "The Laravel Framework.",
    "keywords": ["framework", "laravel"],
    "license": "MIT",
    "type": "project",
    "require": {
        "php": ">=5.5.9",
        "laravel/framework": "5.2.*",
        "guzzlehttp/guzzle": "^6.1"
    },
    "require-dev": {
        "fzaninotto/faker": "~1.4",
        "mockery/mockery": "0.9.*",
        "phpunit/phpunit": "~4.0",
        "symfony/css-selector": "2.8.*|3.0.*",
        "symfony/dom-crawler": "2.8.*|3.0.*"
    },
    "autoload": {
        "classmap": [
            "database"
        ],
        "psr-4": {
            "App\\": "app/"
        }
    },
    "autoload-dev": {
        "classmap": [
            "tests/TestCase.php"
        ]
    },
    "scripts": {
        "post-root-package-install": [
            "php -r \"copy('.env.example', '.env');\""
        ],
        "post-create-project-cmd": [
            "php artisan key:generate"
        ],
        "post-install-cmd": [
            "php artisan clear-compiled",
            "php artisan optimize"
        ],
        "post-update-cmd": [
            "php artisan clear-compiled",
            "php artisan optimize"
        ]
    },
    "config": {
        "preferred-install": "dist"
    }
}
```

App and Testing Namespacing

Install and Update Hooks

See also

- **Composer Docs**: `https://getcomposer.org/doc/`
- **Guzzle (a great way to do API requests and other HTTP requests in PHP)**: `https://packagist.org/packages/guzzlehttp/guzzle`

Making a provider

In the previous section, we used composer to pull in Guzzle, so we're ready to use it in our project. However, we'd rather not have to instantiate the Guzzle client manually every time we invoke it—hardcoding URLs and authentication and settings with each use. A service provider can help to centralize some of this configuration, and later, we will use service providers to help swap in a mock implementation for testing purposes.

Providers can also help us to avoid writing code that directly calls to a service, which is often a very helpful practice. For example, we may make `BillingProvider` that can use either Swipe or `BrightTree` as a billing service. `BillingProvider` allows us to easily switch between different implementations of the billing service.

Getting ready

Follow the steps in the *Working with Composer install command and avoiding composer update* section to pull in Guzzle, and start up your terminal.

How to do it...

The following steps will help you in making a provider:

1. In your terminal (local computer or Homestead), type the following:

```
cd ~/Code/recipes

php artisan make:provider GuzzleClientProvider
```

2. Now in your IDE, you will have a file called `app/Providers/GuzzleClientProvider.php` like this:

```php
<?php

namespace App\Providers;

use Illuminate\Support\ServiceProvider;

class GuzzleClientProvider extends ServiceProvider
{
    /**
     * Bootstrap the application services.
     *
     * @return void
     */
    public function boot()
    {
        //
    }

    /**
     * Register the application services.
     *
     * @return void
     */
    public function register()
    {
        //
    }
}
```

3. Now we will register the client as shown in the following screenshot. Note the two items in the `use` area that import the concrete Guzzle client above the `class` line:

```php
<?php

namespace App\Providers;

use GuzzleHttp\Client;
use Illuminate\Support\ServiceProvider;

class GuzzleClientProvider extends ServiceProvider
{
    public function register()
    {
        $this->app->bind(\App\Interfaces\ClientInterface::class, function($app) {

            $config = [
                'base_uri'          => env('API_CLIENT_URL'),
                'timeout'           => 0,
                'allow_redirects'   => false,
                'verify'            => false,
                'headers'           => [
                    'Content-Type'  => 'application/json'
                ]
            ];

            $client = new Client($config);

            return $client;
        });
    }
}
```

4. Then I make a file called `app/Interfaces/ClientInterface.php`:

```php
<?php

namespace App\Interfaces;


interface ClientInterface
{

}
```

5. Then in `config/app.php`, I register the service:

6. Now, to show it being used, let's plug it into a test:

```
php artisan make:test GuzzleClientTest
```

7. Now you will have a file called `tests/GuzzleClientTest.php`.

8. Then we will use it to hit a testing URL, but first we will edit the `.env` file and add `API_CLIENT_URL=https://en.wikipedia.org/`.

9. Then we will update the test file that we made in step 7, so it looks like this:

```php
<?php

use Illuminate\Foundation\Testing\WithoutMiddleware;
use Illuminate\Foundation\Testing\DatabaseMigrations;
use Illuminate\Foundation\Testing\DatabaseTransactions;
use Illuminate\Support\Facades\App;

class GuzzleClientTest extends TestCase
{
    /**
     * @test
     */
    public function should_query_google()
    {
        $service = App::make(\App\Interfaces\ClientInterface::class);

        $response = $service->request('GET', 'wiki/Main_Page');

        $this->assertEquals(200, $response->getStatusCode());
    }
}
```

10. Then run the following inside Homestead in `/home/vagrant/Code/recipes`:

    `phpunit --filter=should_query_google`

11. You will now see the following:

```
vagrant@homestead:~/Code/recipes$ phpunit --filter=should_query_google
PHPUnit 4.8.24 by Sebastian Bergmann and contributors.

.

Time: 3.6 seconds, Memory: 10.00Mb

OK (1 test, 1 assertion)
vagrant@homestead:~/Code/recipes$
```

How it works...

So, a lot matter just happened previously. Some of this can seem to complicate what you might be used to doing. But as applications grow and you start testing your code, this type of pattern can really pay off.

For example, if we have to change the way we instantiate the client in the application, we can now do this in one place; or if we want to see if we are in `App::environment() ==` `'testing'` and then swap out the provider, we can do this as well.

Let's start with the preceding third item. Here, we register an interface with the Laravel dependency injection system. In our example, the interface is just an empty interface file. We can define methods later on in there, but for now, I am using it as a way to reference the concrete class called `client`. Step 3 sets up some basic configuration settings for Guzzle and then returns it. So, when we inject this interface in the constructors:

```
public function __construct(ClientInterface $client)
{
/////
```

Or when we instantiate it using `App`:

```
App::make(\App\Interfaces\ClientInterface::class);
```

We then get the class that is ready to go as we set it up in the provider.

Also note that I set `env('API_CLIENT_URL')` outside the code. I can then set this in the `.env` file. This makes for an easier deployment workflow, so when I am working locally or on staging, I can hit a staging URL. And when I am working on production, I can hit the production URL. I can swap this out in my `phpunit.xml` file for testing as follows:

```xml
                <directory suffix=".php">app/</directory>
        </whitelist>
    </filter>
    <php>
        <env name="APP_ENV" value="testing"/>
        <env name="CACHE_DRIVER" value="array"/>
        <env name="SESSION_DRIVER" value="array"/>
        <env name="QUEUE_DRIVER" value="sync"/>
        <env name="API_CLIENT_URL" value="https://localhost/any"/>
    </php>
</phpunit>
```

See also

- ▸ **Testing Decoded Great chapters on Providers and Testing**:
  `https://leanpub.com/laravel-testing-decoded`

- ▸ **Laravel—From Apprentice To Artisan**:
  `https://leanpub.com/laravel`

Using the Facade pattern

Using the preceding work, let's take it one step further in how easy it is to use this Client in our code.

Getting ready

Install Guzzle and set up the provider just as we did previously, and you are ready for this next recipe.

How to do it...

1. Make a folder called `Facades` in your `app` folder.

2. Then add a file called `APIClient.php` and make it look like this:

3. Then scroll way down to the `Façade` section of this file, where we can register the Facade in our `config/app.php` file like this:

```
        'Storage' => Illuminate\Support\Facades\Storage::class,
        'URL' => Illuminate\Support\Facades\URL::class,
        'Validator' => Illuminate\Support\Facades\Validator::class,
        'View' => Illuminate\Support\Facades\View::class,
        'APIClient' => App\Facades\APIClient::class,

    ],
```

4. Now, let's see it working in a test by adding the method called `seeing_our_facade_work` to our test:

```
use Illuminate\Foundation\Testing\DatabaseTransactions;
use Illuminate\Support\Facades\App;

class GuzzleClientTest extends TestCase
{
    /**
     * @test
     */
    public function should_query_wikipedia()
    {
        $service = App::make(\App\Interfaces\ClientInterface::class);

        $response = $service->request('GET', 'wiki/Main_Page');

        $this->assertEquals(200, $response->getStatusCode());
    }

    /**
     * @test
     */
    public function seeing_our_facade_work()
    {
        $response = \App\Facades\APIClient::request('GET', 'wiki/Main_Page');

        $this->assertEquals(200, $response->getStatusCode());
    }
}
```

5. Now run the test:

```
>vendor/bin/phpunit --filter=seeing_our_facade_work
PHPUnit 4.8.24 by Sebastian Bergmann and contributors.

.

Time: 608 ms, Memory: 12.25Mb

OK (1 test, 1 assertion)
>
```

How it works...

So, the amount of work is all it takes to make your Provider just as easy to use as View, File, Storage, and all the other Facades that come from Laravel that make it easy and enjoyable to use.

Also, we can change the test to show it being just as easily swapped out. We will cover this in the testing chapter.

See also

▶ **Laracasts and another great video from them**:
  https://laracasts.com/lessons/decoding-facades

Using private packages

Sometimes, you need to use a private repository on GitHub or another location. I will cover here how to set this up in your composer.

Getting ready

We need a private repo, so if you have it and its `composer.json` is set up properly, you will be set from there.

How to do it...

1. First, go to GitHub and navigate to **Settings | Personal access tokens**:

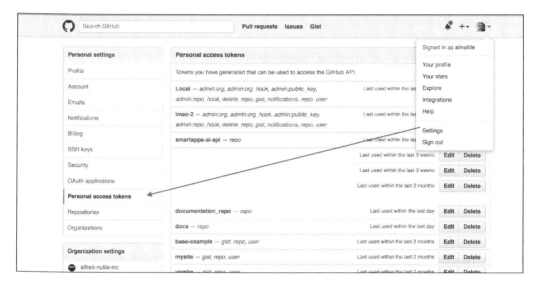

2. At the command line, type this:

```
>composer config -g github-oauth.github.com THE_TOKEN_FROM_ABOVE.
```

3. Then, edit `composer.json` so that there are two new sections:

```
    "require": {
        "php": ">=5.5.9",
        "laravel/framework": "5.2.*",
        "guzzlehttp/guzzle": "^6.1",
        "alfred-nutile-inc/example_private": "dev-master"
    },
    "require-dev": {
        "fzaninotto/faker": "~1.4",
        "mockery/mockery": "0.9.*",
        "phpunit/phpunit": "~4.0",
        "symfony/css-selector": "2.8.*|3.0.*",
        "symfony/dom-crawler": "2.8.*|3.0.*"
    },
    "repositories": [
        {
            "type": "vcs",
            "url": "https://github.com/alfred-nutile-inc/example_private"
        }
    ],
    "autoload": {
        "classmap": [
```

4. Then, let's tell the composer to install this:

```
>rm -rf composer.lock vendor
>composer install
```

How it works...

Alright, let's talk about these steps. The first one is to make sure we are setting up our Homestead or Mac for easy access to the private repository. This is really key as well if you are doing 2FA on your GitHub account (which you should be doing). Step 2 wraps this up by adding it to your ~/.composer configuration.

In the next part, we edit the composer.json file; and here, we see just how powerful Composer really is. It uses conventions and Packagist to easily organize and pull in projects; it also allows you to override this information in the repositories section of the file. Since the repository will not be in Packagist as it is private, the Composer will need to know where to look and this is made possible by this section.

Finally, I do install since I feel it is faster. You can update it or you can do whatever is required as well.

That's it, you will now see this private repository in your vendor/ folder.

See also

▶ **Composer docs**: https://getcomposer.org/doc/05-repositories.md#vcs.

3
Routing

In this chapter, we will cover the following topics:

- ▶ Building an API / JSON based route for searching
- ▶ Testing your route in PHPUnit
- ▶ Building a view based route
- ▶ Testing your view based route in PHPUnit
- ▶ Creating named routes

Introduction

In this chapter, we will cover routing. One thing, in my opinion, that makes a great framework is easy-to-use routing. When I first started in Laravel, coming from Drupal and then Rails, I was really glad to see how easy it is to try ideas in a route and quickly see results.

We will cover testing your routes, API based routes, and naming. By the time you are done I think you will see just how easy routing is in Laravel.

Building an API / JSON based route for searching

In *Chapter 6, Adding Angular to Your App* we will cover Angular and in there I needed to make an API for the widget to talk to. Let's review that again here in more detail.

Getting ready

A fresh install of Laravel will do.

How to do it...

Follow the steps to build an API / JSON route for searching:

1. Add our controller:

    ```
    > php artisan make:controller SearchComics
    ```

2. Add our route:

    ```
    Route::get('/api/v1/search', 'SearchComics@searchComicsByName');
    ```

3. Fill in the controller:

    ```php
    class SearchComics extends Controller
    {
        /**
         * @var MarvelApi
         */
        private $clientInterface;

        public function __construct(ComicClientInterface $clientInterface)
        {
            $this->clientInterface = $clientInterface;
        }

        public function searchComicsByName(Request $request)
        {
            try {
                $name = $request->input('name');

                $offset = $request->input('offset');

                $results = $this->clientInterface->comics($name, $offset);

                return Response::json(['data' => $results['data'], 'message' => "Success Getting Comics"], 200);
            } catch (\Exception $e) {
                return Response::json(
                    ['data' => [], 'message' => sprintf("Error Getting Comics %s", $e->getMessage())], 400);
            }
        }
    }
    ```

4. And in the `ComicClientInterface` class, I handle the `comics` method like this. I will go into more details in the *How it works...* section:

```
34
35    public function comics($title = false, $offset = 0)
36    {
37        $query = ['query' => $this->makeAuth()];
38
39        $query['query'] = array_merge($query['query'], ['offset' => $offset]);
40
41        if ($title) {
42            $query['query'] = array_merge($query['query'], ['titleStartsWith' => $title]);
43        }
44
45        $results = $this->client->request('GET', $this->getApiVersion() . '/comics', $query);
46
47        return json_decode($results->getBody(), true);
48    }
```

5. Show it working at the UI level `http://recipes.dev/api/v1/search`:

```
←  →  C   recipes.dev/api/v1/search

{
    "data": {
        "offset": 0,
        "limit": 20,
        "total": 36908,
        "count": 20,
        "results": [
            {
                "id": 42882,
                "digitalId": 26110,
                "title": "Lorna the Jungle Girl (1954) #6",
                "issueNumber": 6,
                "variantDescription": "",
                "description": null,
                "modified": "2015-10-15T11:13:52-0400",
                "isbn": "",
                "upc": "",
                "diamondCode": "",
                "ean": "",
                "issn": "",
                "format": "Comic",
                "pageCount": 32,
                "textObjects": [],
                "resourceURI": "http://gateway.marvel.com/v1/public/comics/42882",
                "urls": [
                    {
                        "type": "detail",
                        "url": "http://marvel.com/comics/issue/42882/lorna_the_jungl
                    },
                    {
                        "type": "reader",
                        "url": "http://marvel.com/digitalcomics/view.htm?iid=26110&u
                    }
                ],
                "series": {
                    "resourceURI": "http://gateway.marvel.com/v1/public/series/1635
                    "name": "Lorna the Jungle Girl (1954 - 1957)"
```

Figure 1 Example of JSON Response from Search

How it works...

First, I will go over what I did above but then I will show another example to simplify it more.

As usual, I made the controller and plugged in the route. Note I use `api/v1/` as a route prefix. This just helps me later on do a breaking API change at `/api/v2`. There are other ways to do this but for now I like this one.

In the long run, I would normally use `group` to help organize these better:

```php
Route::group(['prefix' => '/api/v1'], function () {
    Route::get('/search', 'SearchComics@searchComicsByName');
});
```

Now for the controller. I complicate things above but here is an even more simple look:

```php
class SearchComics extends Controller
{
    /**
     * @var MarvelApi
     */
    private $clientInterface;

    public function __construct(ComicClientInterface $clientInter
    {
        $this->clientInterface = $clientInterface;
    }

    public function searchComicsByName(Request $request)
    {
        return \App\User::all();
    }
}
```

Figure 2 Example of how easy it is to return JSON

Both examples show how easy it is to return data in JSON. By doing the above simple example, I rely on the fact that the `\Illuminate\Database\Eloquent\Model` implements `\Illuminate\Contracts\Support\Arrayable` and `\Illuminate\Contracts\Support\Jsonable` which automates a lot of this process. In my earlier example, I wanted a bit more control of the response so I took a moment to wrap the results in an error *['data' => array(), 'message' => 'Foo']* so that all my results are the same for all my endpoints. Then I might change the response code a bit to be what I want it to be.

Lastly, my Chrome screenshot is using an extension called JSON Formatter:

Chrome might have this built-in by now. It just makes for a lot nicer output.

See also

▶ **JSON API Spec—Worth reading to get a sense of goals**: `http://jsonapi.org/`.

▶ **Laracasts—Series on API**: `https://laracasts.com/series/incremental-api-development`.

Testing your route in PHPUnit

As seen in the preceding recipe, I used the browser to show that the API is working. Here, I want to show how you can speed up your workflow by using PHPUnit to do this and then, more importantly, you end up with long term testing.

Getting ready

The previous recipes will help show how to lay the foundation. In this one, I will continue from there.

How to do it...

Follow these steps to test your route:

1. Make a test:

```
> php artisan make:test SearchComicsApiTest
```

2. Then, edit the file `tests/SearchComicsApiTest.php`:

```php
class SearchComicsApiTest extends TestCase
{
    /**
     * @test
     */
    public function api_results_from_search_verify_format()
    {
        $this->assertTrue(true);
    }
}
```

3. And run `phpunit`:

```
> phpunit --filter=api_results_from_search_verify_format
```

4. Now let's make it do something by hitting that API:

```php
class SearchComicsApiTest extends TestCase
{
    /**
     * @test
     */
    public function api_results_from_search_verify_format()
    {

        $this->call('GET', '/api/v1/search?name=Wolverine');

        $this->assertResponseOk();

    }
}
```

5. And let's verify some data, first, I will dump the data to my terminal to get a sense of what I can look for:

```php
    /**
     * @test
     */
    public function api_results_from_search_verify_format()
    {

        $results = $this->call('GET', '/api/v1/search?name=Wolverine');

        $this->assertResponseOk();

        var_dump($results->getData(true));
    }
}
```

We will get the following output:

```
PHPUnit 4.8.25 by Sebastian Bergmann and contributors.

./home/vagrant/Code/recipes/tests/SearchComicsApiTest.php:19:
array(2) {
  'data' =>
  array(5) {
    'offset' =>
    int(0)
    'limit' =>
    int(20)
    'total' =>
    int(984)
    'count' =>
    int(20)
    'results' =>
    array(20) {
      [0] =>
      array(29) {
        ...
      }
      [1] =>
      array(29) {
        ...
      }
      [2] =>
      array(29) {
        ...
      }
```

6. Then, I decide to assert a few things:

```php
class SearchComicsApiTest extends TestCase
{
    /**
     * @test
     */
    public function api_results_from_search_verify_format()
    {
        $results = $this->call('GET', '/api/v1/search?name=Wolverine');

        $this->assertResponseOk();

        $results = $results->getData(true);

        $this->assertArrayHasKey('data', $results);

        $this->assertArrayHasKey('limit', $results['data']);

        $this->assertNotNull($results['data']['results']);
    }
}
```

7. That's it, I now know my route is working, without going in the browser, and can now start working with the AngularJS code to display this.

How it works...

Pretty nice how fast PHPUnit makes this. Instead of going from code to browser and reload, I can just iterate more quickly with this workflow.

I start off by using the awesome Artisan command to make a test. Though I am biased since it was my idea ☺. From there, I alter it a bit since I like the syntax where I put `@test` in the annotations instead of in the name of my function `test_some_name_here`.

Then, just to show it working, I run a quick test, then I get back to coding and use the `call` function included in our Laravel PHPUnit testing, and hit the API with a search query. From there, I assert the response is OK. Passing! But keep in mind it is always good to force a fail here since sometimes when a test passes too easily, you might want to force a fail.

Finally, I take the response, which is a result of `Illuminate\Http\JsonResponse`, and `var_dump` the data to the terminal so I can just look it over to see what I have to play with. From there, I use the now converted `$results` as an array and I start to check for keys and values.

That is it, you were able to make an API without hitting the browser.

See also

▸ *Chapter 8, Testing and Debugging Your Application* I will cover how to make fixtures out of this data so you are not hitting the API over and over.

▸ **Laracasts—Incremental APIs—Refactoring tests and traits**: `https://laracasts.com/series/incremental-api-development/episodes/11`.

Building a view based route

In the preceding recipe, we showed how to build a JSON-based API response in a route with a real view. I will show here just how simple it is in routes to output a View. Typically, I would use a controller but in this case I will not, just to show how you can experiment in a route at different levels.

Getting ready

A base install will be fine for this one.

How to do it...

1. Let's add another route for this:

```
Route::get('example_view', function () {

    $data = [
        'label' => "Hello",
        'value' => "World"
    ];

    return view('examples.route_view', compact('data'));
```

2. Then, make a view to handle that route `resources/views/examples/route_view.blade.php`:

```
@extends('layout')

@section('header')

    <h1>Example here</h1>
@endsection

@section('content')



    <h1>{{ $data['label'] }}</h1>
    <h2>{{ $data['value'] }}</h2>


@endsection
```

3. And give it a look `http://recipes.dev/example_view`:

How it works...

Pretty nice how simple this is! I have worked in other frameworks where making routes is a chore in abstraction and speed, or lack of speed.

In this case, we can quickly play with ideas and show results in a view right from the route. You could build an entire API in the route for small microservices.

In this case I just make an array, put it into the view using the php `compact` syntax, and display it. Notice too the dot notation in the `view` function as `examples.route_view` translates into `folder.filename` and the filename did not need the `blade.php` suffix, it is assumed.

And just like in the previous chapter, we could have tested this in PHPUnit! More on that next.

Testing your view based route in PHPUnit

Using the above recipe, I was able to make a view right from the route, now I want to test my view and make sure it is doing what is expected. Typically, I would use Behat but in this example, I will use PHPUnit.

Getting ready

If you follow the above recipe, you will have an example page in place. From here we will start with the testing.

How to do it...

Follow the listed steps for testing your view based route:

1. As usual, make a test:

   ```
   >php artisan make:test ExampleViewTest
   ```

2. Then, in that file `tests/ExampleViewTest.php`, I begin to write a test:

   ```php
   /**
    * @test
    */
   public function example_view()
   {

       $this->visit('/example_view')->see("Hello")->see("World");

       $this->assertResponseOk();

   }
   }
   ```

3. Run the test and it passes:

```
> phpunit --filter=example_view
```

4. Now, to see how we can deal with authentication, add this to the route:

```
Route::group(['middleware' => 'auth'], function() {
    Route::get('example_view', function () {

        $data = ['label' => "Hello", 'value' => "World"];

        return view('examples.route_view', compact('data'));
    });
});
```

5. And what was a passing test is now failing:

```
vagrant@homestead:~/Code/recipes$ phpunit --filter=example_view
PHPUnit 4.8.25 by Sebastian Bergmann and contributors.

F

Time: 4.24 seconds, Memory: 12.00MB

There was 1 failure:

1) ExampleViewTest::example_view
<head>
<title>ICDB: Internet Comic Database</title>
<meta charset="utf-8">
<meta name="viewport" content="width=device-width, initial-scale=1.0">
<meta name="description" content="">
<meta name="author" content="">
<link rel="stylesheet" href="/build/css/all-7343372362.css">
<meta name="theme-color" content="#ffffff">
</head>
<body class="" ng-app="app">

<div id="wrapper">

    <header class="navbar" role="banner"><div class="container">

        <div class="navbar-header">
            <a href="/" class="navbar-brand">
                <h1>ICDB</h1>
```

6. All we have to do is add `$this->actingAs()`:

```
/**
 * @test
 */
public function example_view()
{

    $user = factory(App\User::class)->create();

    $this->actingAs($user)->visit('/example_view')->see("Hello")->see("World");

    $this->assertResponseOk();

}
```

7. And we are back to passing. If you are using `$this->call()` instead of `$this->visit()` then you can use `$this->be()` instead:

```
/**
 * @test
 */
public function example_view()
{

    $user = factory(App\User::class)->create();

    $this->be($user);

    $this->visit('/example_view')->see("Hello")->see("World");

    $this->assertResponseOk();

}
```

How it works...

Pretty nice how Laravel brings all of this into PHPUnit! Keep in mind though it cannot test JavaScript but, in those cases, just use Behat and Selenium.

Also notice in the fail, you get a lot of helpful output. You can even do `dump()`:

```
$this->visit('/example_view')->see("Hello")->see("World")->dump();
```

This gets output whenever you want.

Once again, Laravel makes it easy to test your site even at the view level.

See also

- ▸ **Laravel Docs—Testing**: https://laravel.com/docs/5.2/testing.
- ▸ **Laracasts—TDD Acceptance Testing**: https://laracasts.com/lessons/acceptance-testing-with-tdd.

Creating named routes

From the beginning, even in a small project, I highly suggest naming routes. I will cover a few examples of how and why here.

Getting ready

A base install of Laravel is great. I will use some routes and views from above but you can easily follow along.

How to do it...

Follow the listed steps for creating named routes:

1. To begin with, let's look at some routes I have:

   ```
   > php artisan route:list
   ```

   You will see something like this if you followed along so far, else you will just see the default Laravel route.

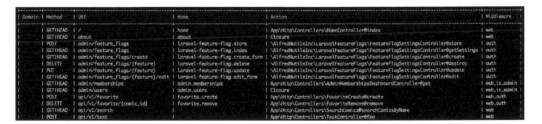

2. Notice the `name` section; that is what we are aiming for here.

3. Note the `admin` section `admin.memberships` and `admin.users` in my app/
   `routes.php` file:

```php
Route::group(['middleware' => ['is_admin']], function () {
    Route::get('/admin/users', function () {
        return "You are here";})
        ->name('admin.users');

    Route::get('/admin/memberships', 'AdminMembershipsDashboardController@get')
        ->name('admin.memberships');
});
```

4. See the `->name()` method at the end of the `Route` facade, it is the cause of
   this magic.

5. Also notice the dot notation naming to help organize a bit more. This is optional but I
   like it for grouping like routes.

6. Here is where it comes in handy though, open up the test and swap out the path for
   the route method:

```php
class ExampleViewTest extends TestCase
{
    /**
     * @test
     */
    public function example_view()
    {

        $user = factory(App\User::class)->create();

        $this->be($user);

        $this->visit(route('example_view'))->see("Hello")->see("World");

        $this->assertResponseOk();

    }
}
```

7. See the following route URL:

```php
Route::group(['middleware' => 'auth'], function() {
    Route::get('example_view', function () {

        $data = ['label' => "Hello", 'value' => "World"];

        return view('examples.route_view', compact('data'));
    })->name('example_view');
});
```

8. Change the route URL to the following:

```
Route::group(['middleware' => 'auth'], function() {
    Route::get('foo', function () {

        $data = ['label' => "Hello", 'value' => "World"];

        return view('examples.route_view', compact('data'));
    })->name('example_view');
});
```

Everything just keeps working, my tests, any links that go there, and so on!

9. Here is an example in my nav `resources/views/nav_layout.blade.php`:

```
        </li>

        <li class="dropdown ">
            <a href="{{ route('admin.memberships') }}">
                Admin Subscriptions
            </a>
        </li>
```

How it works...

As you can see, it is super easy to name our routes. And hopefully, you also see the hours of work this can save you when the client decides to change a URL and all your tests and nav templates start breaking.

Also, when working on a project with others or just yourself, it really is a good way to stay organized:

```
>php artisan route:list | grep WORD_YOU_ARE_LOOKING_FOR
```

This can easily help you find routes, and since routes can be in numerous files, it makes it even more important.

See also

▸ **Laravel Docs—Routing**: https://laravel.com/docs/5.2/routing

4
Building Views and Adding Style

In this chapter, we will cover the following topics:

- ▶ Organizing your Blade files
- ▶ Installing a `WrapBootStrap` theme
- ▶ Making your authentication pages
- ▶ Implementing an error message template
- ▶ Building your main search page
- ▶ Adding static pages

Introduction

Alright, we made it this far without any views. Using the command line and PHPUnit we are able to create much of the backend so that when it is time to make a view, we have the data we want! In this chapter, we will walk though setting up Blade files, installing a theme, making an authentication page, and more.

Organizing your Blade files

To begin, let's look over where our theme files exist per the default Laravel install and do some touch up work to organize them in a *better* way. We are also going to use a scaffolding library to get us going quickly.

Getting ready

If you have been following this far, you are set. Any fresh install of Laravel should be fine too.

How to do it...

1. Install this library, `https://github.com/alnutile/l5scaffold`, as the documents note. Note the extra step, since it is a fork:

```
},
"repositories": [
    {
        "type": "vcs",
        "url": "https://github.com/alnutile/l5scaffold.git"
    }
],
"autoload": {
```

And you may have to add `minimum-stability` at the end of the `composer.json` file:

```
    "post-update-cmd": [
        "php artisan clear-compiled",
        "php artisan optimize"
    ]
},
"config": {
    "preferred-install": "dist"
},
"minimum-stability": "dev"
}
```

2. Then we are going to `scaffold` out a model, migration, views, and more.

```
vagrant@homestead:~/Code/recipes$ php artisan make:scaffold User --schema="name:string,email:string,password:string"
```

3. It will output some info, and the last line will show the route your need to add to your `routes.php` file `Route::resource("users", "UserController"); // Add this` line in `routes.php`.

4. Now we do not need another user migration, so let's delete that one. If you look in the `migration` folder, it is the file at the bottom of that list:

```
▼ ⬚migrations
    ⬚.gitkeep
    📄2014_10_12_000000_create_users_table.php
    📄2014_10_12_100000_create_password_resets_table.php
    📄2016_04_10_165240_create_users_table.php
  ▶ ⬚seeds
    ⬚.gitignore
  ▶ ⬚public
```

Delete the one we just made.

5. Then open your `app/Http/routes.php` file and add the line it told you to add:

```php
<?php

/*...*/

/*
|--------------------------------------------------------------------------
| Application Routes
|--------------------------------------------------------------------------
|
| This route group applies the "web" middleware group to every route
| it contains. The "web" middleware group is defined in your HTTP
| kernel and includes session state, CSRF protection, and more.
|
*/

Route::group(['middleware' => ['web']], function () {

    Route::resource("users","UserController"); // Add this line in routes.php

    Route::get('/', ['as' => 'search',
        'uses' => 'SearchComics@searchComicsByName']);

});
```

6. Now run the migrations, inside of Homestead:

```
>php artisan migrate:refresh --seed
```

7. Now we can see our work if we visit /users, but we have a long way to go:

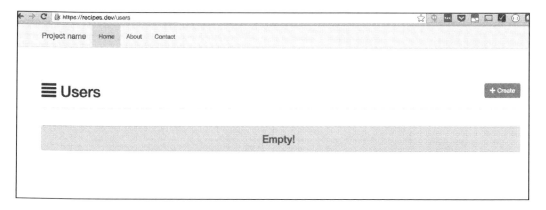

Then, if you want to take a moment to click around—**Create**, **Delete**, **Edit**, and all that is done for you automagically.

8. Now let's review what just happened and see where all these view files are.

How it works...

So, this is about how to organize Blade, but to make the task easier I used a scaffolding library to make all our Blade files see, create, and edit users as well as to see errors on the page, if any.

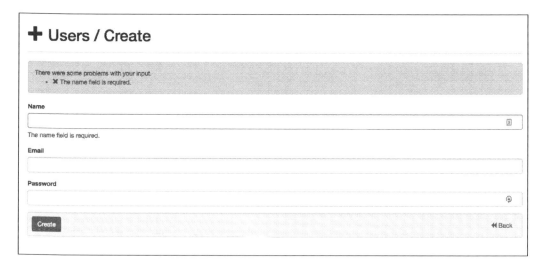

So, where did it put those files, and what files did it make? Let's cover the non-blade related files first.

The migration file we deleted is one file it made. Typically, we would not delete this, but, Laravel already did this one for us.

Then there is the Seeder file `database/seeds/UserTableSeeder.php` we can plug this into the `database/seeds/DatabaseSeeder.php` file if we want.

It would have made a model file `app/User.php` but again, that just happens to come with Laravel.

Then there is the controller, `app/Http/Controllers/UserController.php`, other than validation, you are set to roll.

So now, let's move on to the View/Blade files and how to organize them.

It has made `resources/views/layout.blade.php`, which is the base to all your Blade files. In here, we see `content`.

```
<div class="container">
    @yield('header')
    @yield('content')|
</div><!-- /.container -->
```

This will pull in the content from our files as needed. Let's start with the `user` files made to make our user index, user create, and user edit happen.

```
▼ 🗀 resources
  ▶ 🗀 assets
  ▶ 🗀 lang
  ▼ 🗀 views
    ▶ 🗀 errors
    ▼ 🗀 users
        📄 create.blade.php
        📄 edit.blade.php
        📄 index.blade.php
        📄 show.blade.php
    ▶ 🗀 vendor
      📄 error.blade.php
      📄 layout.blade.php
      📄 welcome.blade.php
```

If we open those files, we can see it is looking for `$user` and showing info based on what we have for that data and what the CRUD step is.

 CRUD (create, read, update, and delete) see more at `https://en.wikipedia.org/wiki/Create,_read,_update_and_delete`.

Notice the `edit` and `create` file reference the `$errors` variable. This exists in Laravel even if there are no `$errors`, but you need to put your route into the `Web Middleware` as we do in the route we showed previously. If you open the Kernel app/Http/`Kernel.php` you can see the reference to `\Illuminate\View\Middleware\ShareErrorsFromSession::class,'`:

```
                        protected $middleware = [
  Kernel.php                  \Illuminate\Foundation\Http\Middleware\CheckForMaintenanceMode::class,
  routes.php              ];
▸ Interfaces
▸ Jobs
▸ Listeners                 /**
▸ Policies                   * The application's route middleware groups.
▸ Providers                  *
  MarvelApi.php              * @var array
  User.php                   */
▸ bootstrap                 protected $middlewareGroups = [
▸ config                        'web' => [
▸ database                          \App\Http\Middleware\EncryptCookies::class,
▸ public                            \Illuminate\Cookie\Middleware\AddQueuedCookiesToResponse::class,
▼ resources                         \Illuminate\Session\Middleware\StartSession::class,
  ▸ assets                          \Illuminate\View\Middleware\ShareErrorsFromSession::class,
  ▸ lang                            \App\Http\Middleware\VerifyCsrfToken::class,
  ▼ views                       ],
    ▸ errors
    ▼ users
      create.blade.php
      edit.blade.php
```

The key here is we are storing our Model/Resource in one folder, `users` later, when we make a `Search` area, I will make a folder called `search`.

Then there is the `Error` file. You will see in the preceding screenshot that the `edit` and `create` files pull this file in.

```
5          <h1><i class="glyphicon glyphicon-edit"></i> Users / Edit #{{$user->id}}</h1>
6      </div>
7   @endsection
8
9   @section('content')
10      @include('error')
11
12      <div class="row">
13          <div class="col-md-12">
14
15              <form action="{{ route('users.update', $user->id) }}" method="POST">
16                  <input type="hidden" name="_method" value="PUT">
17                  <input type="hidden" name="_token" value="{{ csrf_token() }}">
```

Even though these forms have error fields for each form input, there is a top one just in case it is a non-input based error.

Lastly, open the controller and note how it calls to these views:

```
54    /**
55     * Display the specified resource.
56     *
57     * @param int $id
58     * @return Response
59     */
60    public function show($id)
61    {
62        $user = User::findOrFail($id);
63
64        return view('users.show', compact('user'));
65    }
66
```

At this point I am ready to build the rest of my site on this structure. In addition, we can delete the `resources/views/welcome.blade.php` page.

See also

▸ **Laracasts**: `https://laracasts.com/series/laravel-from-scratch/episodes/6`.

▸ **Laravel Documentation**: `https://laravel.com/docs/5.2/blade`

Maybe I have not said this enough, but the docs are really worth reading.

Installing a WrapBootStrap theme

We now have our site up and the `scaffold` command we used in the previous chapter makes the site look clean and simple, using Bootstrap `http://getbootstrap.com/` but here we are going to take it up a notch and add a theme. We will take this nice theme from `http://wrapbootstrap.com/preview/WB0K71344` and put it into place. We will end up with a sidebar, content area, and login pages. One thing that is really helpful is that these themes cost between $7 and $30 making it easy for you to create a good looking site in no time. There are free ones, too, at `http://startbootstrap.com/`, and the same process of putting these in place will carry over! This theme is Bootstrap 2. Ideally, you should go with Bootstrap 3, but the general idea is the same.

Also, note there will be recipes on Gulp which will have an impact on this setup later on.

Getting Started

You can use any of their themes or get a free one from `http://startbootstrap.com/`.

How to do it...

1. Download the theme outside of your application. We only move some parts into the system.

2. Then we are going to make the landing page, broken up into small chunks. So, in the `resources/views` folder, make a `layout.blade.php` file or replace our existing one and we start building into `https://goo.gl/N0yDFK` (because it is such a large page, I will link to the commit).

3. Now we need to get all the files it references and put them into place as well:

   1. Make a folder in public, for now, called `public/css`.

   2. Put the `mvpready-landing.css` file in there.

   3. I also put a `public/css/custom.css` in there for later use.

```
custom.css - recipes - [~/Code/recipes]
.form-inline input.form-control {
    width: 100%;
}

.navbar-brand.custom {
    padding-top: 15px;
    margin-bottom: -15px;
}

div#form-buttons input[type=checkbox] {
    display:none;
}

div#form-buttons input[type=checkbox] + label
{
    opacity: .5;
}

div#form-buttons input[type=checkbox]:checked + label
{
    opacity: 1;
}


.larger p {
    font-size: 155%;
}
```

4. Then we want to grab the `font-awesome.css` file and put it in there. Then the `bootstrap.min.css` file.

5. Then, let's make the `public/js` folder and put some files in there:

   1. Copy `jquery.min.js` into there.

   2. Then `bootstrap.min.js`.

3. Then `mvpready-core.js`.

4. And `mvpready-helpers.js`.

5. And `mvpready-landing.js`.

6. Then, as you can see in the `layout.blade.php` page I linked to `https://goo.gl/N0yDFK`, I break up some files into `partials` using `@include('filename')`:

   1. First, we will do that `resources/views/nav_layout.blade.php` and it will look like the following:

```html
<nav class="collapse navbar-collapse" role="navigation">

    <ul class="nav navbar-nav navbar-right mainnav-menu">

        <li class="dropdown ">
            <a href="/about">
                About
            </a>
        </li>


        <li class="dropdown ">
            <a href="/login">
                Login
            </a>
        </li>


    </ul>

</nav>
```

   2. And lastly, `/resources/views/title.blade.php`, which looks like the following:

```php
@if(isset($title))
    <div class="masthead">
        <div class="container">
            <div class="masthead-subtitle">
                {{ $title }}
            </div>
        </div>
    </div>
@endif
```

7. Then we need to change our home page, right now it returns JSON, we will keep that but move that route to `/api/v1/search` in `app/Http/routes.php`.

```php
Route::group(['middleware' => ['web']], function () {

    Route::get('/', 'HomeController@index');

    Route::resource("users","UserController"); // Add this line in routes.php

    Route::get('/api/v1/search', ['as' => 'search',
        'uses' => 'SearchComics@searchComicsByName']);

});
```

8. Then we will make a new route / again as seen in the preceding image for the `HomeController`.

9. Then we take the lazy way out to make this controller and type:

    ```
    >php artisan make:controller HomeController
    ```

10. And we edit that file so it looks like this:

```php
<?php

namespace App\Http\Controllers;

use ...

class HomeController extends Controller
{

    public function index()
    {

        $title = "Welcome to ICDB";

        return view('home.index', compact("title"));
    }
}
```

11. And a starter Blade file in `resources/views/home/index.blade.php` that looks like:

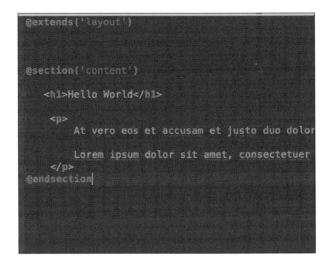

```
@extends('layout')


@section('content')

    <h1>Hello World</h1>

    <p>
        At vero eos et accusam et justo duo dolor

        Lorem ipsum dolor sit amet, consectetuer
    </p>
@endsection
```

12. Then we visit the home page:

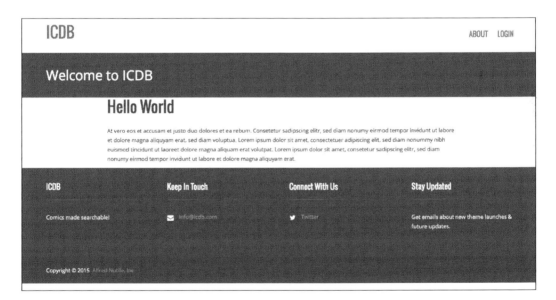

13. How about the user index page?

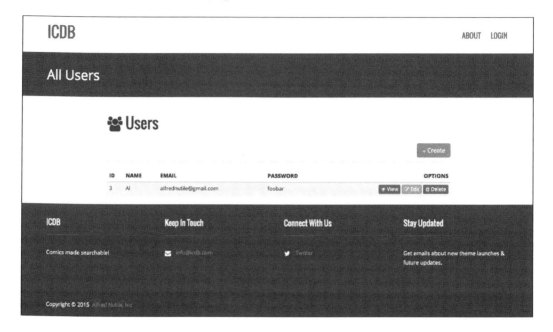

How it works...

As noted, I had to link to GitHub to help show the `layout.blade.php` file at this URL: `https://goo.gl/N0yDFK`. That file is a mix of the original `index.html` they gave me converted into a Blade format. The first step is the name ending in `blade.php`.

Then there is the use of `@include`. Taking time to move out some of the larger bits of code into their own partial is really helpful for reading this code and finding what you are looking for. Need to add a new link to the nav? Great. Open the `nav_layout.blade.php` file. I even tend to take the bottom assets, JavaScript, and the top assets, CSS, and break those into `partials`. But take it too far and you might take the ease out of theming.

Notice too, the use of the word `partials` these are small files that we `@include` in other files. I even do that with forms. Why have one form to create a user and one to edit when you can just have one partial that does both? Easier to maintain, right?

Then I update the route so we can start to show this view on the homepage /. Moving search to `/api/v1/search`, we set it aside for later when we want to talk to it using Angular. For now, we want to talk to our new `HomeController`:

A recent interview with DHH (David Heinemeier Hansson), the creator of Ruby on Rails found on `http://www.fullstackradio.com/32`, made some interesting points on how they lean toward smaller controllers that focus on a task instead of one big controller focusing on a resource.

Then, in there we simply define a `$title` since I show that on pages, and pass that to the `home.index` view. Notice too I made a home folder for just one file. It might be overkill but maybe not. Maybe later we will have a home sidebar and what not.

And that is it. We have a theme installed and we are ready to take on our other pages, like `Users`. Sure, we might simplify the theme a bit for the home page, but you can see how easy it was to move a non-Laravel specific theme into place.

See also

▶ **DHH and Full Stack Radio on Controllers**: `http://david.heinemeierhansson.com/`

▶ **Wrapboot Strap for nice themes**: `https://wrapbootstrap.com/`

▶ **Bootstrap for great foundations to any of your projects**: `http://getbootstrap.com/`

▶ **Foundation (another great theme foundation with way better monsters)**: `http://foundation.zurb.com/`

Making your authentication pages

Laravel 5.2 has made this even easier. You can read `https://laravel.com/docs/5.2/authentication#authentication-quickstart` and you will have all our files, routes and so on. We are just going to make sure it fits in well with our theme and shows the errors as expected.

How to do it...

1. Following the instructions in the Laravel documentation, we have to run:

```
>php artisan make:auth
```

2. Then it will output all this info; these are the files we are going to start checking on:

```
>php artisan make:auth
Created View: /Users/alfrednutile/Code/recipes/resources/views/auth/login.blade.php
Created View: /Users/alfrednutile/Code/recipes/resources/views/auth/register.blade.php
Created View: /Users/alfrednutile/Code/recipes/resources/views/auth/passwords/email.blade.php
Created View: /Users/alfrednutile/Code/recipes/resources/views/auth/passwords/reset.blade.php
Created View: /Users/alfrednutile/Code/recipes/resources/views/auth/emails/password.blade.php
Created View: /Users/alfrednutile/Code/recipes/resources/views/layouts/app.blade.php
Created View: /Users/alfrednutile/Code/recipes/resources/views/home.blade.php
Created View: /Users/alfrednutile/Code/recipes/resources/views/welcome.blade.php
Installed HomeController.
Updated Routes File.
```

3. Then we go to our `resources/views/auth/login.blade.php` Blade file and change the `@extends('layouts.app')` on the top to "`@extends('layout')`"— the one we made.

```
@extends('layout')

@section('content')
<div class="container">
    <div class="row">
        <div class="col-md-8 col-md-offset-2">
            <div class="panel panel-default">
                <div class="panel-heading">Login</div>
                <div class="panel-body">
                    <form class="form-horizontal" role="form" method="POST" a
                        {!! csrf_field() !!}

                        <div class="form-group{{ $errors->has('email') ? ' ha
                            <label class="col-md-4 control-label">E-Mail Addr

                            <div class="col-md-6">
                                <input type="email" class="form-control" name

                                @if ($errors->has('email'))
                                    <span class="help-block">
                                        <strong>{{ $errors->first('email') }}
                                    </span>
                                @endif
                            </div>
                        </div>

                        <div class="form-group{{ $errors->has('password') ? '
                            <label class="col-md-4 control-label">Password</l

                            <div class="col-md-6">
```

 Laravel `auth` scaffolding defaults to making a `layouts` folder and adds an `app.blade.php` file there. This is a convention that makes a lot of sense and sticking to default Laravel conventions is ideal, so feel free to alter the recipe to leave things as the `auth` command set them up as. This package leans toward a different layout name, and that is fine too.

4. Then if we go to `Login` it looks themed, but just not enough. Let's change the column span a bit:

```
@section('content')
<div class="container">
    <div class="row">
        <div class="col-lg-10 col-lg-offset-1 col-md-10 col-md-offset-1">
            <div class="panel panel-default">
                <div class="panel-heading">Login</div>
```

5. Great, now our form works and shows errors:

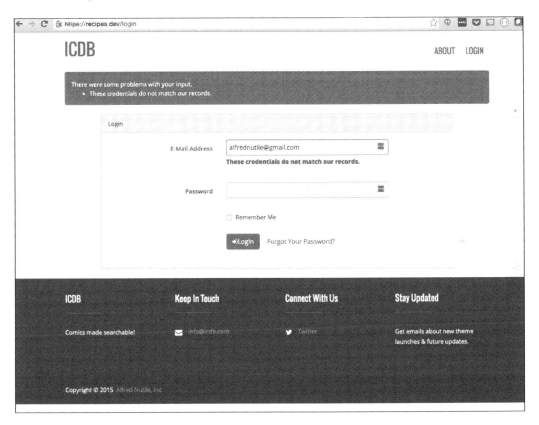

6. Now to fix the other user related authentication pages:

    1. Like the preceding screenshot, rename the top `@extends('layouts.app')` to the following: `@extends('layout')` in `resources/views/auth/passwords/reset.blade.php`

    2. Also—`resources/views/auth/passwords/email.blade.php`

3. And the Register page—`resources/views/auth/register.blade.php`

4. And with Errors:

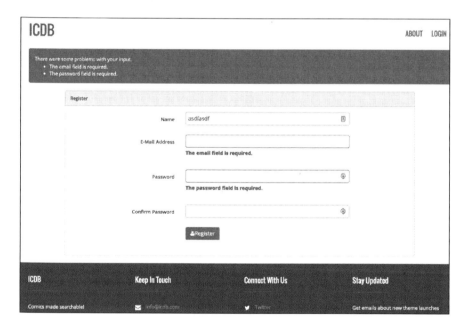

How it works...

Thanks to the Laravel `auth` scaffold it does all the heavy lifting for us! We just took a minute to point to our main layout file and tweak a width setting here and there. This to me is great, because I really just want to get the theme work out of the way, and Laravel does not try and abstract it like other frameworks, but instead lets you do basic HTML right in the template file, with a touch of Blade, which makes it so great.

Moreover, remember our `resources/views/layout.blade.php` has this area:

```
61        </div>
62
63        <div class="row">
64               @yield('header')
65               @yield('content')
66        </div>
67
68    </div> <!-- /#wrapper -->
```

This is what our other files are filling in. They are being wrapped by all the work we did here.

And that is all there is to it!

Implementing an error message template

In this section, I will point out some tips in dealing with errors. I will show how to use them overall, with forms and on different pages.

Getting started...

If you followed this far, you have completed the previous recipes on setting up the layout page and running the Laravel `php artisan auth` scaffold command. So we have two places to think about showing messages, one on the top of pages where you might want to show a message about a user and previous action that was successful, and secondly, in forms. We will cover both here.

But just make sure your main layout page has the following:

```
56
57          <div class="row">
58              <div class="container">
59                  @include('error')
60              </div>
61          </div>
62
63          <div class="row">
64              <div class="container">
65                  @yield('header')
66                  @yield('content')
67              </div>
68          </div>
69
```

And that file `resources/views/error.blade.php` will look like this:

```
CS  Window  Help
    @if (count($errors) > 0)
        <div class="alert alert-danger">
            <p>There where some errors on the page</p>
            <ul>
                @foreach ($errors->all() as $error)
                    <li>{{ $error }}</li>
                @endforeach
            </ul>
        </div>
    @endif
```

How to do it...

The following are the steps to implement an error message template:

1. First, let's make a route that will redirect us to the home page with errors to begin our error output:

```
Route::group(['middleware' => ['web']], function () {

    Route::auth();

    Route::get('/', 'HomeController@index');

    Route::resource("users","UserController"); // Add this line in route

    Route::get('/api/v1/search', ['as' => 'search',
        'uses' => 'SearchComics@searchComicsByName']);

    Route::get('/show_message', function() {
        return redirect('/')->withErrors("Hello There");
    });
});
```

2. Then, if you go to the /show_message page, you will see this:

3. Now let's show a message instead:

```php
Route::group(['middleware' => ['web']], function () {

    Route::auth();

    Route::get('/', 'HomeController@index');

    Route::resource("users","UserController"); // Add this line in routes.php

    Route::get('/api/v1/search', ['as' => 'search',
        'uses' => 'SearchComics@searchComicsByName']);

    Route::get('/show_message', function () {
        return redirect('/')->with("message", "Hello There");
    });
});
```

4. Now we add to our `resources/views/error.blade.php` file:

```php
@if (count($errors) > 0)
    <div class="alert alert-danger">
        <p>There where some errors on the page</p>
        <ul>
            @foreach ($errors->all() as $error)
                <li>{{ $error }}</li>
            @endforeach
        </ul>
    </div>
@endif

@if(Session::get('message'))
    <div class="alert alert-danger">
        <p>{{ Session::get('message') }}</p>

    </div>
@endif
```

This might be a good time to name this file `messages.blade.php` since it is both errors and messages.

5. Let's take a look at the form: `resources/views/users/create.blade.php`.

```
<div class="form-group @if($errors->has('name')) has-error @endif">
    <label for="name-field">Name</label>
    <input type="text" id="name-field" name="name" class="form-control" value="
    @if($errors->has('name'))
        <span class="help-block">{{ $errors->first('name') }}</span>
    @endif
</div>
<div class="form-group @if($errors->has('email')) has-error @endif">
    <label for="email-field">Email</label>
    <input type="text" id="email-field" name="email" class="form-control" value
    @if($errors->has('email'))
        <span class="help-block">{{ $errors->first('email') }}</span>
    @endif
</div>
```

This is the form `php artisan auth` made for us. Notice how it digs into the errors array looking for matching fields. This way you can do it per field and at the top of the form.

How it works...

I started with a `dummy` route to just redirect us and send a message and another error. Once again Laravel makes this super easy. Then we go to the home page and we see the error there. The View has `$error` injected into it, even if there are none, so we are basically iterating over it if it is there.

Then I updated the `error.blade.php` to have a place to get the "`message`" from the Session facade.

And the reset is taken care of by Laravel `auth` scaffolding that made those templates for us.

That is all it took to start injecting styled messages and errors onto our pages.

See also

▶ **Laravel Documents**: `https://laravel.com/docs/5.2/validation#quick-displaying-the-validation-errors`

▶ **Laracast and Flash Messaging**: `https://laracasts.com/series/laravel-5-fundamentals/episodes/20`

▶ **Sessions on Laravel docs**: `https://laravel.com/docs/master/session`

Building your main search page

In this section, I will start to build the search page. To being with, we will add a search bar, and then I will show how to add a form that uses GET to query the API to get comics once the user clicks **Search**. In a later recipe we will convert this to Angular.

Getting started...

The previous two recipes got us going with a home page and a message area, and now we are set to add a form to that page and update the controller.

How to do it...

1. First, we are going to give our route a name, so update your `routes.php` file:

```
Route::get('/', ['as' => 'home', 'uses' => 'HomeController@index']);

Route::resource("users","UserController"); // Add this line in routes.php
```

2. Now, when you run `php artisan route:list`, you will see home as a name:

```
vagrant@homestead:~/Code/recipes$ php artisan route:list
+--------+-----------+-------------------------+---------------+----------------------------------------------------------------+-------------+
| Domain | Method    | URI                     | Name          | Action                                                         | Middleware  |
+--------+-----------+-------------------------+---------------+----------------------------------------------------------------+-------------+
|        | GET|HEAD  | /                       | home          | App\Http\Controllers\HomeController@index                      | web         |
|        | GET|HEAD  | api/v1/search           | search        | App\Http\Controllers\SearchComics@searchComicsByName           | web         |
|        | GET|HEAD  | login                   |               | App\Http\Controllers\Auth\AuthController@showLoginForm         | web,guest   |
|        | POST      | login                   |               | App\Http\Controllers\Auth\AuthController@login                 | web,guest   |
|        | GET|HEAD  | logout                  |               | App\Http\Controllers\Auth\AuthController@logout                | web         |
|        | POST      | password/email          |               | App\Http\Controllers\Auth\PasswordController@sendResetLinkEmail| web,guest   |
|        | POST      | password/reset          |               | App\Http\Controllers\Auth\PasswordController@reset             | web,guest   |
|        | GET|HEAD  | password/reset/{token?} |               | App\Http\Controllers\Auth\PasswordController@showResetForm     | web,guest   |
|        | GET|HEAD  | register                |               | App\Http\Controllers\Auth\AuthController@showRegistrationForm  | web,guest   |
|        | POST      | register                |               | App\Http\Controllers\Auth\AuthController@register              | web,guest   |
|        | GET|HEAD  | show_message            |               | Closure                                                        | web         |
|        | GET|HEAD  | users                   | users.index   | App\Http\Controllers\UserController@index                      | web         |
|        | POST      | users                   | users.store   | App\Http\Controllers\UserController@store                      | web         |
|        | GET|HEAD  | users/create            | users.create  | App\Http\Controllers\UserController@create                     | web         |
|        | GET|HEAD  | users/{users}           | users.show    | App\Http\Controllers\UserController@show                       | web         |
|        | PUT|PATCH | users/{users}           | users.update  | App\Http\Controllers\UserController@update                     | web         |
|        | DELETE    | users/{users}           | users.destroy | App\Http\Controllers\UserController@destroy                    | web         |
|        | GET|HEAD  | users/{users}/edit      | users.edit    | App\Http\Controllers\UserController@edit                       | web         |
+--------+-----------+-------------------------+---------------+----------------------------------------------------------------+-------------+
```

3. Now we will use that route name for our form in the `resources/views/home` folder add `resources/views/home/_search.blade.php`.

```
File  Edit  View  Navigate  Code  Refactor  Run  Tools  VCS  Window  Help
1      <form action="{{ route('home') }}" method="GET" class="form-horizontal">
2          <div class="input-group">
3              <input type="text" name="search" class="form-control col-lg-10"
4                  placeholder="Search for your comic...">
5              <span class="input-group-btn">
6                  <button type="submit" class="btn btn-primary">Search</button>
7              </span>
8
9          </div>
10     </form>
11     |
```

4. Now let's update our home index page to show all this at: `resources/views/home/index.blade.php`:

```
@extends('layout')

@section('content')
    <div class="container">
        <div class="row">
            <div class="col-lg-8 col-lg-offset-2">

                @include('error')

                @include('home._search')

                <hr>

                <div class="panel panel-default">
                    <div class="panel-heading">Find some comics!</div>
                    <div class="panel-body">
                        What are you waiting for?
                    </div>
                </div>

            </div>
        </div>
    </div>
@endsection
```

5. Now if we go to the home page we should see this:

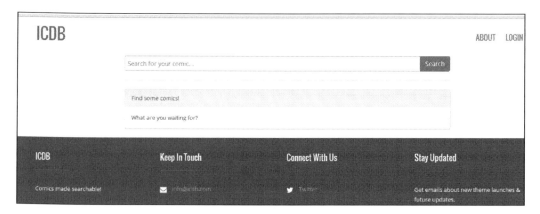

6. Now let's make the **Search** button do some work! First, update the HomeController at app/Http/Controllers/HomeController.php so the constructor looks like this:

```php
<?php

namespace App\Http\Controllers;

use App\Http\Requests;
use App\Interfaces\ComicClientInterface;
use App\MarvelApi;
use Illuminate\Http\Request;

class HomeController extends Controller
{

    /**
     * @var MarvelApi
     */
    private $clientInterface;

    public function __construct(ComicClientInterface $clientInterface)
    {
        $this->clientInterface = $clientInterface;
    }
}
```

7. Then in our method to render the page, let's keep an eye out for the `search` form query string in the incoming Request so that it looks like this in `app/Http/Controllers/HomeController.php`:

```php
 *
 * @return \Illuminate\Http\Response
 */
public function index(Request $request)
{
    $name = '';

    if($request->input('search')){
        $name = $request->input('search');
        $message = sprintf("Your results for %s", $name);
        Session::flash('status', $message);
    }

    $results = $this->clientInterface->comics($name);

    $results = $this->transformResults($results);

    return Response::view('home.index', compact('results'));
}

private function transformResults($results)
{
    if(isset($results['data']))
        return $results['data'];

    return $this->returnEmptyResults();
}

private function returnEmptyResults()
{
    $results = [
        'results'   => [],
        'offset'    => 0,
        'limit'     => 20,
        'total'     => 0,
        'count'     => 0
    ];

    return $results;
}
```

8. Then we add some logic and style to our `index.blade.php` page so that it looks like the following screenshot or visit `https://goo.gl/OmDqyD`.

```
@extends('layout')

@section('content')
  <div class="container">
    <div class="row">
      <div class="col-lg-8 col-lg-offset-2">

        @include('home._search')
        <hr>

        <div class="panel panel-default">
          <div class="panel-heading">Find some comics!</div>
          <div class="panel-body">
            @if(empty($results['results']))
              <p>What are you waiting for?</p>
            @else
              @foreach($results['results'] as $result)
                <div class="media">
                  <div class="media-left col-lg-2">
                    <a href="{{ $result['urls'][0]['url'] }}">
                      @if(isset($result['thumbnail']['path']))
                        <img class="media-object img-thumbnail img-responsive"
                          src="{{ $result['thumbnail']['path'] . '.' . $result['thumbnail']['extension'] }}"
                          alt="...">
                      @else
                        <img class="media-object" src="/images/placeholder.jpg" alt="...">
                      @endif
                    </a>
                  </div>
                  <div class="media-body">
                    <h4 class="media-heading">{{ $result['title'] }}</h4>
                    {{ $result['description'] }} <a
                      href="{{ $result['urls'][0]['url'] }}">more...</a>
                  </div>
                </div>
              @endforeach

            @endif

          </div>
        </div>

      </div>
    </div>
  </div>
@endsection
```

9. Now we do a search, and our page looks like this:

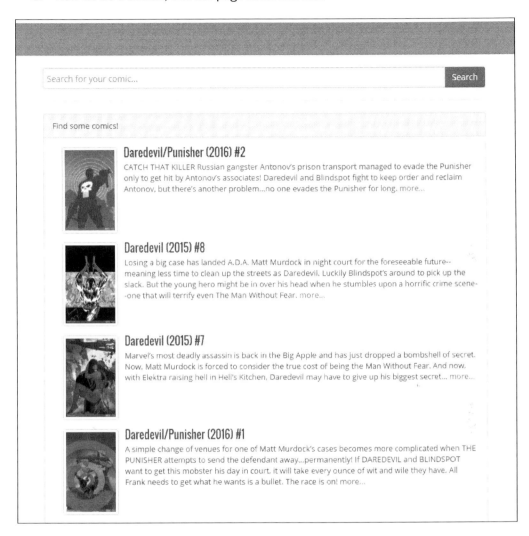

How it works...

First, I started by adding the route name. Why? Overall it is just a good habit. This way, if you move this URL you do not have to change any of the routes in this file since you are using the name of the route.

Then, in the Controller, I did a few odd things. First of all, I would rather not have my controller this busy, but I'm just trying to keep this simple for now. The index method looks for `search` in the Request, and if it finds it, it will use the input to query the API. Maybe if there is none, we should default to another API feature like "Latest Comics" or `/v1/public/events` and get their latest events!

Then I transform the results. Keep in mind the client I made transformed the results, so in this case I am just guarding my application from changes the API might make for output. Also, later if I want to switch to another API, I still have the same output to the UI and API. One part of this is the `returnEmptyResults` so I can have a consistent result set even if empty. One of my main goals here is keeping logic out of the View. The View layer should just iterate over the data and have as little info as possible about all the edge cases of the data and so on.

Finally, I pass a flash message to let the user know how the search went. And that is it - you have a form fetching results from the API.

See also

▶ **Laracast—Flashing to the Session**: `https://laracasts.com/series/laravel-5-from-scratch/episodes/15`

Adding a static page

I will cover how easy it is to add a static page. We will look at several approaches.

Getting started...

We have a base install from all the previous work done and an *About* link. We are going to make that work.

How to do it...

1. I will show three ways. This first way, we just put a file in the public folder called `about.html` and just type in there `Foo`. Then visit `https://recipes.dev/about.html` and you see something not that elegant, but it shows you how easy it is to bypass Laravel altogether. It's a good example of making an error message or site is down for maintenance message.

2. The next one is a bit more common. We will make a route that will just return `Foo` to the page.

```
Route::group(['middleware' => ['web']], function () {

    Route::auth();

    Route::get('/', ['as' => 'home', 'uses' => 'HomeController@index']);

    Route::get('/about', ['as' => 'about', function(){
        return "Foo";
    }]);
});
```

3. Then, finally, we use a real View placing the file here: `resources/views/about.blade.php`.

4. And then make the file look like the following:

```
@extends('layout')

@section('content')

    <p>
        At vero eos et accusam et justo duo dolores et ea

        Lorem ipsum dolor sit amet, consectetuer adipisc
    </p>

@endsection
```

5. Then update the route file to return this view, no need for a controller for this:

```
Route::group(['middleware' => ['web']], function () {

    Route::auth();

    Route::get('/', ['as' => 'home', 'uses' => 'HomeController

    Route::get('/about', ['as' => 'about', function(){
        $title = "About";
        return view('about', compact('title'));
    }]);
```

6. Then visit `https://recipes.dev/about` and you should see this (could use some serious copy help!).

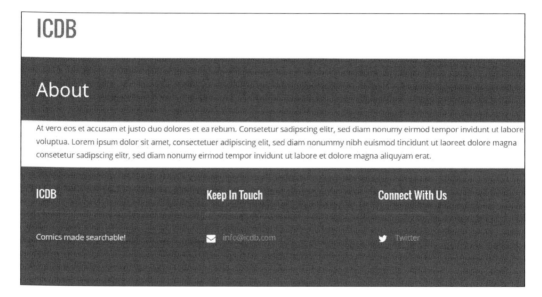

How it works...

That's it! Pretty easy really. I have seen some frameworks make this terribly hard, but now you have full control to manage some pages as needed, simply in the route, or a full HTML file.

5
Working with Data

In this chapter, we will cover the following topics:

- ▸ Setting up users and running migrations
- ▸ Altering a migration
- ▸ Using factories for migrations and tests
- ▸ Using a generator to scaffold your user wishlist area
- ▸ Seeding so you can see how your app looks
- ▸ Adding a file upload to user profile
- ▸ Validating file upload
- ▸ Saving files to S3

Introduction

In this chapter, I will take a look at common workflows, gotchas, and other tips and tricks around Laravel and data or *state*, which in this case will include files.

Setting up users and running migrations

Here, we will take a look at users, model, and migration as well as some steps for running them on your machine and more.

Getting ready

The base install of Laravel should make setting up for this easy. Just make sure to update your .env file for the correct database name and then make sure to provision your Vagrant box and you are ready. Also, we will be running this work from within our Vagrant box since the migrations will talk to the database on the default port.

How to do it...

1. Set up your .env file to look like the following:

```
APP_ENV=local
APP_DEBUG=true
APP_KEY=Xidkr59zYNuPVKWqHLiWwppEgK3EfYrJ
APP_URL=https://recipes.dev

DB_HOST=127.0.0.1
DB_PORT=3306
DB_DATABASE=recipes_local
DB_USERNAME=homestead
DB_PASSWORD=secret
```

2. Laravel comes with user migration so this is the easy part. All you need to do is run:

    ```
    >php artisan migrate
    ```

    And that is it!

3. To rollback this work, you can type:

    ```
    >php artisan migrate:rollback
    ```

How it works...

Laravel 5.x made this super easy. You can see the migrations in the database/migration folder. You will see one in there to help with passwords as well. Don't want users? Just delete them. Many sites might not have users, for example, an API that just takes tokens.

See also

▸ **Laracasts (building user profies)**: `https://laracasts.com/lessons/building-user-profiles`

Altering a migration

Migration workflows are one more thing that makes Laravel such a great framework for teams as well as the lone developer. In this recipe, we are going to show the proper way to change a migration.

Getting ready

Even a fresh install will get you started, we just need a migration and then we will alter it. In this case, we are going to alter the `users` table.

How to do it....

Follow these steps to alter the `users` table:

1. Inside Vagrant, run your migration if you have not already. We talked about setting up Vagrant in *Chapter 1*, *Setting Up and Installing Laravel*.

2. Then type:

```
>php artisan make:migration alter_users_table_add_twitter_name_field
```

3. Now you will have the file in your `database/migrations` folder—edit that so it looks like the following:

```php
class AlterUsersTableAddTwitterNameField extends Migration
{
    /**
     * Run the migrations.
     *
     * @return void
     */
    public function up()
    {
        //
    }

    /**
     * Reverse the migrations.
     *
     * @return void
     */
    public function down()
    {
        //
    }
}
```

4. Then we need to modify it to add the actual logic to alter the table `users`. In this case by adding a field:

```php
class AlterUsersTableAddTwitterNameField extends Migration
{
    public function up()
    {
        Schema::table('users', function(Blueprint $table)
        {
            $table->string('twitter')->nullable();
        });
    }

    /**
     * Reverse the migrations.
     *
     * @return void
     */
    public function down()
    {
        Schema::table('users', function(Blueprint $table)
        {
            if(Schema::hasColumns('users', ['twitter']))
                $table->dropColumn('twitter');
        });
    }
}
```

5. Then run the migration:

    ```
    >php artisan migrate
    ```

6. That's it, you now have a new field to save twitter names too!

How it works...

Looks like a lot of work! Why not just alter the previous file and rerun our migrations? That is a good question and sometimes, when you are just starting a project, have not deployed it to any servers, or have no one else working with you then that works. Here, though, we see how to deal with changes as a project grows in features and shrinks in features (ideally).

In this example, you will see I named the file a certain way, prefixing it with `alter_` this helps when you open up the `migration` folder to more easily see what the files are for. Also note the class name Laravel made for us: `AlterUsersTableAddTwitterNameField` it took our lowercase underscores and made a class out of it. That means you cannot name two migrations the same. One more thing that is harder to do when you are giving more descriptive names like `create_users_table` or `alter_users_table_add_foo_bar`.

Also you will see me set the field to `nullable`. I will talk about feature flags in another recipe but this makes it possible to not use this field till the feature is ready. Also, I personally like to keep some of this logic in the code.

See also

 ▸ **Laracast:** migrations: `https://laracasts.com/series/laravel-5-fundamentals/episodes/7`

Using factories for migrations and tests

Factories are a newer feature in Laravel 5.1. It makes it very easy to populate models with Faker data: `https://github.com/fzaninotto/Faker`. I will cover using factories in tests. In the *How it works...* section of the same recipe, I will explain more about the process, including why we use it.

Getting ready

A fresh install of Laravel, Homestead setup for migrations is needed. Then follow the prior recipe for altering a migration:

```php
class User extends Authenticatable
{
    /**
     * The attributes that are mass assignable.
     *
     * @var array
     */
    protected $fillable = [
        'name', 'email', 'password', 'twitter',
    ];

    /**
     * The attributes excluded from the model's JSON form.
     *
     * @var array
     */
    protected $hidden = [
        'password', 'remember_token',
    ];
}
```

How to do it...

Follow these steps to use factories:

1. First, we will show this in a test so let's type:

```
>php artisan make:test ExampleFactoryTest
```

2. Then, open that file and we will create a user-related factory:

```php
<?php

use ...

class ExampleFactoryTest extends TestCase
{

    use DatabaseTransactions;
    /**
     * @test
     */
    public function should_have_twitter_name()
    {
        $user = factory(\App\User::class)->create();

        $this->assertEquals('foo', $user->twitter);

    }
}
```

3. Then we can run our test to watch if it fails. I will go into more details in *How it works...* section of the same recipe:

```
vagrant@homestead:~/Code/recipes$ vendor/bin/phpunit --filter=should_have_twitter_name
PHPUnit 4.8.24 by Sebastian Bergmann and contributors.

E

Time: 4.82 seconds, Memory: 12.00Mb

There was 1 error:

1) ExampleFactoryTest::should_have_twitter_name
ErrorException: Undefined property: Illuminate\Database\Eloquent\FactoryBuilder::$twitter

/home/vagrant/Code/recipes/tests/ExampleFactoryTest.php:17

FAILURES!
Tests: 1, Assertions: 0, Errors: 1.
vagrant@homestead:~/Code/recipes$
```

4. Now I will open the factory file `database/factories/ModelFactory.php` and add that field:

```php
<?php

/* ... */

$factory->define(App\User::class, function (Faker\Generator $faker) {
    return [
        'name' => $faker->name,
        'email' => $faker->safeEmail,
        'twitter' => str_random(10),
        'password' => bcrypt(str_random(10)),
        'remember_token' => str_random(10),
    ];
});
```

5. Then run the test again:

```
> vendor/bin/phpunit --filter=should_have_twitter_name
```

6. Then I will get a different error. The red *F* which shows we have a failing test:

```
vagrant@homestead:~/Code/recipes$ vendor/bin/phpunit --filter=should_have_twitter_name
PHPUnit 4.8.24 by Sebastian Bergmann and contributors.

F

Time: 4.34 seconds, Memory: 12.00Mb

There was 1 failure:

1) ExampleFactoryTest::should_have_twitter_name
Failed asserting that two strings are equal.
--- Expected
+++ Actual
@@ @@
-'foo'
+'OApKlFcjNC'

/home/vagrant/Code/recipes/tests/ExampleFactoryTest.php:18

FAILURES!
Tests: 1, Assertions: 1, Failures: 1.
vagrant@homestead:~/Code/recipes$
```

7. So now I need to take control of the Twitter name so I know what to expect, so I update it to look like the following. This is one really nice feature of the `factory` function you can override the fields as needed:

```php
use ...

class ExampleFactoryTest extends TestCase
{

    use DatabaseTransactions;
    /**
     * @test
     */
    public function should_have_twitter_name()
    {
        $user = factory(\App\User::class)->create(['twitter' => 'foo']);

        $this->assertEquals('foo', $user->twitter);
    }

}
```

8. Now run our test and see green!

```
vagrant@homestead:~/Code/recipes$ vendor/bin/phpunit --filter=should_have_twitter_name
PHPUnit 4.8.24 by Sebastian Bergmann and contributors.

.

Time: 3.99 seconds, Memory: 12.00Mb

OK (1 test, 1 assertion)
vagrant@homestead:~/Code/recipes$ |
```

9. We can take this further and make more data in the system by just setting the number in the factory:

```
use ...

class ExampleFactoryTest extends TestCase
{
    use DatabaseTransactions;
    /**
     * @test
     */
    public function should_have_twitter_name()
    {
        $user = factory(\App\User::class, 5)->create(['twitter' => 'foo']);

        $this->assertEquals('foo', $user->twitter);
    }
}
```

Of course they should not all have the same Twitter handle.

How it works...

Why use factories and not just seed the site? Over time, I have stopped using seeding to set up the application for testing. I only use seeding for making the UI show data for the product owner to see the features they asked for. What I try to do is set up the state, data, or the application right in the Behat or PHPUnit test. For example, if I needed to test a number of users in the system and pagination, I would make sure, in my test, to start with a clean slate for users, not wiping the entire database and then using the factory method to set them up.

One thing to keep in mind, if you use factory in seeding or migrations, it will not work on production since the Faker library is only loaded with composer on non-production environments. So if you are going to use them there, which is not out of the ordinary really since sometimes you need to migrate new data into the system or seed production when you first set it up for a project, consider that particular issue.

See also

▸ **Laravel docs:**

`https://laravel.com/docs/5.2/seeding#using-model-factories`

`https://laravel.com/docs/5.2/testing#model-factories`

▸ **Laracasts:**

`https://laracasts.com/series/whats-new-in-laravel-5-1/episodes/5`

Using a generator to scaffold your user wishlist area

In *Chapter 4, Building Views and Adding Style,* I covered the user area in some detail, I will extend that here as I focus more on the wishlist area and using Scaffolding to build that out. There are many options out there to scaffold your view files, migrations, controllers, and routes. I will use l5scaffolding package: `https://packagist.org/packages/alnutile/l5scaffold` because I know it, since I forked it and used it in another few projects. While these lessons will focus specifically on using the l5scaffolding package, the basic concepts will be applicable to any of the available packages. Scaffolding is particularly useful when building a proof of concept, when you need to have something done fast and then wait until it is approved before spending time focusing on the quality of code.

In this lesson, we're going to create a *wishlist* feature that allows users to create personalized lists of comics. We need to make this wishlist item hold enough information so we can get the comic, as needed, from the Marvel API at a later date, or better yet just save the data there so the query is super quick.

So with that in mind, I will make a new model called `favorites` with these fields:

Name of field	Type	Notes
id	Integer	Auto incrementing
comic_data	JSON	Using the newer Laravel cast feature
user_id	Integer	So it links back to a user
created_at		Typical created at updated at fields
updated_at		Typical created at updated at fields

Getting ready

This recipe relies on the work done in the previous recipes on users and migrations, so make sure that you've completed those before proceeding.

How to do it...

1. We first, inside Homestead, run our `make:schema` command:

   ```
   >php artisan make:scaffold WishList --schema="comic_
   data:json,user_id:integer"
   ```

2. Then, after we run that, we should see the following:

```
vagrant@homestead:~/Code/recipes$ php artisan make:scaffold WishList --schema="comic_data:json,user_id:integer"
Configuring WishList...
Migration created successfully.
Seed created successfully.
Model created successfully.
Controller created successfully.
Skip Layout, because already exists.
Skip Error, because already exists.
Views created successfully.
Dump-autoload...
Route::resource("wish_lists","WishListController"); // Add this line in routes.php
vagrant@homestead:~/Code/recipes$
```

3. Now let's run our migration:

```
>php artisan migrate
```

```php
<?php

use |

class CreateWishListsTable extends Migration {

    /**
     * Run the migrations.
     *
     * @return void
     */
    public function up()
    {
        Schema::create('wish_lists', function(Blueprint $table) {
            $table->increments('id');
            $table->json('comic_data');
            $table->integer('user_id');
            $table->timestamps();
        });
    }

    /**
     * Reverse the migrations.
     *
     * @return void
     */
    public function down()
    {
        Schema::drop('wish_lists');
    }

}
```

4. Make sure to update your `factory` class as well `database/factories/ModelFactory.php` so it looks like this:

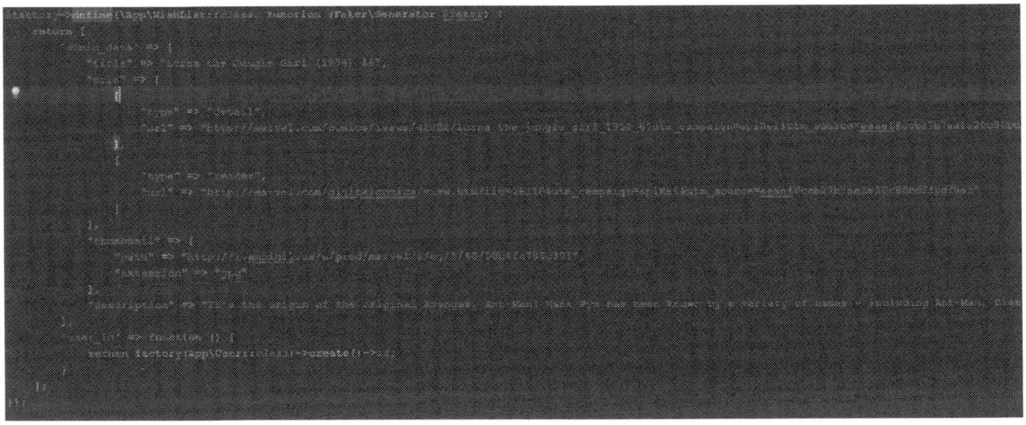

Figure 1 ModelFactory

Notice I pulled the data I want out of some factory data I got from an API request.

5. Now add the route we saw in the output from step 2 to our `routes` file:

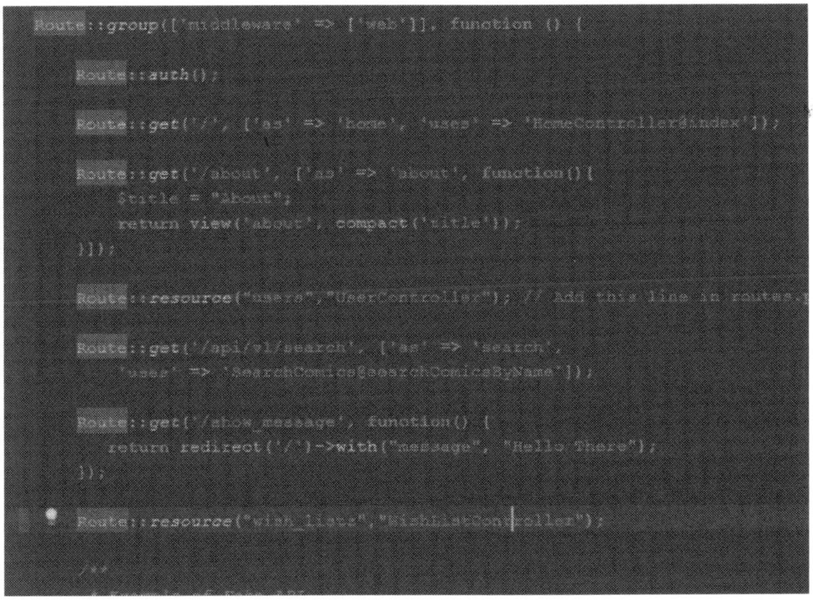

6. Let's look at all the files it made in the `views` folder `resources/views/wish_lists`:

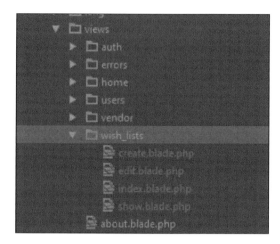

7. Now, if you log in and visit `/wish_lists`, you see the following:

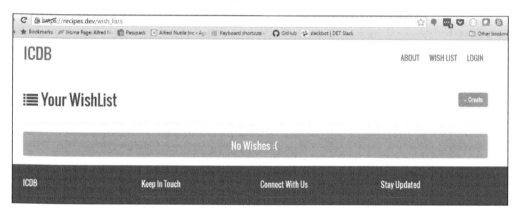

8. Since later we will be making an Angular widget to add these from the home page, we can remove the `create.blade.php` file but otherwise you have this full form to edit, create, and delete items.

How it works...

Now to review all the steps and reasons behind them. First I make a test. In this case, it is a nice way to help work though all the setup steps I need to take. Then I make a factory, because as you will see in the next section, they are a great habit to get into using for your day to day workflow, both in testing and seeding your project. Finally, I show using factories in a test. We see how easy it is to make one resource or many. It really is a key workflow for you to grasp.

See also

▶ **Laracast (database seeding and model factories):** `https://laracasts.com/ series/intermediate-laravel/episodes/9`

Seeding so you can see how your app looks

The wishlist area we made previously is really tough for me or a product owner to sign off on without some data in there. What I will do in this recipe is show how to seed that area of your website so you can then have a more realistic look at the feature with data.

Getting ready

Just follow the previous recipe called *Using factories for migration and tests*. After you are done there, the page `/wish_lists` should look like this:

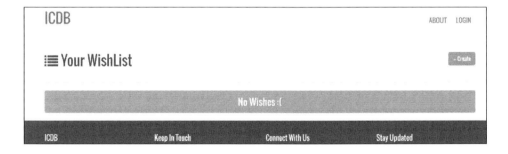

How to do it...

1. The scaffolding from the previous recipe created a new file called `database/seeds/WishListTableSeeder.php`. If you're not using scaffolding, you can easily make these on your own by typing:

   ```
   >php artisan make:seeder WishListTableSeeder
   ```

2. Edit that file so it looks like the following:

   ```php
   <?php

   use App\User;
   use Illuminate\Database\Seeder;


   class WishListTableSeeder extends Seeder {

       public function run()
       {
           $user = User::first();

           factory(\App\WishList::class, 20)->create(['user_id' => $user->id]);
       }

   }
   ```

3. Now we need to include that in the core `DatabaseSeeder` file `database/seeds/DatabaseSeeder.php`:

   ```php
   <?php

   use Illuminate\Database\Seeder;

   class DatabaseSeeder extends Seeder
   {
       /**
        * Run the database seeds.
        *
        * @return void
        */
       public function run()
       {
           $this->call(UserTableSeeder::class);
           $this->call(WishListTableSeeder::class);
       }
   }
   ```

4. Now we are ready to run the seeder:

    ```
    >php artisan migrate:refresh --seed
    ```

5. Now log in and check out that user interface:

How it works...

Alright, now we have seeded the database. That means we can show this to the product owner without having to click 21 times to show the pagination working!

I could take this so much further. For example, the repetition of comic data can easily be replaced with any of those 100 comics we have in our fixture data. Also, I could make a PHPUnit or Behat test to show that; this works not only at the pagination level, but the user will not see items that are not theirs.

Heck, let's do that now really quickly, we set up Behat in *Chapter 3*, *Routing*, so using that we can make our `behat.yml` as seen here: `https://github.com/alnutile/recipes/blob/master/behat.yml#L15.`

Add the domain context and write the test:

`https://github.com/alnutile/recipes/blob/master/features/wishlist/wishlist.feature`

Then write the `DomainContext` file for that:

`https://github.com/alnutile/recipes/blob/master/features/bootstrap/WishListPageDomainContext.php`

We now have a passing Behat test!

```
vagrant@homestead:~/Code/recipes$ vendor/bin/behat -swishlist_domain --append-snippets
Feature: Setting up WishList area
    Show users withlist items but not other users
    As an logged in user
    So I can manage them but not see others

  Scenario: User visits wishlist page and sees only their wishlists
    Given I login and visit the wishlist page
    Then I should see Lorna but not see Spiderman

1 scenario (1 passed)
2 steps (2 passed)
0m0.76s (18.55Mb)
vagrant@homestead:~/Code/recipes$
```

Now let's back it up with a Behat UI context page. Once again, add this to your `behat.yml` file:

`https://github.com/alnutile/recipes/blob/master/behat.yml#L18`

Then add the UI context file:

`https://github.com/alnutile/recipes/blob/master/features/bootstrap/WishListPageUIContext.php`

And we have a passing test there too! Simple!

One thing to keep in mind is that the Faker library is not loaded in a production environment, so factories that rely on Faker for model data won't work in production and tests that rely on that factory data will fail.

See also

 ▸ **Laracasts (database seeding and model factories):** `https://laracasts.com/series/intermediate-laravel/episodes/9`
 ▸ **Laravel docs (never hurts to read these):** `https://laravel.com/docs/5.2/seeding`

Adding a file upload to user profile

Now the user has a profile. We are going to add file upload. I will walk through the process, like previously, using Behat so we can see the process from the "outside in", for example, how the product owner sees the feature and builds from the "inside out", for example, where the classes take a message and process it to make a response.

Getting ready

The previous recipe will help set up the profile area but honestly any form you are working on will do.

How to do it...

1. Let us first write our Behat user story as a starter point. This will help take on that task in a more "test-first" process. So our test file `features/profile/profile_ image.feature` looks like this:

```
@javascript
Feature: User can upload image to profile
  Can upload an image to their profile
  Any authenticated user
  So the site will have a sense of community

  @cleanup_user_profile
  Scenario: Can upload image to profile page edit page
    Given I am on the page to edit my profile
    Then I should be able to upload an image file
    And then see it on my profile view page
```

2. Then our `behat.yml` is made aware of this new "suite" to test:

```
profile_image_domain:
    paths: [ %paths.base%/features/profile]
    contexts: [ ProfileImageDomainContext ]
profile_image_ui:
    paths: [ %paths.base%/features/profile]
    contexts: [ ProfileImageUIContext ]
```

3. Then, just like before, we make the Behat context file for that in `features/bootstrap/ProfileImageDomainContext.php`, setting it up for Behat to fill in the blanks for us:

```php
class ProfileImageDomainContext extends MinkContext implements Context, SnippetAcc
{

    use \Illuminate\Foundation\Testing\DatabaseTransactions, WishListTrait, LoginT

    private $baseUrl;
    private $profile;

    /**
     * @var \App\Repositories\ProfileRepository
     */
    private $repo;

    public function __construct()
    {
        $this->baseUrl = env('APP_URL');
    }

}
```

4. Now I will run the `behat` command:

```
alfrednutile@ubuntu:~/Code/recipes$ vendor/bin/behat -sprofile_image_domain --append-snippets
@javascript
Feature: User can upload image to profile
  Can upload an image to their profile
  Any authenticated user
  So the site will have a sense of community

  @cleanup_user_profile
  Scenario: Can upload image to profile page edit page
    Given I am on the page to edit my profile
    Then I should be able to upload an image file
    And then see it on my profile view page

1 scenario (1 undefined)
3 steps (3 undefined)
0m1.55s (20.46Mb)

u features/bootstrap/ProfileImageDomainContext.php - `I am on the page to edit my profile` definition added
u features/bootstrap/ProfileImageDomainContext.php - `I should be able to upload an image file` definition added
u features/bootstrap/ProfileImageDomainContext.php - `then see it on my profile view page` definition added
alfrednutile@ubuntu:~/Code/recipes$
```

5. Now the file has the methods stubbed out for me!

```
/**
 * @var \App\Repositories\ProfileRepository
 */
private $repo;

public function __construct()
{
    $this->baseUrl = env('APP_URL');
}

/**
 * @Given I am on the page to edit my profile
 */
public function iAmOnThePageToEditMyProfile()
{
    throw new PendingException();
}

/**
 * @Then I should be able to upload an image file
 */
public function iShouldBeAbleToUploadAnImageFile()
{
    throw new PendingException();
}

/**
 * @Then then see it on my profile view page
 */
```

6. I will use the first step to set up the state or "world" we need, the user, and the profile, and make sure we have a fixture file:

```
/**
 * @Given I am on the page to edit my profile
 */
public function iAmOnThePageToEditMyProfile()
{
    //using this step to setup the "world"
    // User
    // User's Profile
    // Image fixtures in place
    $this->user = factory(\App\User::class)->create();

    Auth::login($this->user);

    if(!File::exists(base_path('tests/fixtures/example_profile.jpg')))
        File::copy(base_path('tests/fixtures/profile.jpg'), base_path('tests/fixtures/example_profile.jpg'));

    //make sure I have a profile
    factory(\App\Profile::class)->create(['user_id' => $this->user->id]);
}
```

7. Then we will build the `Request`, note; we can fake a request! This means, as you will see later, we will be ready to plug the methods into the controller since we already handle the request here just as it will come in to the controller:

```
/**
 * @Then I should be able to upload an image file
 */
public function iShouldBeAbleToUploadAnImageFile()
{
    //make file payload request since i will have the repository deal with it
    $request = new \Illuminate\Http\Request();
    $file = new \Symfony\Component\HttpFoundation\FileBag();
    $path = base_path('tests/fixtures/example_profile.jpg');
    $originalName = 'example_profile.jpg';
    $upload = new \Illuminate\Http\UploadedFile($path, $originalName, null, null, null, TRUE);
    $file->set('profile_image', $upload);
    $request->files = $file;
    $this->repo = new \App\Repositories\ProfileRepository();
    $results = $this->repo->uploadUserProfileImage($request);

    PHPUnit::assertTrue($results, "Repo did not return true");

    PHPUnit::assertTrue(File::exists(public_path($this->user->id . '/example_profile.jpg')), "File Not found");
}
```

8. Notice right here we can make our `Repository` class take the request and do that work, leaving the soon to be made controller with not much to do or test!

```
$this->repo = new \App\Repositories\ProfileRepository();
$results = $this->repo->uploadUserProfileImage($request);
```

9. Now to look at the class managing the request. I will go into more detail in the *How it works...* section of the same recipe:

```php
class ProfileRepository
{

    public function getProfileForAuthenticatedUser()
    {
        return Profile::where('user_id', Auth::user()->id)->firstOrFail();
    }

    public function uploadUserProfileImage(Request $request)
    {
        if($request->file('profile_image') && $request->file('profile_image')->isValid())
        {

            Log::info("Going to save the file");

            $request->file('profile_image')->move(public_path(Auth::user()->id), 'example_profile.jpg');
            return true;
        }

        Log::info("No file :(");

        return false;
    }
}
```

10. Then I wrap up the test with the following example, as I get the data from the `ProfileRepository` class and verify it has what I expect:

```php
/**
 * @Then then see it on my profile view page
 */
public function thenSeeItOnMyProfileViewPage()
{
    //Reloading the profile to see if it now has the image
    $this->profile = $this->repo->getProfileForAuthenticatedUser();
    PHPUnit::assertArrayHasKey('profile_image', $this->profile->toArray(), "Key for image not found with profile");
    PHPUnit::assertTrue($this->profile->toArray()['profile_image'], "File not found with profile");
}
```

11. The `ProfileRepository` class is pretty simple really; it will return `profile_image`:

```php
public function getProfileForAuthenticatedUser()
{
    return Profile::where('user_id', Auth::user()->id)->firstOrFail();
}
```

12. Done with our domain-level work! Your classes are ready for the controller to use! Now to focus on the UI and make this work, just like previously we use `--init` to stub out the file `features/bootstrap/ProfileImageUIContext.php`.

13. We will start hitting that in a moment but let's make our controller:

```
>php artisan make:controller ProfileEditController
```

14. We simply plug into the controller what we did in the domain previously, letting the controller do very little as it only managed good and bad responses!

```php
class ProfileEditController extends Controller
{
    public function getAuthenticatedUsersProfileToEdit(ProfileRepository $repository)
    {
        try
        {
            $profile = $repository->getProfileForAuthenticatedUser();

            if(!Gate::allows('edit-profile', $profile))
                return redirect()->route('home')->with('message', "This is not your profile :

            return view('profile.edit', compact('profile'));
        }
        catch (ModelNotFoundException $e)
        {
            return redirect()->route('home')->with('message', "Could not find your profile :
        }
        catch (\Exception $e)
        {
            return redirect()->route('home')->with('message', "Error getting profile :(");
        }
    }
}
```

15. Now for the route:

```
Route::group(['middleware' => ['web']], function () {

    Route::auth();

    Route::get('profile/edit', 'ProfileEditController@getAuthenticatedUsersProfileToEdit')->name('profile.edit');
    Route::put('profile/edit', 'ProfileEditController@updateAuthenticatedUsersProfile')->name('profile.update');
```

16. And the page to show the form for the `get` route previously: `resources/views/profile/edit.blade.php`

```
@section('content')

    <div class="row">
        <div class="col-md-8 col-lg-offset-2">
            <form action="{{ route('profile.update') }}" method="POST" enctype="multipart/form-data">
                <input type="hidden" name="_method" value="PUT">
                <input type="hidden" name="_token" value="{{ csrf_token() }}">

                <div class="form-group @if($errors->has('profile_image')) has-error @endif">
                    <label for="profile_image">Profile Image</label>
                    <input type="file" id="profile_image" name="profile_image"/>
                    <p>Upload your image?</p>
                    @if($errors->has('profile_image'))
                        <span class="help-block">{{ $errors->first('profile_image') }}</span>
                    @endif
                </div>
                <div class="well well-sm">
                    <button type="submit" class="btn btn-primary">Save</button>
                    <a class="btn btn-link pull-right" href="{{ route('profile') }}"><i class="fa fa-backward"></i> Back</a>
                </div>
            </form>
        </div>
    </div>
@endsection
```

17. Finally, the method to handle the upload or the `PUT` request in our controller from step 14, which talks to the `app/Repositories/ProfileRepository.php` repository, I showed previously during the Domain work:

```
public function updateAuthenticatedUsersProfile(Requests\ProfileEditRequest $request, ProfileRepository $repository)
{
    try
    {
        /**
         * We do auth at the ProfileRequest level
         */
        $repository->uploadUserProfileImage($request);

        return redirect()->route('profile')->with('message', 'Image Updated');
    }
    catch (ModelNotFoundException $e)
    {
        return redirect()->route('home')->with('message', 'Could not find your profile ');
    }
    catch (\Exception $e)
    {
        return redirect()->route('home')->with('message', 'Error getting profile ');
    }
}
```

18. And we fill in the UI test to run against the site to show the whole thing just working, you can see that file here: `https://github.com/alnutile/recipes/blob/master/features/bootstrap/ProfileImageUIContext.php`:

```
vagrant@homestead:~/Code/recipes$ vendor/bin/behat -sprofile_image_ui
@javascript
Feature: User can upload image to profile
  Can upload an image to their profile
  Any authenticated user
  So the site will have a sense of community

  @cleanup_user_profile
  Scenario: Can upload image to profile page edit page
    Given I am on the page to edit my profile
    Then I should be able to upload an image file
    And then see it on my profile view page

1 scenario (1 passed)
3 steps (3 passed)
0m13.95s (18.16Mb)
vagrant@homestead:~/Code/recipes$ |
```

19. Since it is running Selenium2, it pops open Chrome and I can see the following output:

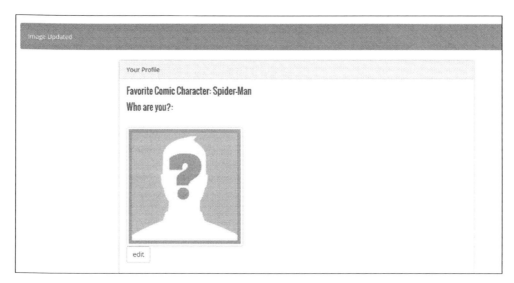

How it works...

OK, there is a lot here—let me cover the file part first and then I will go into some details.

The file upload part really only came down to a few things. One, the form is a multipart form under `enctype`:

```
        <div class="col-md-8 col-lg-offset-2">
            <form action="{{ route('profile.update') }}" method="POST" enctype="multipart/form-data">
```

Notice in the following that we set the method to `PUT`. `PUT` being better for dealing with updating a record:

```
<form action="{{ route('profile.update') }}" method="POST" enctype="multipart/form-data">
    <input type="hidden" name="_method" value="PUT">
    <input type="hidden" name="_token" value="{{ csrf_token() }}">
```

Then the input field has the ID of `profile_image`, which is what we set the input field in the domain tests as to what I was looking for the file in:

```
        <div class="form-group @if($errors->has('profile_image')) has-error @endif">
            <label for="profile_image">Profile Image</label>
            <input type="file" id="profile_image" name="profile_image"/>
            <p>Upload your image?</p>
            @if($errors->has('profile_image'))
                <span class="help-block">{{ $errors->first('profile_image') }}</span>
            @endif
        </div>
```

Then I save the image, using the `Request` method seen in the controller to talk to the file and move it to where I want to store it.

The controller's only job in all of this is to take the request, pass it to the correct class and method, and deal with the response, good or bad. This makes our testing so much easier and we can fully build this out and plug it in with total confidence.

The rest of this just shows again how we can work on code inside tests both to help us think through the steps we need to perform, to write our classes out before we even get to the controller or route, and also to help our code read better overall.

▸ Laracasts: file upload 101: `https://laracasts.com/lessons/file-uploads-101`

Validating the file upload

With all the previous work in place for the file upload, now I want to cover file validation. For this, we will let the Laravel `request` method handle the logic for us. This way, we can deal with all of this outside the controller, so when we plug it in we will be ready to go. I will cover checking file size and type.

Getting ready

Use the previous recipe to set up sound groundwork. I will use that recipe to then create a test around size and type of file.

How to do it...

1. Make the custom form validation request:

    ```
    >php artisan make:request ProfileUploadRequest
    ```

2. Now add to our Behat feature `features/profile/profile_image.feature` some of the things we are looking for:

    ```
    Scenario: Dealing with edge cases
      Given I upload a non jpg file I should get an error message
      Given I upload a file that is too large I should get an error message
    ```

3. Then we run the step in the following image to stub out our steps in the context file. This is due to the `--append-snippets` switch:

```
vagrant@homestead:~/Code/recipes$ vendor/bin/behat --sprofile_image_domain --append-snippets --name="Dealing"
@javascript
Feature: User can upload image to profile
  Can upload an image to their profile
  Any authenticated user
  So the site will have a sense of community

  Scenario: Dealing with edge cases
    Given I upload a non jpg file I should get an error message
    Given I upload a file that is too large I should get an error message

1 scenario (1 undefined)
2 steps (2 undefined)
0m0.42s (14.63Mb)

u features/bootstrap/ProfileImageDomainContext.php - `I upload a non jpg file I should get an error message` definitio
u features/bootstrap/ProfileImageDomainContext.php - `I upload a file that is too large I should get an error message
tion added
vagrant@homestead:~/Code/recipes$
```

And we are set to start writing the code needed to handle this!

4. Our test will look like this as it verifies the file type, in this case, I pass in png but in my form request I set it to jpg:

```
/**
 * @Given I upload a non jpg file I should get an error message
 */
public function iUploadANonJpgFileIShouldGetAnErrorMessage()
{
    $request = new \App\Http\Requests\ProfileUploadRequest();

    $file = new \Symfony\Component\HttpFoundation\FileBag();
    $path = base_path('tests/fixtures/example_profile.png');
    $originalName = 'example_profile.png';
    $upload = new \Illuminate\Http\UploadedFile($path, $originalName, null, null, null, TRUE);
    $file->set('profile_image', $upload);
    $request->files = $file;

    $rules = $request->rules();

    $validator = Validator::make($request->all(), $rules);

    $fails = $validator->fails();

    PHPUnit::assertTrue($fails);
}
```

5. You can see the form request here:

```php
class ProfileUploadRequest extends Request
{

    protected $kilobytes = 2000;
    /**
     * Determine if the user is authorized to make this request.
     *
     * @return bool
     */
    public function authorize()
    {
        return false;
    }


    /**
     * Get the validation rules that apply to the request.
     *
     * @return array
     */
    public function rules()
    {
        return [
            'profile_image' => 'mimes:jpeg,jpg|between:0,' . $this->getKilobytes(),
        ];
    }


    /**
     * @return int
     */
    public function getKilobytes()
    {
        return $this->kilobytes;
    }


    /**
     * @param int $kilobytes
     */
    public function setKilobytes($kilobytes)
    {
        $this->kilobytes = $kilobytes;
    }

}
```

6. And then I add one more "step" into the context file to cover the file size:

```php
/**
 * @Given I upload a file that is too large I should get an error message
 */
public function iUploadAFileThatIsTooLargeIShouldGetAnErrorMessage()
{
    $request = new \App\Http\Requests\ProfileUploadRequest();

    $file = new \Symfony\Component\HttpFoundation\FileBag();
    $path = base_path('tests/fixtures/example_profile.jpg');
    $originalName = 'example_profile.jpg';
    $upload = new \Illuminate\Http\UploadedFile($path, $originalName, null, 10000, null, TRUE);
    $file->set('profile_image', $upload);
    $request->files = $file;

    $request->setKilobytes(4);
    $rules = $request->rules();

    $validator = Validator::make($request->all(), $rules);

    $fails = $validator->fails();

    var_dump($validator->errors());

    PHPUnit::assertTrue($fails);
}
```

7. Then run our test to know it is working and we are done!

```
@javascript
Feature: User can upload image to profile
  Can upload an image to their profile
  Any authenticated user
  So the site will have a sense of community

  Scenario: Dealing with edge cases
    Given I upload a non jpg file I should get an error message

    Given I upload a file that is too large I should get an error message

        /home/vagrant/Code/recipes/features/bootstrap/ProfileImageDomainContext.php:141:
        class Illuminate\Support\MessageBag#4326 (2) {
          protected $messages =>
          array(1) {
            'profile_image' =>
            array(1) {
              [0] =>
              string(52) "The profile image must be between 0 and 4 kilobytes."
            }
          }
          protected $format =>
          string(8) ":message"
        }

1 scenario (1 passed)
2 steps (2 passed)
0m0.51s (16.05Mb)
vagrant@homestead:~/Code/recipes$
```

8. That's it, we already had the `Requests\ProfileUploadRequest` plugged into the controller, as we inject it right at the top of this method!

```
public function updateAuthenticatedUsersProfile(Requests\ProfileUploadRequest $request, ProfileRepository $repository)
{
    try
    {
        /**
         * We do auth at the ProfileRequest level
         */
        $repository->uploadUserProfileImage($request);

        return redirect()->route('profile')->with('message', "Image Updated");
    }
    catch (ModelNotFoundException $e)
    {

        return redirect()->route('home')->with('message', "Could not find your profile :(");
    }
    catch (\Exception $e)
    {
        return redirect()->route('home')->with('message', "Error getting profile :(");
    }
}
```

How it works...

Pretty neat how simple Laravel makes this! With the form validation request, we made, we can protect the controller method and validate incoming data before it even hits the inside of that method. And with this form request class we see how "easy" it is to test outside the controller!

Then we use the validation feature built into Laravel to quickly apply rules to the `profile_image`.

See also

- ▶ Laravel docs: `https://laravel.com/docs/5.2/requests`
- ▶ Laravel validation: `https://laravel.com/docs/5.2/validation`

Saving files to S3

With the previous recipe, I covered how to upload and save files. I will show how easy it is to get those onto S3. By the time we are done, we will have our files uploaded to S3 and when needed for testing our app will deal with the local switch for us. I will show this both at the upload level and the view level.

Getting ready

If you did the previous recipe, you will have the basic classes you need to make this happen. Also, you need to make an S3 bucket on AWS. I will cover this a bit *but* read more on their website, since doing this right is a skill and you should not be using your AWS key and AWS secret in your app. You should use a set made for the app; for a user you make just for this app.

How to do it...

1. We need a bucket! Log into AWS and make a user. Then download the API key and secret you get with that user:

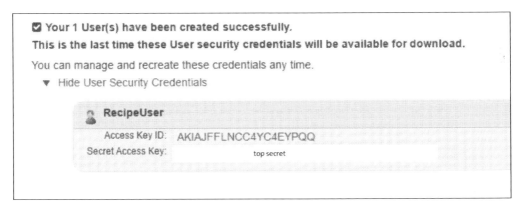

2. Save those to your local machine and enter them like this into your .env file, making sure to match the key name just as it is here:

```
AWS_REGION=us-east-1
AWS_SECRET_ACCESS_KEY=topsecret
AWS_ACCESS_KEY_ID=AKIAJFFLNCC4YC4EYPQQ
```

3. Now update your `config/filesystems.php` file to use the following:

```php
<?php

return [

    'default' => env('FILESYSTEM_DEFAULT', 's3'),

    'cloud' => 's3',

    'disks' => [

        'local' => [
            'driver' => 'local',
            'root' => storage_path('app'),
        ],

        'public' => [
            'driver' => 'local',
            'root' => storage_path('app/public'),
            'visibility' => 'public',
        ],

        's3' => [
            'driver' => 's3',
            'key' => env('AWS_ACCESS_KEY_ID'),
            'secret' => env('AWS_SECRET_ACCESS_KEY'),
            'region' => 'us-east-1',
            'bucket' => env('PROFILE_IMAGE_BUCKET'),
        ],

    ],

];
```

4. We are setting s3 to the default. Later, I will explain why in the *How it works...* section. Add to your `.env` file, this line but note it is marked out for now:

    `#FILESYSTEM_DEFAULT=local`

5. Back to AWS, go to the S3 bucket and make a bucket called `recipes-book` and add that to your `.env` as well like this:

    `PROFILE_IMAGE_BUCKET='recipes-book'`

6. And let's install the library needed to talk to AWS:

    `>composer require league/flysystem-aws-s3-v3 ~1.0`

7. Now we need to make sure the user we made has a policy to access this bucket. Go to that user and look for the **Permissions** tab:

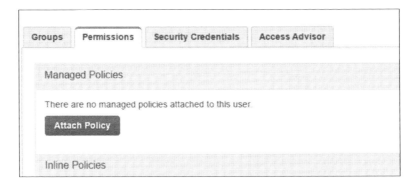

8. Attach this policy for starters:

```
{
    "Version": "2012-10-17",
    "Statement": [
        {
            "Effect": "Allow",
            "Action": [
                "s3:ListBucket"
            ],
            "Resource": [
                "arn:aws:s3:::recipes-book"
            ]
        },
        {
            "Sid": "Stmt1482005994000",
            "Effect": "Allow",
            "Action": [
                "s3:GetObject",
                "s3:PutObject"
            ],
            "Resource": [
                "arn:aws:s3:::recipes-book/*"
            ]
        }
    ]
}
```

9. Alright, setup is done! Let's change some code, starting from the inside with `app/Repositories/ProfileRepository.php`:

```php
*/
class ProfileRepository
{

    public function getProfileForAuthenticatedUser()
    {
        return Profile::where('user_id', Auth::user()->id)->firstOrFail();
    }

    public function uploadUserProfileImage(Request $request)
    {
        if($request->file('profile_image') && $request->file('profile_image')->isValid())
        {

            Log::info("Going to save the file");

            $contents = file_get_contents($request->file('profile_image')->getRealPath());

            Storage::put($this->isLocalOrS3() . Auth::user()->id . '/example_profile.jpg', $contents);

            return true;
        }

        Log::info("No file :(");

        return false;
    }

    protected function isLocalOrS3()
    {
        return (env('FILESYSTEM_DEFAULT') == 'local') ? 'public' : '';
    }

}
```

More on this will be in the *How it works...* section.

That is it! When you now upload a file, it will be on S3! How do we show the file?

10. Let's now update how we show the file, open the `app/Profile.php` and we are going to update this to consider S3 or local:

```php
class Profile extends Model
{
    protected $fillable = [
        'favorite_comic_character'
    ];

    protected $appends = ['profile_image'];

    public function getProfileImageAttribute()
    {

        $path    = (!Auth::guest()) ? Auth::user()->id . '/example_profile.jpg' : false;

        if(Auth::guest()) {
            $image = false;
        }
        elseif(is_local_or_s3()) {
            $image = (Storage::exists(is_local_or_s3() . $path)) ? Storage::url($path): false;
        }
        else {
            $image = (Storage::exists($path)) ? $this->getSignedUrl($path, 10): false;
        }

        return $this->attributes['profile_image'] = $image;
    }

    public function scopeMyProfile($query)
    {
        return $query->where('user_id', Auth::user()->id)->firstOrFail();
    }

    public function getSignedUrl($filename_and_path, $expires_minutes = '10', $bucket = false)
    {
        /**
         * @var S3MultiRegionClient $client
         */
        $client    = Storage::getDriver()->getAdapter()->getClient();
        $bucket    = ($bucket)?:env('PROFILE_IMAGE_BUCKET');

        $command = $client->getCommand('GetObject', [
            'Bucket' => $bucket,
            'Key' => $filename_and_path
        ]);

        $request = $client->createPresignedRequest($command, Carbon::now()->addMinutes($expires_minutes));

        return (string) $request->getUri();
    }
}
```

I will explain `getSignedUrl` in the *How it works...* section as well.

11. Now the view has exactly what it needs to display the URL to the image, whether it is local or S3. Here is the final code for the view `resources/views/profile/show.blade.php`:

```
@extends('layout')

@section('content')
    <div class="container">
        <div class="row">
            <div class="col-lg-8 col-lg-offset-2">
                <div class="panel panel-default">
                    <div class="panel-heading">Your Profile</div>
                    <div class="panel-body">

                        <ul class="list-unstyled">
                            <li>
                                <H4>Favorite Comic Character: {{ $profile->favorite_comic_character }}</H4>
                            </li>

                            <li><h4>Who are you?:</h4> <br>
                                @if ($profile->profile_image)
                                    <img src="{{$profile->profile_image }}" alt="" class="img-thumbnail img-responsive">
                                @endif
                            </li>
                            <li>
                                <a href="{{ route('profile.edit') }}" class="btn btn-default">edit</a>
                            </li>
                        </ul>

                    </div>
                </div>

            </div>
        </div>
    </div>
@endsection
```

12. Then set up a symlink as noted in the `https://laravel.com/docs/5.2/filesystem` docs in your public folder to the `storage/app/public` as storage. This is only needed, though, for public images which we are not really using here except to test this out but you can see how it can work if needed.

How it works...

Now for the nitty-gritty details! First we make a user in AWS. Why? Because if your info leaks out, it is better to have it be the key and secret for one application/user and not for your entire account! As you build more apps, including staging areas, you will only have to change this one application's credentials if there is an issue. So please do this!

Then we save that key and secret as needed per the Amazon and Laravel guidelines by using, in the `.env` file, the key, region, and secret `AWS_REGION`, `AWS_SECRET_ACCESS_KEY`, and `AWS_ACCESS_KEY_ID` syntax. And since the `.env` *never goes to GitHub* but only on your machine and the machine you deploy to, your credentials are safe.

Then we set up the policy for the user. Amazon recommends attaching these to groups and putting users into groups so do that later, but for now we can just do this. Note the policy is very focused, we limit the user's access to this bucket—very cool how this works.

I then move on to the repository, having it now talk to `Storage`. I still use `$request` to get the file's content but then, using storage I can stream it right to AWS. I use a method here to help with one thing and that is to know if we are dealing with local, if we are then I will put the file into `public/`, which seems to be the default for Laravel per the docs I link to below. I could choose not use this and put it into the `storage` folder but then how would I show it on the page? Later, I will turn this into a helper.

Now that it is working how do we get the file? That is when I open back up the model `Profile` and update the code I had there to deal with showing the file. Let's break it down:

Figure 6 S3 Signed URL

I use this method to get the file and in here, with the helper, I decide if we are local or S3. At that point, I can use `Storage` to get the URL for display purposes.

Now, if it is on S3, I want a signed URL. Of course, I could just use the `url()` method and that is fine if I set the bucket to static website under properties in the AWS console as seen here:

But in this case I want to protect these files and only show them for 10 minutes. Okay, so a profile file is a bad example but the point is "wow, this is powerful".

Here is the method to deal with getting the signed URL:

```
public function getSignedUrl($filename_and_path, $expires_minutes = '10', $bucket = false)
{
    /**
     * @var S3MultiRegionClient $client
     */
    $client     = Storage::getDriver()->getAdapter()->getClient();
    $bucket     = ($bucket)?:env('PROFILE_IMAGE_BUCKET');

    $command = $client->getCommand('GetObject', [
        'Bucket' => $bucket,
        'Key' => $filename_and_path
    ]);

    $request = $client->createPresignedRequest($command, Carbon::now()->addMinutes($expires_minutes));

    return (string) $request->getUri();
}
```

Pretty amazing we can get a URL that will offer access for x minutes! Using this, we can have secure content on our site, and of course we just benefit from having our files on S3, more on that in a moment.

Here is the helper btw is this file here `app/helpers.php`:

```php
<?php

if(! function_exists('is_local_or_s3'))
{
    function is_local_or_s3()
    {
        return (env('FILESYSTEM_DEFAULT') == 'local') ? 'public/' : '';
    }
}
```

I register this with `composer.json` like so:

```json
    ],
    "autoload": {
        "classmap": [
            "database"
        ],
        "psr-4": {
            "App\\": "app/"
        },
        "files": [
            "app/helpers.php"
        ]
    },
```

Also note, when we set up our `config/filesystems.php`, I made the bucket name part of the `.env` file. Ideally, you will have a bucket for *staging* and one for *production* to make your process safer and cleaner. By defaulting to `s3`, I did not have to write `Storage::disk('s3')` in the app. Though I could have made the helper swap this out for me, I think the other way was a bit cleaner, especially when `s3` is my main goal here.

Overall, using S3 is a huge win. You separate your files off the server so there are no worries if you need to rebuild the server or scale. You get re-visioning on S3 if you want and auto backups! It really is a good practice to get into.

See also

> ▸ Laravel docs: filesystem: `https://laravel.com/docs/5.2/filesystem`

6
Adding Angular to Your App

In this chapter, we will cover the following topics:

- ▸ Adding Angular search to our search page
- ▸ Handling Angular and Ajax requests
- ▸ Paginating our Angular results
- ▸ Testing an Angular page with Behat
- ▸ Creating a relationship with favorites
- ▸ Building a favorites Ajax widget in Angular
- ▸ Validating incoming input
- ▸ Using the CORS protection
- ▸ Using Elixir and Gulp to set up Angular

Introduction

I will show you how easy it is to get Angular into your application. I will also go over some workflow tips and tricks. When you are done with this chapter, you will have an easier time installing and plugging in Angular, as a widget into any part of your site!

Let's start by installing Angular 1.5. I will use this version over 2.x as it will be supported for quite some time, and the usage paradigm of it more closely follows what I am used to in Vue and other great JavaScript frameworks.

Getting ready

Any base installation of Laravel will work. In our case, we will be using the one from all the previous recipes.

How to do it...

1. Let's install bower to help us install Angular:

    ```
    >sudo npm install -g bower
    ```

2. Then, we need to initialize our app's bower file:

    ```
    >bower init
    ```

    Just answer default to all the questions.

3. Let's install bower to help us get Angular:

    ```
    >bower install angular
    ```

4. Then, by starting simple, I will copy over the file called `bower_compontents/ angular/angular.js` into my `public/js` folder. Later, we will use Gulp for this:

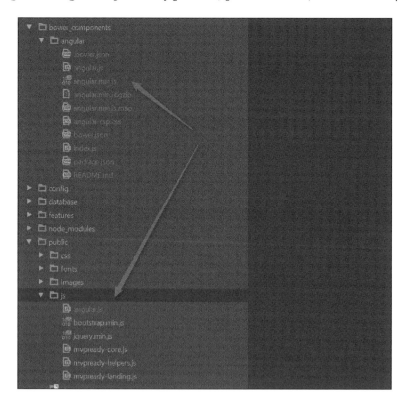

5. Alright, let's put `angular.js` into the layout page:

```
<!-- Bootstrap core JavaScript

<!-- Core JS -->
<script src="/js/jquery.min.js"></script>
<script src="/js/angular.js"></script>
<script src="/js/bootstrap.min.js"></script>
```

Note that it is under jQuery that I pulled in during the theme recipe, you need to put jQuery first so that Angular does not try and use its lite version of jQuery.

6. Now, let's add one more file called `app.js` for our code in the `public/js` folder; and register it under the `angular.js` include file:

```
<!-- Bootstrap core JavaScript

<!-- Core JS -->
<script src="/js/jquery.min.js"></script>
<script src="/js/angular.js"></script>
<script src="/js/app.js"></script>
<script src="/js/bootstrap.min.js"></script>
```

7. We will have a simple Controller to register `angular.module`.

```
(function(){
    'use strict';

    angular.module('app', []);

    function MainController()
    {
        var vm = this;
        vm.open = open;

        activate();

        function activate()
        {
            console.log("Here is angular");
        }

    }

    angular.module('app')
        .controller('MainController', MainController);

})();
```

8. Not much yet! But now, go to the browser and open the JavaScript Console by going here in Chrome:

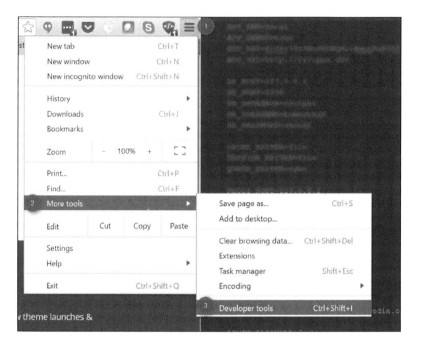

9. Then, click on the **Console** tab:

10. Add `np-app` to the body tag on `resources/views/layout.blade.php` so that it looks like this:

```
<body ng-app="app">
```

11. Now, add the controller to your home page, `resources/views/home/_search.blade.php` partial:

12. Now, reload the page, and you will see this:

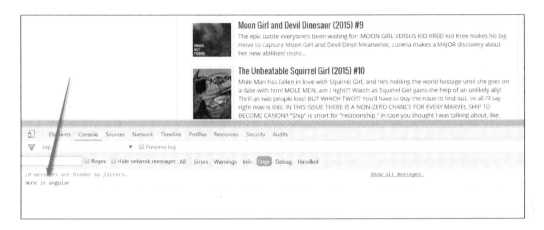

13. We are now ready to build a widget or some other feature on our site using Angular!

How it works...

The first part of this is the installation, thanks to Homestead, most of this is ready to go, npm, node and so on. Then I use bower, though I would prefer not to use bower; but `npm install angular` was not working to install angular, or at least, pull it down. Bower made a `bower.json` file, so other teammates can get the setup just as easily. You should include these steps in `readme.md` so that they will know to get started by running `bower install`. But in this case, I am going to include bower's folder in GitHub. Yes, I do not want to run it on every CI build, I do not want to add that time to my builds and add that point of failure. And overall, I am not going to use a ton of JavaScript on this app. Later, I will use bower installer and will no longer need bower components.

Next, I will add the files to the `layouts` blade page, putting jQuery above Angular. As noted, this is key since it needs to let jQuery take care of the things it takes care of.

Then, I copied it over to public. Later on, Gulp will do this for me as I work, but for now, I just want to keep it simple at the recipe level. Then, my `app.js` file comes after it. In this file, I do three very key things:

```
(function() {
    'use strict';

    angular.module('app', []);          ①


    function MainController()            ②
    {
        var vm = this;
        vm.open = open;

        activate();

        function activate()
        {
            console.log("Here is angular");
        }

    }

    angular.module('app')
        .controller('MainController', MainController);   ③

})();
```

1. First, I instantiate the `angular.module` calling it `app` you will see me later on use in the `body` tag.

```
<body class="" ng-app="app">
```

If I called the app called `foo`, then I would put it in the body as `foo`. It is best to wrap this up above the level of work you are doing, not at the same level.

2. Second, I make a controller: a scope on the page that will render all the Angular-related markup between the opening and closing div. This it what it will look like:

```
(function() {
    'use strict';

    angular.module('app', []);


    function MainController()
    {
        var vm = this;
        vm.hello = "Hello Angular";

        activate();

        function activate()
        {
            console.log("Here is angular");
        }

    }

    angular.module('app')
        .controller('MainController', MainController);

})();
```

3. Plug it into `resources/views/home/_search.blade.php` as follows:

```
<form action="{{ route('home') }}" method="GET" class="form-horizontal" ng-controller="MainController as vm">
    <div class="input-group">
        <input type="text" name="name" class="form-control col-lg-10"
            placeholder="Search for your comic...">
        <span class="input-group-btn">
            <button type="submit" class="btn btn-primary">Search</button>
        </span>
        <div class="help-block">@{{ vm.hello }}</div>
    </div>
</form>
```

4. Then you will see this:

Third, I register my Controller with the `app` so when `ng-app` takes over it, will have my Controllers in its objects.

We will make something happen with this in the next recipe!

See also

▸ **Laracasts—Vue, nice alternative to Angular**: `https://laracasts.com/series/learning-vue-step-by-step`

▸ **John Papa—required reading as it helps you find a consistent style**: `http://www.johnpapa.net/angular-style-guide/`

Adding Angular search to our search page

In this section, we are going to convert the search to be Angular-based. What this means is that when the users will type in a word to search, they will then press **Search** and instead of reloading the page, we will do a request using Ajax and take the response of this request. I am not doing it because they type, due to API limitations at Marvel, but you could do this.

I need to also consider pagination later on and other odds and ends later on to this API.

Getting ready

It would be good to setup Angular as I did in the preceding recipe so that you are ready to start updating the `MainController` and your custom js file.

How to do it...

1. First, we set up `MainController` to look like this:

```
window Help
    (function(){
        'use strict';

        angular.module('app', []);


        function MainController()
        {
            var vm = this;
            vm.hello = "Hello Angular";
            vm.search = '';
            vm.searchFor = searchFor;
            vm.disableSearch = disableSearch;
            activate();

            function activate()
            {
                console.log("Here is angular");
            }

            function disableSearch()
            {
                return vm.search.length < 3;
            }

            function searchFor() {
                console.log("This is what I want to search for " + vm.search);
            }

        }

        angular.module('app')
            .controller('MainController', MainController);

    })();
```

I will create the `searchFor` method, and then define it in my `vm` area.

> *Placing bindable members at the top makes it easy to read and helps
> you to instantly identify which members of the controller can be bound
> and used in the View—John Papa Guide*

Then, I add `disableSearch` so that the button cannot be clicked before the user has some characters typed into the search input. And as mentioned previously, I pull it up into the `vm` area, since I will be using this in the View layer as well.

2. Now, I go into the `resources/views/home/_search.blade.php` View that I made and update the form to be controlled by Angular:

In this case, I add `novalidate` so that Angular can handle it and bypass the HTML validation. Then, I add the `vm.search` model so that we can bind this input to the model that I defined in the controller.

Now on `Submit`, I attach `ng-click` and `vm.searchFor`. I also set this to disable using `ng-disable` and the `vm.disableSearch()` function so that the user does not over-hit the Marvel API.

Lastly, just for effect, I add `help-block` to show the results of `vm.search` as the user types the text.

3. Now, when users type a word and click on `Search`, they see this:

4. Now, we need to send this request someplace! So, let's add `$http` to our `MainController` so that we can do a `GET` request to the backend.

```
function MainController($http)
{
    var vm = this;
    vm.hello = "Hello Angular";
    vm.search = '';                          2
    vm.searchFor = searchFor;
    vm.disableSearch = disableSearch;
    vm.searching = false;
    vm.error = false;
    vm.api_results = [];

    activate();

    function activate()
    {
        console.log("Here is angular");
    }

    function disableSearch()
    {
        return vm.search.length < 3;
    }

    function searchFor() {
        searchApiForComics(vm.search);
    }

    /**
     * @NOTE we can pull this out into a service as well
     */
    function searchApiForComics()          1
    {
        vm.searching = true;
        vm.error = false;
        $http.get('/api/v1/search')
            .success(function(response) {
                console.log(response);
                vm.searching = false;
                vm.api_results = response.data;
            })
            .error(function(response) {
                console.log("Error getting results");
                vm.error = true;
                vm.searching = false;
                console.log(response);
            });
    }
}
```

In *section 1* of the image, I add the function, which I will explain more thoroughly later on. But notice that in *section 2* , I do not introduce this to vm since the View layer does not need to access this.

5. When we run this, we get an error:

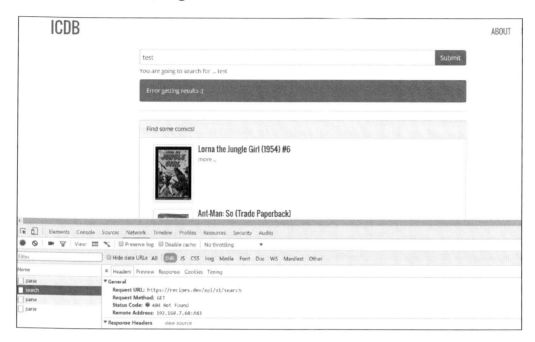

This is because we have not built it yet; see the next recipe for this one.

6. That's it; we officially have most of the setup that we need to make requests and handle the responses. Next recipe will go into how to output the response in Laravel, and then on the frontend how to handle the response on the frontend.

   We will also deal with the *Success* and *Error* of the response so that we can react as needed. In this case, I will show you an error. On Success, we will see later on how we can show this message and, of course, the results.

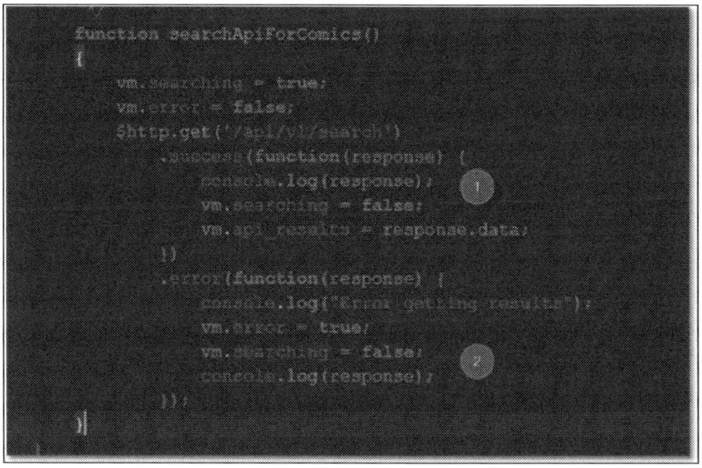

Figure 1 HTTP Success and Error

7. One more thing; I want to make sure to add my query string to the request and clearly define the type of request it is, for example, JSON.

Here, I update my GET function:

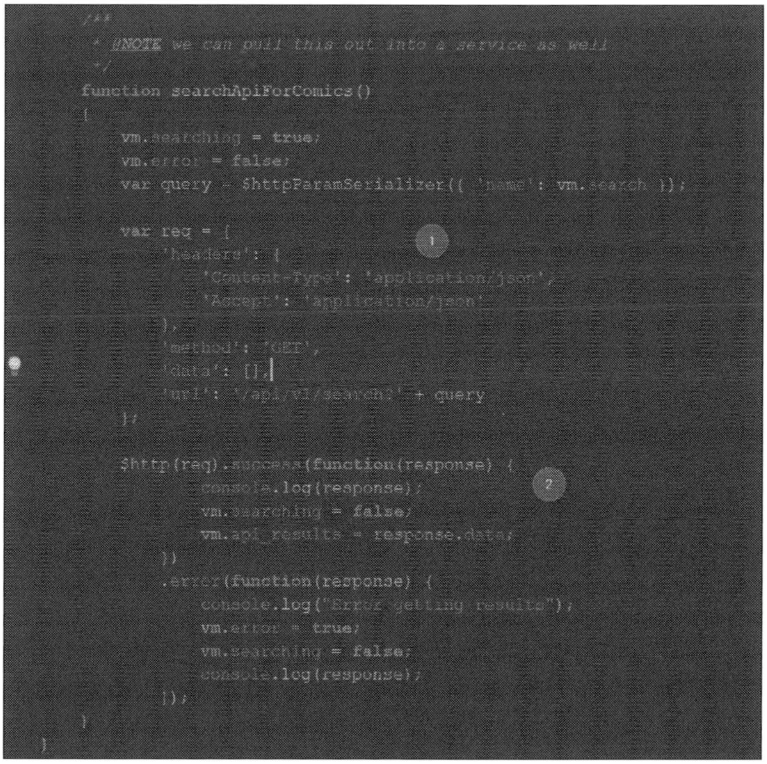

Here, we see the results, which I will cover in the *How it works...* section.

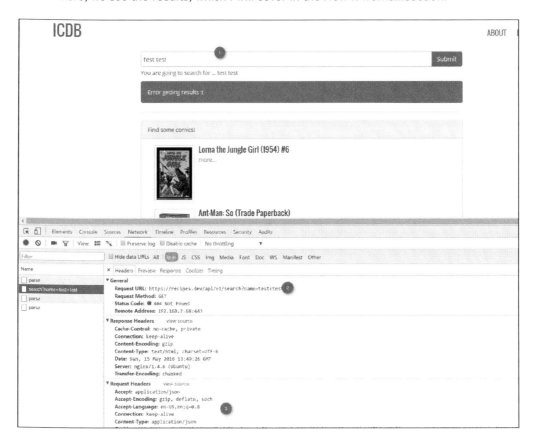

How it works...

To begin with, we set up our `MainController` to have some more `vm` state that `View` will later have access to. For example, `vm.searchFor` will be a method that I will introduce into the `View`, as well as `vm.disableSearch` to return `true` or `false` on the button to disable it or not.

Then, I go into the View called `resources/views/home/_search.blade.php` and add all of these methods and register `ng-model=vm.search`. This is the act of binding the input value to an Angular model for saving state and returning, in real time, any changes. We will see this in `help-block` later on.

I add `ng-click` to the submit area, so we take over it as well, leaving Angular to manage this form instead of HTML. As the page is rendered, HTML and then Angular kicks in and takes over the re-rendering of the content in the HTML. This is due to the `ng-app` that we registered earlier in the `resources/views/layout.blade.php` body tag and the `ng-controller` that we register here.

Using `ng-if`, I can set some hide and show features, and then turn them on and off throughout the process of the user's interaction with the form and the results of the backend.

Finally, I use the built-in the `$http` and `GET` Angular to send a request to the API, which does not exist yet. Now, I could talk directly to the Marvel API, but this would pass some `API KEY` and `PASSWORD` secrets into the browser that I do not want the user to see; therefore, I will make later on a Laravel API route just for this interaction. Also, you often get CORS issues going back and forth with APIs that are not in the same domain as your Angular application.

Notice too that I inject `$http` into the Controller. This is the Angular Dependency Injection service in action. Just like Laravel, it has a great DI to help inject these needed services:

```
MainController.$inject = ['$http', '$httpParamSerializer'];

function MainController($http, $httpParamSerializer)
{
    var vm = this;
    vm.hello = "Hello Angular";
```

Here is an updated version that I make sure to `$inject` it in as well so that later on, it will survive any minification work we do—`https://docs.angularjs.org/api/auto/service/$injector#usage`.

Note that I can take this further, as we learn with PHP designs, to make a controller just for this search, make a Service that talks to the Model and holds the business logic away from the controller, and so on. A lot of your knowledge of good design in PHP will carry over. I will links in the *See also* section to some items around this.

See also

- **John Papa guide controller as with VM**: `https://github.com/johnpapa/angular-styleguide/blob/master/a1/README.md#controlleras-with-vm`

- **John Papa guide and services**: `https://github.com/johnpapa/angular-styleguide/blob/master/a1/README.md#style-y035`

- **John Papa guide and keeping controllers focused**: `https://github.com/johnpapa/angular-styleguide/blob/master/a1/README.md#keep-controllers-focused`

Handling Angular and Ajax requests

In this recipe, we will build both the backend sections in Laravel to take an Angular request, and then respond back to Angular. We will output the information into the Angular frontend.

First, I will update the initial controller that lays out the page so that we can share both the initial layout and the response results layout instead of having one driven by Laravel and another driven by Angular.

Getting ready

See the previous recipe on setting up the request. In this section, we will just continue from there.

How to do it...

The following are the steps for handling Angular and Ajax requests:

1. I will install this `https://github.com/laracasts/PHP-Vars-To-Js-Transformer` library to begin with and use it in my Laravel controller:

    ```
    >composer require "Laracasts/utilities":"~2.0"
    ```

2. Then, I follow all the installation steps seen on their GitHub page:

    1. Run vendor publish, so I can alter the `config` file:

        ```
        >php artisan vendor:publish
        ```

2. Alter the `config` file `config/javascript.php` file; add a footer file and include it in the layout:

```
return [

    /*
    |--------------------------------------------------------------------------
    | View to Bind JavaScript Vars To
    |--------------------------------------------------------------------------
    |
    | Set this value to the name of the view (or partial) that
    | you want to prepend all JavaScript variables to.
    | This can be a single view, or an array of views.
    | Example: 'footer' or ['footer', 'bottom']
    |
    */
    'bind_js_vars_to_this_view' => 'footer',

    /*
    |--------------------------------------------------------------------------
    | JavaScript Namespace
    |--------------------------------------------------------------------------
    |
    | By default, we'll add variables to the global window object. However,
    | it's recommended that you change this to some namespace - anything.
    | That way, you can access vars, like "SomeNamespace.someVariable."
    |
    */
    'js_namespace' => 'window'

];
```

I will set `footer` for the bind.

3. Then, I will add the footer file as needed to `resources/views/footer.blade.php` so that it looks like this:

Figure 2 Footer Place Holder

There is not much there yet, more later!

3. Then, I will update our Controller, called `app/Http/Controllers/HomeController.php`, to set up the JavaScript `window` object to have our `api_results` right when the user visits this page. We will show this later:

```php
public function index(Request $request)
{
    $name = '';

    if ($request->input('name')) {
        $name = $request->input('name');
    }

    $results = $this->searchComicsRepository->getComicsByName($name);

    \JavaScript::put([
        'api_results' -> $results
    ]);

    return Response::view('home.index', compact('results'));
}
```

4. Then, I clean up the View to move the Angular scope up a level, so the form can live with the search results scope:

   1. I pull all the previous Laravel work into a partial `resources/views/home/_laravel_search_results.blade.php` so that it looks like this. I may never use this, but I just wanted to pull it out as a reference for later purposes.

```php
@if(empty($results['results']))
    <p>What are you waiting for?</p>
@else
    @foreach($results['results'] as $result)
        <div class="media">
            <div class="media-left col-lg-2 col-mg-2 col-sm-2">
                <a href="{{ $result['urls'][0]['url'] }}">
                    @if(isset($result['thumbnail']['path']))
                        <img class="media-object img-thumbnail img-responsive"
                            src="{{ $result['thumbnail']['path'] . '.' . $result['thumbnail']
                            alt="...">
                    @else
                        <img class="media-object" src="/images/placeholder.jpg" alt="...">
                    @endif
                </a>
            </div>
            <div class="media-body">
                <h4 class="media-heading">{{ $result['title'] }}</h4>
                {{ $result['description'] }} <a
                    href="{{ $result['urls'][0]['url'] }}">more...</a>
            </div>
        </div>
    @endforeach

@endif
```

2. Then, I create new file for the Angular template logic just to keep my files from getting too big—`resources/views/home/_angular_search_results.blade.php`:

```
<div class="panel panel-default">
    <div class="panel-heading">Find some comics!</div>
    <div class="panel-body">

        <div ng-repeat="result in vm.api_results.results">
            <div class="media">
                <div class="media-left col-lg-2 col-mq-2 col-sm-2">
                    <a href="@{{ $result['urls'][0]['url'] }}">
                        <img ng-if "result['thumbnail']['path']" class="media-object img-thumbnail img-responsive"
                            src="@{{ result['thumbnail']['path'] + '.' + result['thumbnail']['extension'] }}"
                            alt="...">
                        <img ng-if "!result['thumbnail']['path']" class="media-object" src="/images/placeholder.jpg"
                            alt="...">
                    </a>
                </div>
                <div class="media-body">
                    <h4 class="media-heading">@{{ result['title'] }}</h4>
                    @{{ result['description'] }} || <a
                        href="@{{ result['urls'][0]['url'] }}">more...</a>
                </div>
            </div>
        </div>
    </div>
</div>
```

I will cover more in the *How it works...* section.

3. Then, `resources/views/home/_search.blade.php` will look like this:

```
<div ng-controller="MainController as vm">

    <form method="GET" class="form-horizontal" novalidate>
        <div class="input-group">
            <input type="text" name="name" class="form-control col-lg-10"
                placeholder="Search for your comic..." ng-model="vm.search">
        <span class="input-group-btn">
            <input type="submit" class="btn btn-primary" ng-click="vm.searchFor()" ng-disabled=
        </span>
        </div>
        <div class="help-block">You are going to search for ... @{{ vm.search }}</div>
        <div class="alert alert-info" ng-if="vm.searching">Searching for results will be right 
        <div class="alert alert-danger" ng-if="vm.error">Error getting results :( </div>
    </form>
    <hr>
    @include('home._angular_search_results')
</div>
```

This now just includes that inside the `MainConroller` scope. Notice that I pulled `ng-controller` out into a wrapper div, so it surrounds both my form and these results.

4. Finally, for the view, I update the main file that Laravel renders on the home page, called `resources/views/home/index.blade.php`, so that it includes these files:

```
@extends('layout')

@section('content')
    <div class="container">
        <div class="row">
            <div class="col-lg-8 col-lg-offset-2">

                @include('home.search')

            </div>
        </div>
    </div>
@endsection
```

Now, when you reload the home page, Angular is in charge of the default output.

Also note that `window.api_results` has data too.

Figure 3 Google Console

Now, on the page load, we are ready for the data that comes in from the backend, and we are seeing exactly what we saw before with Blade and Laravel.

5. Now, I need to set up the backend; I will handle the `GET` request coming in:

    1. Add the controller logic called `app/Http/Controllers/SearchComics.php`:

```
public function searchComicsByName(Request $request)

    try {
        $name = $request->input('name');

        $results = $this->clientInterface->comics($name);

        return Response::json(['data' => $results['data'], 'message' => "Success Getting Comics"], 200);
    } catch (\Exception $e) {
        return Response::json(
            ['data' => [], 'message' => sprintf("Error Getting Comics %s", $e->getMessage())], 400);
    }
}
```

2. Add the route you see here:

```
Route::get('/api/v1/search', ['as' => 'search',
    'uses' => 'SearchComics@searchComicsByName']);
```

3. Then, you are set to go and make a request! I will go over the numbers in the *How it works...*section:

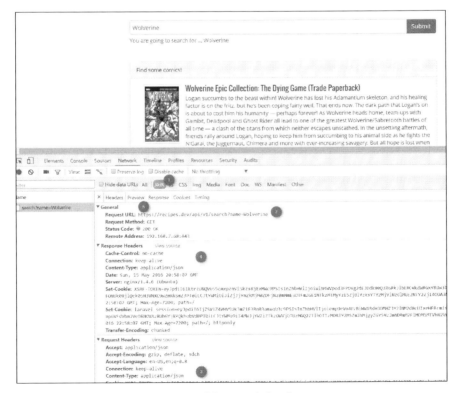

Figure 4 Requests in Detail

6. After this is done, I plug into `MainController` to show it taking on the response:

    1.   Note first how we are getting the response:

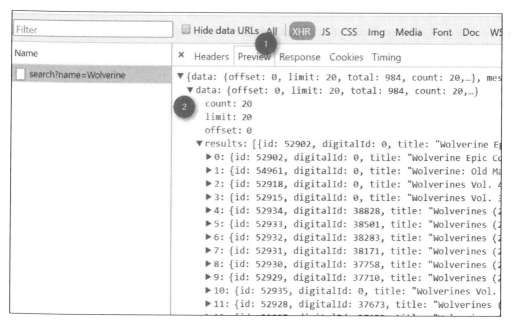

Figure 5 Preview Tab, nice look at JSON output

We click on the Preview window, and then see that the date key has results and much more.

    2.   Then, note that we will just use this as the initial load:

```
function activate()
{
    console.log("Here is angular");
    vm.api_results = $window.api_results;   1
    console.log(vm.api_results);
}


function disableSearch()
{
    return vm.search.length < 3;
}

function searchFor() {
    searchApiForComics(vm.search);
}

/**
 * @NOTE we can pull this out into a service as well
 */
function searchApiForComics()
{
    vm.searching = true;
    vm.error = false;
    var query = $httpParamSerializer({ 'name': vm.search })

    var req = {
        'headers': {
            'Content-Type': 'application/json',
            'Accept': 'application/json'
        },
        'method': 'GET',
        'data': [],
        'url': '/api/v1/search?' + query
    };

    $http(req).success(function(response) {
            console.log(response);
            vm.searching = false;
            vm.api_results = response.data;   2
    })
        .error(function(response) {
            console.log("Error getting results");
            vm.error = true;
            vm.searching = false;
            console.log(response);
    }));
}
```

Just like with the `action` area, [1], we take the response and set the `data` part of it to `vm.api_results` in section [2].

3. That's it, the page looks just as before, but there's no reload on the results!

7. One more thing, by changing `resources/views/home/_search.blade.php`, we can show a spinning gear while the page is searching.

```
<div class="help-block">You are going to search for ... @{{ vm.search }}</div>
<div class="alert alert-info" ng-if="vm.searching">
    <i class="fa fa-gear fa-spin"></i> Searching for results will be right back...</div>
<div class="alert alert-danger" ng-if="vm.error">Error getting results :( </div>
</form>
```

How it works...

First things first, pull in the JavaScript transformer. I find this a really easy way to set up the Angular widget to have content as soon as the page is loaded. Of course, we could have just made the request after the fact, but then the user would be looking at a loading icon, and it is not needed in this case.

After this is installed, we set up the Laravel Controller to use it, passing, for now, just the `api_results` into the `$window`, and returning the view.

From here, I move out the old Laravel Blade rendering of this data, and I move in an Angular formatted template using `ng-repeat`, the `@{{` curly bracket template parsers, and more. But if you look at it, it is not too far off from the original Laravel Blade layout. I also choose to break these up into smaller files for easier reading; this really is the only reason they can both exist just fine in the same files.

That's it! When I reload the page, we are ready to see the data I injected into `$window`, and from here, we can start making API calls. Note that when doing the backend work, I no longer need to reload the browser to see any changes.

Once the backend is in place, you will be able to search as the following screenshot. Note that in the screenshot, I am on the `Network` area of Chrome Developer Tools and that I am filtering by `XHR (1)`. Once in there, I can dig into `Request URL (2)`, `Content-Type (3)`, and `Preview (5)` the format of results if needed.

Figure 6 Google Network Tab

All of this now works the moment I press **Submit**, and the results of the response will place the `response.data` object into `vm.api_results` just as the original page loads.

There is just a slight amount of repetition in the two controllers.

The one to render the home page `app/Http/Controllers/HomeController.php`:

```php
class HomeController extends Controller
{

    /**
     * @var SearchComicsRepository
     */
    private $searchComicsRepository;

    public function __construct(SearchComicsRepository $searchComicsReposi
    {
        $this->searchComicsRepository = $searchComicsRepository;
    }

    /**
     * Show the application dashboard.
     *
     * @return \Illuminate\Http\Response
     */
    public function index(Request $request)
    {
        $name = $request->input('name');

        $results = $this->searchComicsRepository->getComicsByName($name);

        \JavaScript::put([
            'api_results' => $results
        ]);

        return Response::view('home.index', compact('results'));
    }
}
```

Figure 7 Home Controller

And the one to return API requests `app/Http/Controllers/SearchComics.php`:

```
class SearchComics extends Controller
{
    /**
     * @var MarvelApi
     */
    private $clientInterface;

    public function __construct(ComicClientInterface $clientInterface)
    {
        $this->clientInterface = $clientInterface;
    }

    public function searchComicsByName(Request $request)
    {
        try {
            $name = $request->input('name');

            $results = $this->clientInterface->comics($name);

            return Response::json(['data' => $results['data'], 'message' => "Success Getting Comics"], 200);
        } catch (\Exception $e) {
            return Response::json(
                ['data' => [], 'message' => sprintf("Error Getting Comics %s", $e->getMessage())], 400);
        }
    }
}
```

This is all it took to convert this area to Angular and start using its templates mixed in with Blade; thanks to the @ symbol that this is cake.

See also

▶ **Laracasts and API work**: https://laracasts.com/series/incremental-api-development

There are many quick ways to build APIs and standards that you can follow:"

▶ **Building APIs You Won't Hate by Phil Sturgeon**: https://apisyouwonthate.com/

Paginating our Angular results

Now we have a ton of results, 730, as seen in this request:

```
Name                          ×  Headers  Preview  Response  Cookies  Timing
☐ search?name=Spider-Man      ▼{data: {offset: 0, limit: 20, total: 730, count: 20,…}, message: "Success Getting Comics"}
                                ▼data: {offset: 0, limit: 20, total: 730, count: 20,…}
                                    count: 20
                                    limit: 20
                                    offset: 0
                                ▶results: [{id: 52564, digitalId: 0, title: "Spider-Man/Deadpool (2016) #6", issueNumber: 6,…},…]
                                    total: 730
                                message: "Success Getting Comics"
```

Since we cannot show all 730 at once, and since the API gives us 20 at a time, let's paginate through their APIs.

Getting ready

Use a fresh Laravel installation and follow these steps.

How to do it...

1. Install a library that helps with pagination and tons of other things:

   ```
   >npm install angular-ui-bootstrap --save
   ```

2. Then, load the library into our public folder by copying it over to `public/js` and `public/css`. Later, we will optimize this part of the workflow:

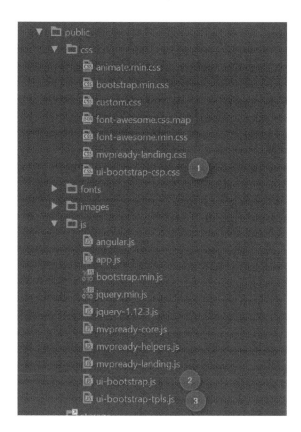

3. You will find all of these here:

4. Then into the top of `resources/views/layout.blade.php`:

```
<!-- App CSS -->
<link rel="stylesheet" href="/css/mvpready-landing.css">
<link rel="stylesheet" href="/css/ui-bootstrap-csp.css">

<link rel="stylesheet" href="/css/custom.css">
<link href="/css/animate.min.css" rel="stylesheet">
<!-- <link rel="stylesheet" href="/css/custom.css"> -->
```

5. And at the bottom of the same file:

```
<!-- Core JS -->
<script src="/js/jquery-1.12.3.js"></script>
<script src="/js/angular.js"></script>
<script src="/js/ui-bootstrap.js"></script>
<script src="/js/ui-bootstrap-tpls.js"></script>
<script src="/js/app.js"></script>
<script src="/js/bootstrap.min.js"></script>
```

6. Now, in our `public/js/app.js`, we load the library:

```
(function(){
    'use strict';

    angular.module('app', ['ui.bootstrap']);
```

7. Now that we have loaded the libraries, let's use the Pagination buttons at the top and bottom of `resources/views/home/_angular_search_results.blade.php`:

```
<div class="panel-body">
    <uib-pagination max-size="vm.maxSize" total-items="vm.api_results.total" ng-model="vm.currentPage" ng-change="vm.paginate()"></uib-pagination>

    <div ng-repeat="result in vm.api_results.results">
        <div class="media">
            <div class="media-left col-lg-2 col-md-2 col-sm-2">
                <a href="@{{ result['urls'][0]['url'] }}">
                    <img ng-if="result['thumbnail']['path']" class="media-object img-thumbnail img-responsive"
                        src="@{{ result['thumbnail']['path'] + '.' + result['thumbnail']['extension'] }}"
                        alt="...">
                    <img ng-if="!result['thumbnail']['path']" class="media-object" src="/images/placeholder.jpg"
                        alt="...">
                </a>
            </div>
            <div class="media-body">
                <h4 class="media-heading">@{{ result['title'] }}</h4>
                @{{ result['description'] }} <a
                    href="@{{ result['urls'][0]['url'] }}">more...</a>
            </div>
        </div>
    </div>

    <uib-pagination max-size="vm.maxSize" total-items="vm.api_results.total" ng-model="vm.currentPage" ng-change="vm.paginate()"></uib-pagination>
```

8. Let's take a closer look:

```
<uib-pagination max-size="vm.maxSize" total-items="vm.api_results.total"
                ng-model="vm.currentPage" ng-change="vm.paginate()">

</uib-pagination>
```

9. The Angular Controller now needs to consider this new API query string and data points:

```
/**
 * @NOTE we can pull this out into a service as well
 */
function searchApiForComics()
{
    vm.offset = (vm.currentPage - 1) * vm.totalPerRequest;    ①
    vm.searching = true;
    vm.error = false;
    var query = $httpParamSerializer({ 'name': vm.search });

    var req = {
        'headers': {
            'Content-Type': 'application/json',
            'charset': 'utf-8',
            'Accept': 'application/json'
        },
        'method': 'GET',
        'data': [],                                           ②
        'url': '/api/v1/search?offset=' + vm.offset + '&' + query
    };

    $http(req).success(function(response) {
        console.log(response);
        vm.searching = false;
        vm.api_results = response.data;
    })
    .error(function(response) {
        console.log("Error getting results");
        vm.error = true;
        vm.searching = false;
        console.log(response);
    });
}
```

I will go into the details of each of these in the *How it works...* section.

The top of the file looks like the following screenshot:

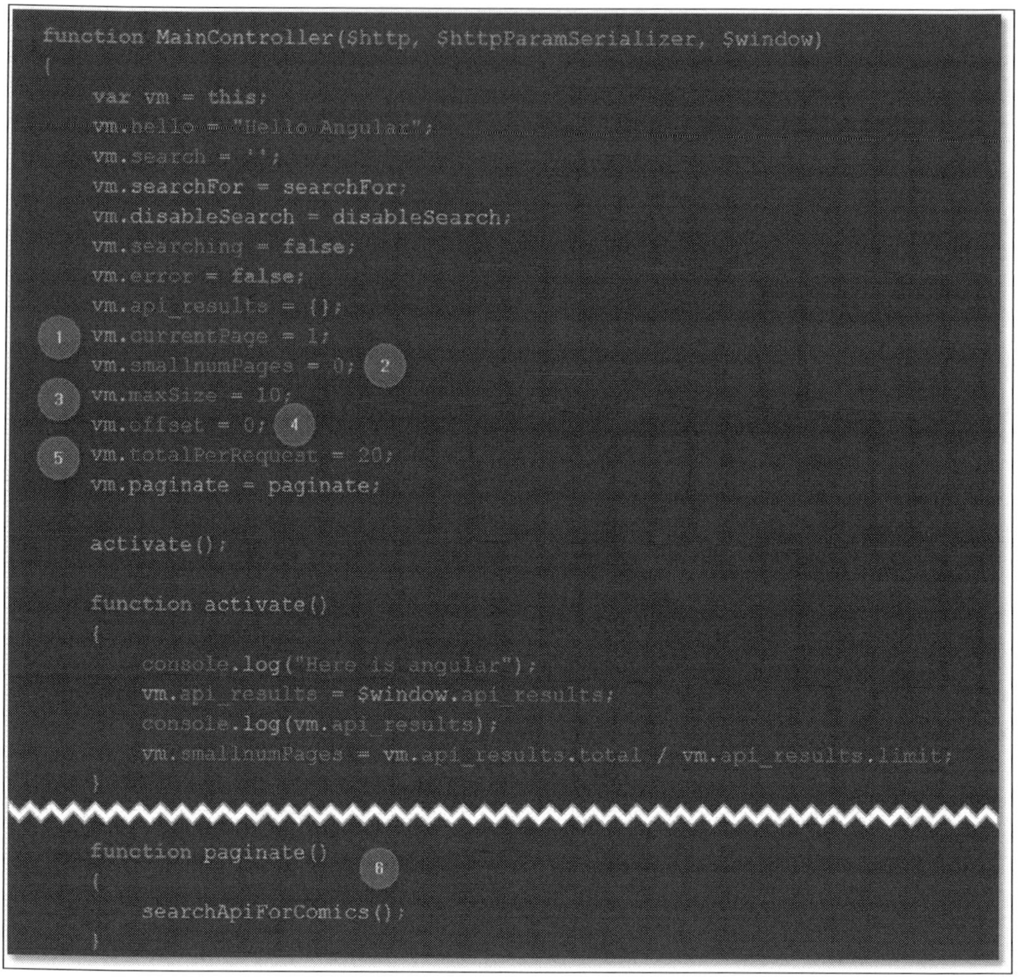

```
function MainController($http, $httpParamSerializer, $window)
{
    var vm = this;
    vm.hello = "Hello Angular";
    vm.search = '';
    vm.searchFor = searchFor;
    vm.disableSearch = disableSearch;
    vm.searching = false;
    vm.error = false;
    vm.api_results = {};
    vm.currentPage = 1;
    vm.smallnumPages = 0;
    vm.maxSize = 10;
    vm.offset = 0;
    vm.totalPerRequest = 20;
    vm.paginate = paginate;

    activate();

    function activate()
    {
        console.log("Here is angular");
        vm.api_results = $window.api_results;
        console.log(vm.api_results);
        vm.smallnumPages = vm.api_results.total / vm.api_results.limit;
    }

    function paginate()
    {
        searchApiForComics();
    }
}
```

10. Make sure to update the Laravel `app/Http/Controllers/SearchComics.php` controller to pass the new offset.

```php
public function searchComicsByName(Request $request)
{
    try {
        $name = $request->input('name');

        $offset = $request->input('offset');

        $results = $this->clientInterface->comics($name, $offset);

        return Response::json(['data' => $results['data'], 'message' => "Success Getting Comics"], 200);
    } catch (\Exception $e) {
        return Response::json(
            ['data' => [], 'message' => sprintf("Error Getting Comics %s", $e->getMessage())], 400);
    }
}
```

11. And now the Service, `app/Providers/MarvelApiClient.php`.

```php
public function comics($title = false, $offset = 0)
{
    $query = ['query' => $this->makeAuth()];

    $query['query'] = array_merge($query['query'], ['offset' => $offset]);

    if ($title) {
        $query['query'] = array_merge($query['query'], ['titleStartsWith' => $title]);
    }

    $results = $this->client->request('GET', $this->getApiVersion() . '/comics', $query);

    return json_decode($results->getBody(), true);
}
```

12. Then, add the `public/css/custom.css` file:

```css
.nav, .pagination, .carousel, .panel-title a { cursor: pointer; }
```

13. Now paginate away! It will all work after this, unless there is not much to see:

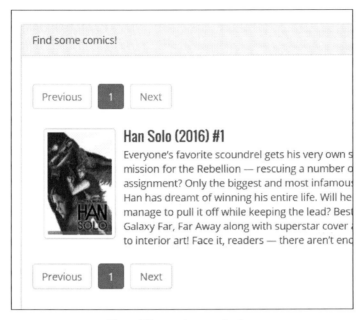

Figure 8 Now we have pagination

How it works...

It's amazing how easy the Bootstrap UI library makes my work! It is a great set of directives for common UI needs.

First, there are a number of files we have to move over to public. Though its not ideal, there is another recipe later on in the book where this workflow is *fixed*.

Then, we add the `uib-pagination` directive to the Blade template. A directive is a very powerful feature of Angular but is very confusing at first, and after. This directive expects some information to be set, and I set this information in the `vm` scope.

Later, I update the `searchApiForComics` function to update the offset. I subtract 1 since I do not want to offset the first page. Then, I add this to the query string.

After this, I go to the top of the `app.js` file and make sure to make these available to `view` and set them as needed on the top and in `activate`. Also note the `paginate` method. This is called from the `uib-pagination` directive.

That is it! It is really so simple to paginate, almost as simple as in Laravel.

▶ UI Bootstrap for Angular: `https://angular-ui.github.io/bootstrap/`

Tons of helpful Angular Directives; almost all that you need are here.

Testing an Angular page with Behat

How about testing these Angular pages? In the previous recipes, I set up Behat and showed how to use this tool to not only test your site but also to help you write code. I will now show how easy it is to test it using Behat over other tools such as Protractor, since with Behat, we get the benefit of Gherkin-based tests that can both test the UI and do Integration-level tests.

Getting ready

In the previous recipes, I installed Behat. I will go over it again, so a base Laravel install should be enough.

How to do it...

1. Install Behat using composer; your `composer.json` will look like this:

```
"require": {
    "php": ">=5.5.9",
    "laravel/framework": "5.2.*",
    "guzzlehttp/guzzle": "^6.1",
    "laralib/l5scaffold": "dev-master",
    "behat/mink": "^1.7",
    "behat/behat": "^3.1",
    "behat/mink-extension": "dev-master",
    "laracasts/behat-laravel-extension": "^1.0",
    "behat/mink-selenium2-driver": "^1.3",
    "league/flysystem-aws-s3-v3": "^1.0",
    "laracasts/utilities": "~2.0"
```

2. Run `composer update`, or if you are impatient like me, run `rm -rf vendor composer.lock`, and then `composer install`

3. Run Behat `init` to set things up:

   `>vendor/bin/behat --init`

4. Make a `behat.yml` file at the root of your app like this:

```
dow Help
    default:
        suites:
            home_ui:
                paths: [ %paths.base%/features/home]
                contexts: [ HomePageUiContext ]
        extensions:
            Laracasts\Behat:
                env_path: .env.behat
            Behat\MinkExtension:
                default_session: laravel
                base_url: https://recipes.dev
                laravel: ~
                selenium2:
                    wd_host: "http://selenium.dev:4444/wd/hub"
                browser_name: chrome

    travis:
        extensions:
            Laracasts\Behat:
                env_path: .env.travis
            Behat\MinkExtension:
                base_url: http://localhost:8000
                default_session: laravel
                laravel: ~
                selenium2:
                    wd_host: 'http://127.0.0.1:4444/wd/hub'
                browser_name: chrome
```

5. Run Behat again to set up these files (`-s` tells it what suite to use, and `--init` will set up the context class for us):

    ```
    >vendor/bin/behat --init -shome_ui
    ```

6. Now, add the `features/home/search.feature` file:

```
Feature: Search using Angular from the Home page
  Searching Marvel using Angular
  As a user on the sight
  So the results are fast

  Scenario: Search for Wolverine
    Given I am on the homepage
    And I search for "Wolverine"
    Then I should see a ton of results about him
    And if I click the Next in the Pagination I can see even more
```

7. Now, let's run this, so Behat does a ton of work for us:

```
>vendor/bin/ behat -shome_ui --append-snippets
```

8. Great, now it made this `features/bootstrap/HomePageUiContext.php` file for us and appended a ton of methods for us to go through:

```php
/**
 * @Given I search for :arg1
 */
public function iSearchFor($arg1)
{
    $this->searching_for = $arg1;
    $this->assertPageNotContainsText($arg1);
    $this->fillField("name", $arg1);
    $this->pressButton("search");
    sleep(3);
}

/**
 * @Then I should see a ton of results about him
 */
public function iShouldSeeATonOfResultsAboutHim()
{
    $this->assertPageContainsText($this->searching_for);
}

/**
 * @Then if I click the Next in the Pagination I can see even more :arg1
 */
public function ifIClickTheNextInThePaginationICanSeeEvenMore2($arg1)
{
    $this->clickLink("Next");
    sleep(4);
    $this->assertPageContainsText($arg1);
}
```

9. Before we run the test, let's add `id=search` to `resources/views/home/_ search.blade.php`:

```
<input type="text" name="name" c
            placeholder="Search for y
<span class="input-group-btn">
    <input type="submit" id="search"
</span>
</div>
```

Figure 9 Add ID to search

10. Then, run your test:

```
ubuntu@ubuntu:~/Code/recipes$ behat -shome_ui --append-snippets
@javascript
Feature: Search using Angular from the Home page
  Searching Marvel using Angular
  As a user on the sight
  So the results are fast

  Scenario: Search for Wolverine
    Given I am on the homepage
    And I search for "Wolverine"
    Then I should see a ton of results about him
    And if I click the Next in the Pagination I can see even more "Wolverines (2015) #5"

1 scenario (1 passed)
4 steps (4 passed)
0m12.26s (22.00Mb)
ubuntu@ubuntu:~/Code/recipes$
```

How it works...

Not too bad! We got Behat installed with just three commands, and we are ready to start. Well, we are kind of ready to start. Remember, I am in my virtual machine, so this had to be set up. And I had to install *Selenium* on my Windows machine from `https://www.npmjs.com/package/selenium-standalone`, which is not too bad really. Then, I had to run it before I ran the previous one.

Also note that the `behat.yml` file is looking for `selenium.dev`, which is set in my virtual machine's `/etc/hosts` file as follows:

```
192.168.7.57    selenium.dev
127.0.0.1       localhost
127.0.1.1       ubuntu
192.168.7.68    alsblog5.dev
```

This is the IP of my Windows box that the virtual machine is a guest of.

After this, I add `@javascript` to the `search.feature` file. This tells Behat to talk to selenium for this test and interact with a browser; else this will not work since it requires JavaScript. By default, we are using the *Symfony BrowserKit 2* driver, which is able to parse JavaScript. You can put this at the `Scenario` level too if needed so that `Scenarios` can run faster without JavaScript if not needed.

As far as the test goes, it is just some simple interactions with the web page. I added `id=search` to make this super easy for entering data into this field. I could have just as easily set the `name` instead.

Then, I add `sleep` since the Marvel API sometimes has a delay, and I did not want to have a timeout on it. I could have added a wait for an element to appear on the page, which would be a safer bet, such as waiting for the message box to go away.

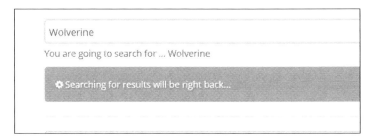

See also

▸ Laracasts—Laravel 5 and Behat—BFFs: `https://laracasts.com/lessons/laravel-5-and-behat-bffs`

Creating a relationship with favorites

This is an Angular section, but I will take a moment to create a simple relationship, which we will later build a widget around. In this case, I am going to add a `favorites` table to the system and relate this to a user. It will hold the information I need to show a comic from Maravel.

Getting ready

A base installation of Laravel with the User model migrated is required here.

How to do it...

1. Run this inside the virtual machine console:

   ```
   >php artisan make:migration create_favorites_table
   ```

2. Open this file, and add the `database/migrations/2016_05_16_220136_create_favorites_table.php` fields:

```php
class CreateFavoritesTable extends Migration
{
    public function up()
    {
        Schema::create('favorites', function (Blueprint $
            $table->increments('id');
            $table->string('user_id');
            $table->text('comic');
            $table->timestamps();
        });
    }

    /**
     * Reverse the migrations.
     *
     * @return void
     */
    public function down()
    {
        Schema::drop('favorites');
    }
}
```

3. Then, make a model for this file:

   ```
   >php artisan make:model Favorite
   ```

4. In this file, we can add a relationship back to the user:

```php
<?php

namespace App;

use Illuminate\Database\Eloquent\Model;

class Favorite extends Model
{
    protected $fillable = [
        'comic'
    ];

    protected $casts = [
        'comic' => 'array'
    ];

    public function user()
    {
        return $this->belongsTo(\App\User::class);
    }
}
```

5. Then, open the user file called `app/User.php` to relate back to the `favourites`:

```php
public function favorites()
{
    return $this->hasMany(\App\Favorite::class);
}
```

6. Now, we are ready to build this UI.

How it works...

This is a fairly normal migration with a relationship with just a little extra. For one, notice the plural name of the `favorites` table, this is a Laravel convention. Then, for the model class, I name that using singular notation since that again is a Laravel convention.

In there, I cast the `comic` field to array because I am going to dump the entire JSON object there; this way, I do not need to make an API call to show the user's Favorites!

Also notice the name of the `create_` file; this again is the convention in Laravel. Creating or Altering this also helps others on your team to know what the file is about.

Also, I protect `favorites` from the Mass Assignment attack by not allowing `user_id` to be done via a parameter that is passed in.

This is pretty much it; we are now ready to make a widget.

See also

- ▶ Laravel Docs—Mass Assignment: `https://laravel.com/docs/5.2/eloquent#mass-assignment`
- ▶ Laravel Docs—Migrations: `https://laravel.com/docs/5.2/migrations`

Building a favorites Ajax widget in Angular

What I will cover in this section is adding the ability for a user to click on a `star` next to the comic, and then it will be saved to the database, and added it as a `Favorite` via a widget on the page.

This is what they will see on the search results page:

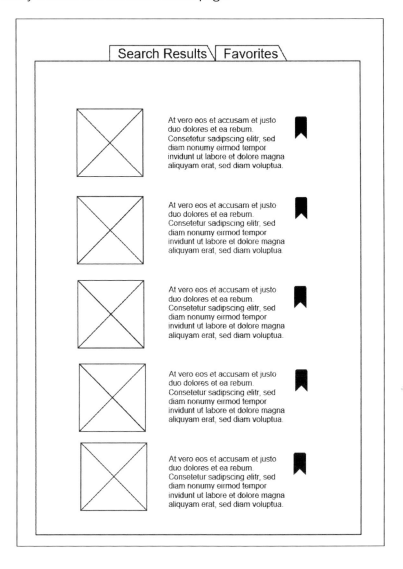

When they click on the `Favorites` Tab, they see only their `Favorites` and can remove them:

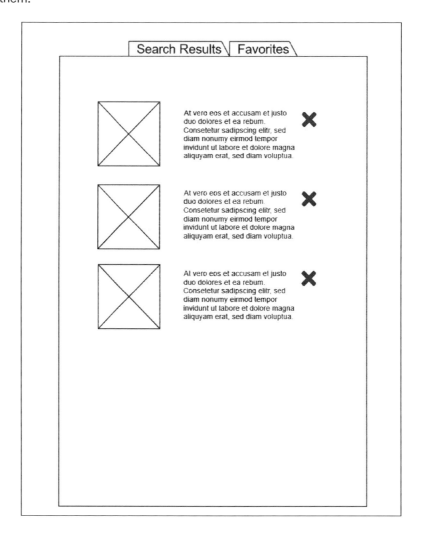

This way you can see and remove `Favorites`. And since I am using a lot of the same layout, it should save me time.

Getting ready

See the previous recipe for setting up the model or just follow along.

How it works...

1. Return `favorites` into the Home Page JavaScript:

```php
public function index(Request $request)
{
    $name = $request->input('name');

    $results = $this->searchComicsRepository->getComicsByName($name);


    \JavaScript::put([
        'api_results' => $results,
        'user' => $this->getUserInfo()
    ]);

    return Response::view('home.index', compact('results'));
}
```

The `getUserInfo` method is here:

```php
use Illuminate\Support\Facades\Auth;

trait UserTrait
{

    public function getUserInfo()
    {
        if(Auth::guest())
            return [];

        $user = Auth::user()->load('favorites');
        return $user->toArray();
    }

}
```

2. Then, make a tab area on the home page to show this `resources/views/home/` `index.blade.php` data:

```
@extends('layout')

@section('content')
    <div class="container" ng-controller="MainController as vm">
        <div class="row">
            <div class="col-lg-8 col-lg-offset-2">
                <div class="panel panel-default">
                    <div class="panel-heading">Find some comics!</div>
                    <div class="panel-body">
                        <uib-tabset active="active">
                            <uib-tab index="0" >
                                <uib-tab-heading>
                                    <i class="fa fa-search"></i> Search Results
                                </uib-tab-heading>
                                @include('home._search')
                            </uib-tab>

                            <uib-tab index="2">
                                <uib-tab-heading>
                                    <i class="fa fa-star"></i> Favorites
                                </uib-tab-heading>

                                @include('home._favorites')

                            </uib-tab>
                        </uib-tabset>
                    </div>
                </div>
            </div>
        </div>
    </div>
@endsection
```

3. Then, we update the template called `resources/views/home/_search.blade.` `php`:

```
<div>
    <form method="GET" class="form-horizontal" novalidate>
        <div class="input-group">
            <input type="text" name="name" class="form-control col-lg-10"
                placeholder="Search for your comic..." ng-model="vm.search">
            <span class="input-group-btn">
                <input type="submit" id="search" class="btn btn-primary" ng-click="vm.searchFor()" ng-disabled="vm.disableSearch()">Search</input>
            </span>
        </div>
        <div class="help-block">You are going to search for ... @{{ vm.search }}</div>
        <div class="alert alert-info" ng-if="vm.searching">
            <i class="fa fa-gear fa-spin"></i> Searching for results will be right back...</div>
        <div class="alert alert-danger" ng-if="vm.error">Error getting results !</div>
    </form>
    <hr>
    @include('home._angular_search_results')
</div>
```

We also update `resources/views/home/_favorites.blade.php`:

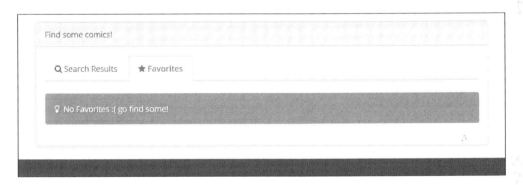

4. Now, when users click on **Favorites**, they will see them (but there are none):

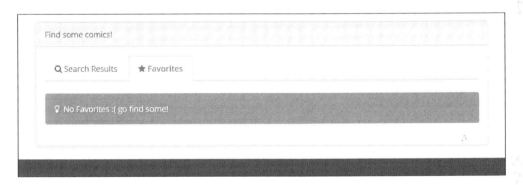

5. Now, add a button to the results coming in, so when I click it, it will make a POST request to the API called `resources/views/home/_laravel_search_results.blade.php`:

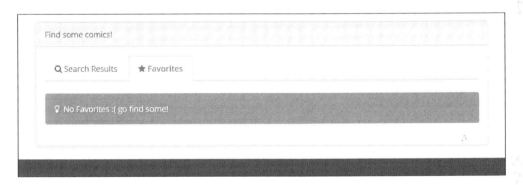

6. The `vm.favorite` in `public/js/app.js` to handle the request:

```javascript
function favorite(comic)
{
    var req = {
        'headers': {
            'Content-Type': 'application/json',
            'charset': 'utf-8',
            'Accept': 'application/json'
        },
        'method': 'POST',
        'data': [ { 'comic': comic } ],
        'url': '/api/v1/favorite'
    };

    $http(req).success(function(response) {
        console.log(response);
    })
    .error(function(response) {
        console.log("Error creating favorite");
        vm.error = true;
        console.log(response);
    });
}
```

7. Now, let's add the `favorite` create controller called `app/Http/Controllers/FavoriteCreate.php`:

```php
class FavoriteCreate extends Controller
{
    public function create(Request $request)
    {
        $comic = $request->input('comic');

        $favorite = Favorite::create(
            [
                'comic' => $comic
            ]
        );

        $favorite->user_id = Auth::user()->id;

        $favorite->save();

        return Response::json(['data' => $favorite->toArray(), 'message' => "Favorite Added"], 201);
    }
}
```

8. Let's create the route called `app/Http/routes.php`:

```
Route::post('api/v1/favorite', 'FavoriteCreate@create')->name('favorite.create');
```

9. Now, for the delete button in the HTML called `resources/views/home/_favorites.blade.php`, do as follows:

```
<h4 class="media-heading">@{{ favorite.comic['title'] }}
    <span ng-click="vm.favoriteRemove(favorite.id, $index)"><i class="fa fa-trash" style="..."></i></span>
</h4>
```

10. Add the `vm.favoriteRemove` method to `public/js/app.js`:

```javascript
function favoriteRemove(comic_id, index) {

    var req = {
        'headers': {
            'Content-Type': 'application/json',
            'charset': 'utf-8',
            'Accept': 'application/json'
        },
        'method': 'DELETE',
        'data': [],
        'url': '/api/v1/favorite/' + comic_id
    };

    $http(req).success(function(response) {

            //Was having an issue with splice off
            //so resorted to this for now
            angular.forEach(vm.favorites, function(v,i) {
                if(i == index)
                {
                    vm.favorites.splice(i, 1);
                }
            })
        })
        .error(function(response) {
            vm.error = true;
        });
}
```

11. Then, create the backend delete controller in Laravel `app/Http/Controllers/FavoriteRemove.php`.

```php
class FavoriteRemove extends Controller
{
    public function remove(Request $request, $id)
    {

        $fav = $fav = Favorite::find($id);

        if($fav && $fav->user_id == Auth::user()->id) {
            $fav->delete();
            return Response::json(['data' => null, 'message' => "Favorite Deleted"], 200);
        }

        return Response::json(['data' => null, 'message' => "Error deleting Favorite"], 304);
    }
}
```

12. And create the backend delete route:

13. That is it, we have a working API and widget that, other than lacking a notification system to show the user that the favorite was created, works well.

How to do it...

Let's go down this long list of steps one at a time. First we populate some more information in the JavaScript that we are pushing into the `$window` of the browser `app/Http/Controllers/HomeController.php`. This information will let us know more about the user, but more importantly, the favorites, if any.

Then, using the Angular Bootstrap UI directive for Tabs, I set this up as well, which is super easy. With this, I can show and hide these two panes when the user clicks it. I could even load data by clicking on the tab to make this page load faster, but for now, I am fine with the way it is.

After this, I break my Blade files up a bit; Index now pulls in search and favorites and each one of these fills in what is needed. It is just nice to keep these files small.

Then, I begin to add `spans` to trigger actions when the user clicks them, thanks to `ng-click`.

Now, I get into making the CREATE and DELETE methods in app.js. This is pretty simple still POST and DELETE with POST having the comic object, and DELETE just needs the ID. Then, I deal with the response for the POST method called favorite by pushing it into the existing vm.favorites model, which then dynamically updates the UI. As for DELETE, I just remove the matching index from vm.favorites. I could have pulled in lodash here since I was having trouble with splice.

I am not doing enough with failed responses, but this could be some later work. This would go well with https://github.com/CodeSeven/toastr as I could also show the user that the favorite is being added.

Finally, we need a route to talk to and a controller to handle the request. The routes are straight forward and the Controllers are as well. Note that I use one controller per action just to try and keep them small. If there was much repeat in them, I would make a base called FavoriteController for them to share. Both of them return JSON, and I then alter the default response code as I wish.

By the way, CORS is missing, and I will cover it shortly.

See also

  ▶ UI Bootstrap—Making life easy: https://angular-ui.github.io/bootstrap/#/tabs

      Toastr is a JavaScript library for non-blocking notifications. jQuery is required. The goal here is to create a simple core library that can be customized and extended—https://github.com/CodeSeven/toastr.

  ▶ Response codes Explore vendor/symfony/http-foundation/Response.php

Validating incoming input

The previous work did not cover validation. We could check for comic, and then check that the user is the owner. What I will do here is show how to use Form Request Validation to validate the incoming request.

Getting ready

If you have been following along, you have the app/Http/Controllers/ FavoriteCreate.php controller in place, so we are going to add validation to it.

How to do it...

1. Add toastr so that we can notify people as needed (https://github.com/ Foxandxss/angular-toastr); you will see in the next layout that I had to move several files from the bower_components/angular-toastr to the public/js and public/css folders.

2. I also install the Angular animate:

   ```
   >bower install angular-toastr#0.4.1 -S
   ```

3. Add it to resources/views/layout.blade.php:

   ```
   <!-- App CSS -->
   <link rel="stylesheet" href="/css/mvpready-landing.css">
   <link rel="stylesheet" href="/css/ui-bootstrap-csp.css">
   <link rel="stylesheet" href="/css/angular-toastr.css">

   <link rel="stylesheet" href="/css/custom.css">
   <link href="/css/animate.min.css" rel="stylesheet">
   <!-- <link rel="stylesheet" href="/css/custom.css"> -->
   ```

   Add it at the bottom of the file as well:

   ```
   <!-- Bootstrap core JavaScript
   ==================================== -->
   <!-- Core JS -->
   <script src="/js/jquery-1.12.3.js"></script>
   <script src="/js/angular.js"></script>
   <script src="/js/angular-animate.js"></script>
   <script src="/js/ui-bootstrap.js"></script>
   <script src="/js/ui-bootstrap-tpls.js"></script>
   <script src="/js/angular-toastr.js"></script>
   <script src="/js/angular-toastr.tpls.js"></script>
   <script src="/js/app.js"></script>
   <script src="/js/bootstrap.min.js"></script>
   ```

4. Register it with the app called public/js/app.js:

   ```
   angular.module('app', ['ui.bootstrap', 'ngAnimate', 'toastr']);

   MainController.$inject = ['$http', '$httpParamSerializer', '$window', 'toastr'];
   ```

5. Then, add it to our handle error area:

```
.error(function(response) {
    toastr.error('Error Adding Favorite', 'Error');

    angular.forEach(response, function(v, i) {

        angular.forEach(v, function(message, index) {
            toastr.error(message, 'Error');
        })
    });
});
```

6. Let's make the form called `request`:

   >php artisan make:request FavoriteCreateRequest

7. Then, add what we need to validate, `app/Http/Requests/`
   `FavoriteCreateRequest.php`:

```
class FavoriteCreateRequest extends Request
{
    public function authorize()
    {
        return true;
    }

    public function rules()
    {
        return [
            'comic' => 'required'
        ];
    }
}
```

8. Finally, add this to the controller:

```
public function create(Requests\FavoriteCreateRequest $request)
{
    $comic = $request->input('comic');

    $favorite = Favorite::create(
        [
            'comic' => $comic
        ]
    );
```

9. Now, make sure to catch it and send the error to the screen:

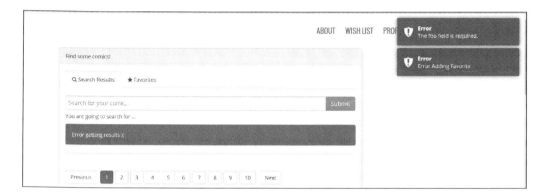

10. That's it! Maybe you can add it now to the success notice when adding `favorites`.

How it works...

Pretty simple; using "Form Request Validation", we can validate the Controller method before anything happens in there. With this in place, we are ready to reject incoming requests that are not valid without adding any more code to our Controller.

Then, in the angular side of things, we just handle the errors and show the message. You will see that I iterate over the array of errors just in case there is more than one.

Notice that in the toastr docs, you can configure these messages as needed.

See also

▸ **Toastr Demo**: `http://foxandxss.github.io/angular-toastr/`
▸ **Laravel Docs**: `https://laravel.com/docs/5.2/validation#form-request-validation`

Using the CORS protection

So far, even though the routes for this app are protected by the `auth` middleware, I am not dealing with CORS, because I am in the same domain as the login session and Angular has the benefits of sessions and XSRF.

You can see here that it is injecting it into the request for me as I use `$http`:

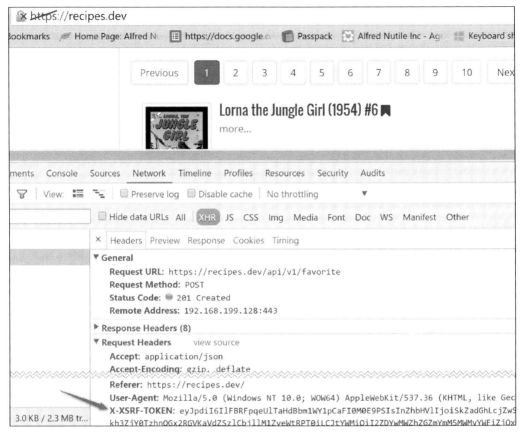

Figure 10 XSRF

So, if I went to another site in the same browser, the site cannot use the session from the site that I am coming from to make a request. In this case, if my request was using jQuery, for example, I would need to include this information. Here is an example using jQuery, so we can see a more manual approach to this.

Getting ready

For now, we will create a couple of routes with a basic jQuery Ajax request, and the POST request will be handled as well. I will cover this here, so just have a Laravel installation ready.

How to do it...

1. We will make a new View that is really simple:

```html
<!DOCTYPE html>
<html lang="en">
<head>
</head>
<body class="">
<div>

    You are here...

    <div id="here"></div>

    <script src="/js/jquery-1.12.3.js"></script>
    <script src="/js/examplecors.js"></script>
</div>
</body>
</html>
```

2. Then, we make our Route file to serve these example routes:

```php
Route::group(['middleware' => ['web']], function () {

    Route::auth();

    Route::post('/api/v1/test', 'TestController@foo');

    Route::get('/api/v1/token', function() {
        return csrf_token();
    });

    Route::get('/test_cors', 'TestController@view');
```

3. We make a test controller called `app/Http/Controllers/TestController.php` just to show the example:

```php
class TestController extends Controller
{
    public function view()
    {
        return view('test');
    }

    public function foo()
    {
        return Response::json("Here", 200);
    }
}
```

4. Now back to the JavaScript, first we are going to do this without _token:

```javascript
(function($){
    $(document).ready(function(){
        post();

        function success(response){
            console.log('made request');
        }

        function post(){
            $.ajax({
                type: "POST",
                url: '/api/v1/test',
                data: [] ,
                success: success
            });
        }
    });
})(jQuery);
```

5. This is what we get:

6. Then, when we add the token:

```
(function($){
    $(document).ready(function(){
        var token = false;
        $.ajax({
            type: "GET",
            url: '/api/v1/token',
            data: [],
            success: successToken
        });

        function successToken(response){
            token = response;
            post();
        }

        function success(response){
            console.log('made request');
        }

        function post(){
            $.ajax({
                type: "POST",
                url: '/api/v1/test',
                data: { '_token': token } ,
                success: success
            });
        }
    });
})(jQuery);
```

7. We get this:

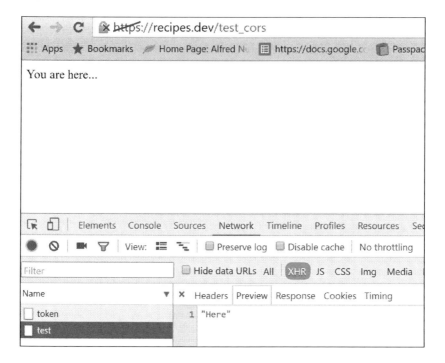

How it works...

It's a good thing Laravel and Angular take some of this work out of the way. But previously, I showed a very basic example of how this can work in a more manual way.

The hard part of this example is that it is an API, but really, it is just for this widget. If I was making a public API, it would be `stateless` and expect you to pass a secret in with the request.

Also notice that in the Laravel docs they talk about even for any form that are doing a `POST` or `PUT`—`https://laravel.com/docs/5.2/quickstart-intermediate#authentication-routing`.

```
@section('content')

    <!-- Bootstrap Boilerplate... -->

    <div class="panel-body">
        <!-- Display Validation Errors -->
        @include('common.errors')

        <!-- New Task Form -->
        <form action="{{ url('task') }}" method="POST" class="form-horizontal">
            {{ csrf_field() }}

            <!-- Task Name -->
            <div class="form-group">
                <label for="task-name" class="col-sm-3 control-label">Task</label>
```

See also

▸ Alfred Nutile—CSRF Tokens and `Angular.js`: `https://alfrednutile.info/posts/110`

Using Elixir and Gulp to set up Angular

After all the manual installation work at the start of this chapter, I want to step back and automate this with Elixir. I will use Gulp via Elixir to put my files in place for me and aggregate them as I work on them.

This means I will start to keep my assets in `resources/assets"` not `"public` and then aggregate them, as I edit them, to the correct areas.

To be clear, I am, by far, no Gulp expert. The system here just helped me to put in place a decent workflow, filling in some of the blanks I did not see in the Laravel docs.

Getting ready

If you did not follow the start of this chapter, you might not have all the files I am about to move into different places. If not, no big deal; you will still get a sense of how this all works.

How to do it...

1. Move all CSS files into `resources/css"` and JavaScript `"resources/js` so that your folders look like this:

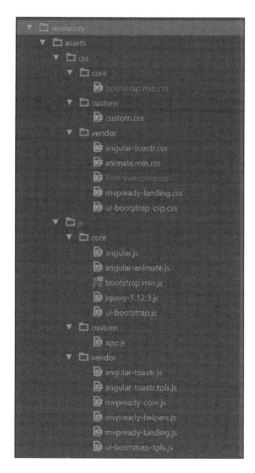

2. Then, move all the CSS calls out of the layout, so it looks just like this:

```
<head>
    <title>ICDB: Internet Comic Database</title>

    <meta charset="utf-8">
    <meta name="viewport" content="width=device-width, initial-scale=1.0">
    <meta name="description" content="">
    <meta name="author" content="">

    <link rel="stylesheet" href="{{ elixir('css/all.css') }}">

    <meta name="theme-color" content="#ffffff">

</head>
```

3. Then, I will do the same for the footer and all the previous JavaScript files:

```
<script src="{{ asset('js/all.js', true) }}"></script>
```

4. Now, we need to set up `gulpfile.js` to deal with all those files we moved, so it can make `all.js` and `all.css` that we referenced previously:

```
var elixir = require('laravel-elixir');

elixir(function(mix) {
    mix
        .styles(
            [
                "vendor/*.css",
                "core/bootstrap.min.css",
                "custom/custom.css"
            ], "public/css/all.css")
        .scripts(
            [
                "core/jquery-1.12.3.js",
                "core/angular.js",
                "core/angular-animate.js",
                "core/bootstrap.min.js",
                "core/ui-bootstrap.js",
                "vendor/*.js",
                "custom/app.js"
            ], "public/js/all.js")
        .version( ["css/all.css", "js/all.js"]);
});
```

5. During this Gulp run, there is going to be a folder created in `public` called `build`. I am going to make this ahead of time and dump all the fonts in there.

6. Then, at the command line, inside your virtual machine, run Gulp and you will see this output:

```
>gulp
```

```
ubuntu@ubuntu:~/Code/recipes$ gulp
[06:13:36] Using gulpfile /mnt/hgfs/Code/recipes/gulpfile.js
[06:13:36] Starting 'default'...
[06:13:36] Starting 'styles'...

Fetching Styles Source Files...
    - resources/assets/css/vendor/*.css
    - resources/assets/css/core/bootstrap.min.css
    - resources/assets/css/custom/custom.css


Saving To...
    - public/css/all.css

[06:13:39] Finished 'default' after 3.52 s
[06:13:39] gulp-notify: [Laravel Elixir] Stylesheets Merged!
[06:13:39] Finished 'styles' after 3.62 s
[06:13:39] Starting 'scripts'...

Fetching Scripts Source Files...
    - resources/assets/js/core/jquery-1.12.3.js
    - resources/assets/js/core/angular.js
    - resources/assets/js/core/angular-animate.js
    - resources/assets/js/core/bootstrap.min.js
    - resources/assets/js/core/ui-bootstrap.js
    - resources/assets/js/vendor/*.js
    - resources/assets/js/custom/app.js


Saving To...
    - public/js/all.js

[06:13:43] gulp-notify: [Laravel Elixir] Scripts Merged!
[06:13:43] Finished 'scripts' after 3.69 s
[06:13:43] Starting 'version'...

Fetching Version Source Files...
    - public/css/all.css
    - public/js/all.js


Saving To...
    - public/build

[06:13:43] Finished 'version' after 281 ms
ubuntu@ubuntu:~/Code/recipes$
```

7. Reload the page; it all works:

Figure 11 All our JS is there

8. Finally, I leave `gulp watch` running, so as I edit the JS files and CSS files, they are updated for me on the fly!

How it works...

Wow, we reduced all these files to two! Now is the time to cover the details.

First, I moved them into folders: `core`, `custom`, and `vendor`. I used this to manage the order later on in the `gulpfile.js`. I might have been able to manage the order just by prefixing their names with numbers, for example, `0_angular.js`; that might be worth trying. Then, I can use `*` to just put them all together in one call. As far as order goes, it just is the same problem that we had to deal with before. jQuery needed to go before Angular, and Angular before my custom work, and so on.

After this, I removed all these items from the `layout.blade.php` file, and for CSS, I use the `elixir` method. This, as you can see with the preceding screenshot, helps to `cache bust` (cool term, had to write it) by creating a dynamic name for this CSS file. Above it is `all-xxxxxxxxx.css`, and this will change every time your run `gulp` or `gulp watch`. And for the JS assets, I used the `asset` function to pull it in and set `true`, so it is `https`.

The `gulpfile.js` is where I just have to break up the files into `styles` and `scripts` and deal with order. The more I can fit into `*.js` or `*.css`, the better since it is less work for me.

The last part you have to do once (or automate it) is move the fonts. For me, I just copied them into the `build` folder so that it was the relative path of the CSS file, which now lives in `public/build/css`, so it will still just work with this font's folder at the same level.

Then, as you work, leave `gulp watch` running, and with almost no delay, you can edit your files, go to the browser, reload, and see your changes. Some people would even auto-reload the browser too, but you would have to run Gulp on your local box.

In the end, we took almost 20 files and turned them into two files! Later, with minifications, we reduce it even more. This means saving a lot on loading time, since the browser is getting less assets. Later, as we minify things, we will save bandwidth too on mobile devices.

See also

- ▶ Laracasts—Laravel and the |Front-End: `https://laracasts.com/series/laravel-5-and-the-front-end`
- ▶ Laravel Docs: `https://laravel.com/docs/5.2/elixir`

7

Authentication, Security, and Subscriptions

In this chapter, we will cover the following topics:

- ▶ Using policies and guard to protect user pages
- ▶ Adding feature flags to hide features from users
- ▶ Implementing Socialite to allow users to login with Facebook
- ▶ Adding custom middleware to protect the user admin area
- ▶ Using Laravel to set up a subscription site
- ▶ Creating an interface for the user to manage subscriptions
- ▶ Creating an admin interface for subscriptions

Introduction

This chapter will cover many of the day-to-day workflows that are needed to protect your site, manage subscriptions, and administer users.

By the time you are done, you will have a better understanding of how these features work and when to use them.

Using policies and guard to protect user pages

Here, I am going to show how we can use gate to keep users from deleting other people's Favorites.

Getting ready

A fresh install of Laravel will do. But if you have followed along this far, you will have all the routes and controllers in place.

How to do it...

1. Using Artisan, we will make a policy as follows:

    ```
    > php artisan make:policy FavoriteDeletePolicy
    ```

2. It will create a file called `app/Policies/FavoriteDeletePolicy.php`.

3. Then, we register it with the `app/Providers/AuthServiceProvider.php` class:

```
protected $policies = [
    \App\Favorite::class => \App\Policies\FavoriteDeletePolicy::class
];
```

Register Policy

4. Now, we update the policy to have `delete` just as `model`:

```php
use App\Favorite;
use App\User;
use Illuminate\Auth\Access\HandlesAuthorization;

class FavoriteDeletePolicy
{
    use HandlesAuthorization;

    /**
     * Create a new policy instance.
     *
     * @return void
     */
    public function __construct()
    {
        //
    }

    public function delete(User $user, Favorite $favorite)
    {
        return $user->id == $favorite->user_id;
    }
}
```

5. Then, we will plug the gate into the controller called `app/Http/Controllers/FavoriteRemove.php`:

```php
public function remove(Request $request, $id)
{
    $fav = $fav = Favorite::find($id);

    if (Gate::denied('delete', $fav)) {
        return Response::json(['data' => null, 'message' => "Error You do not own this favorite"], 403);
    }

    if ($fav && $fav->user_id == Auth::user()->id) {
        $fav->delete();
        return Response::json(['data' => null, 'message' => "Favorite deleted"], 200);
    }

    return Response::json(['data' => null, 'message' => "Error deleting favorite"], 304);
}
```

6. Once this is done, you will see how users are rejected if they do not own Favorite; for a moment, I will update the policy to be this—the opposite of what we really want—just for example:

```
public function delete(User $user, Favorite $favorite)
{
    return $user->id != $favorite->user_id;
}
```

This is the response that they will get:

Failed Response

7. You will see that it works correctly if we put it back to `==`, and if they do own Favorite:

201 Response

How it works...

It seems like a lot of work just to write this logic. Why not just check for it here in the controller? Well, you are organizing your policies for one. This helps as an app grows. Also, you can use this same gate logic in your `@can` views, for example, to hide and show buttons as needed on a page.

Also, it really is best to keep your controllers slim. Moving code into services, and in this case, a policy can make it easier to reuse. You really do not want to get into a case, ever, where you have to use a method in another controller rather than the one you are working in. It is a sign that it is time to break these methods into a sharable class.

See also

▸ Laravel Docs at `https://laravel.com/docs/master/authorization`

Adding feature flags to hide features from users

Now that we did gate, let's use a library with gate Laravel feature flag, so we can show and hide features based on the user who logs in!

This can really be a big deal. Say, I am not ready to show any user, but myself, a feature, then when I login, I can see it working. But when I am ready for another user to see it, I can then add features to the list of people who can see it.

Getting ready

I am going to use the install from the start of this recipe book, but you can just jump in as we just need two users to try this out.

How to do it...

1. First, I will make sure I have two users.

2. Then, I will install the library per it's instructions:

   ```
   > composer require alfred-nutile-inc/laravel-feature-flag
   ```

3. Now, let's load the provider:

   ```
   Laracasts\Utilities\JavaScript\JavaScriptServiceProvider::class,
   AlfredNutileInc\LaravelFeatureFlags\FeatureFlagsProvider::class,
   ```

4. Let's run the migration for this library:

   ```
   >php artisan vendor:publish --\ provider="AlfredNutileInc\
   LaravelFeatureFlags\FeatureFlagsProvider" --tag='migrations'
   ```

5. Now, let's add a migration based on their example to put this in place. Here is a link to the code https://github.com/alfred-nutile-inc/laravel-feature-flag/blob/master/database/migrations_example/2016_01_25_005027_alter_users_table_add_twitter.php:

   ```
   >php artisan make:migration add_favorites_feature_flag
   ```

Now, set it up:

```
> php artisan migrate
```

```php
class AddFavoritesFeatureFlag extends Migration
{
    /**
     * Run the migrations.
     *
     * @return void
     */
    public function up()
    {

        $feature = new \AlfredNutileInc\LaravelFeatureFlags\FeatureFlag();
        $feature->key = 'add-favorite';
        $feature->variants = ["users" => ['me@alfrednutile.info']];
        $feature->save();

    }

    /**
     * Reverse the migrations.
     *
     * @return void
     */
    public function down()
    {

    }

}
```

6. I had to fix my `resources/views/error.blade.php` file so that it does not care if the libraries templates did not have the `$errors` variable:

```blade
@if (isset($errors) && count($errors) > 0)
    <div class="alert alert-danger">
        <p>There where some errors on the page</p>
        <ul>
            @foreach ($errors->all() as $error)
                <li>{{ $error }}</li>
            @endforeach
        </ul>
    </div>
@endif
```

7. Then, I will show it working in `/admin/feature_flags`:

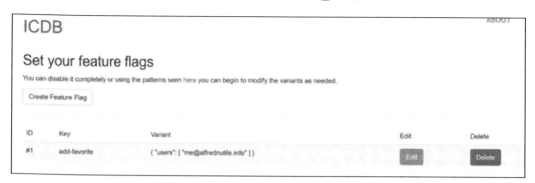

8. Now, let's plug it into our theme called `resources/views/home/_angular_search_results.blade.php`:

```
<div class="media-body">
    <h4 class="media-heading">@{{ result['title'] }}
        @can('feature-flag', 'add-favorite')
            <span ng-click="vm.favorite(result)"><i class="fa fa-bookmark" style="..."></i></span>
        @endcan
    </h4>
        @{{ result['description'] }} <a
        href="@{{ result['urls'][0]['url'] }}">more...</a>
```

9. Then, I will add the other user, and check whether he can see `database/seeds/UserTableSeeder.php` or not:

```
class UserTableSeeder extends Seeder
{

    public function run()
    {
        // TestDummy::times(20)->create('App\Post');
        factory(\App\User::class)->create(
            [
                'email' => 'me@alfrednutile.info',
                'password' => bcrypt(env('ADMIN_PASSWORD'))
            ]
        );
        factory(\App\User::class)->create(
            [
                'email' => 'demo@foo.com',
                'password' => bcrypt(env('DEMO_PASSWORD'))
            ]
        );
    }
}
```

10. If we login as `me@alfrednutile.info` all is well:

11. But if we login as `demo@foo.com`, it is gone!

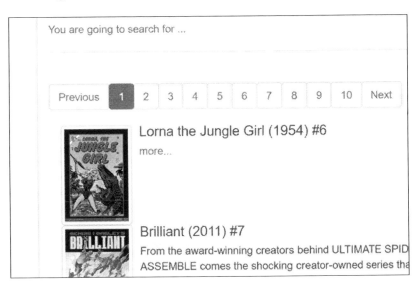

12. Then, I will turn it on and off simultaneously:

How it works...

Keep in mind that this is not security. This just happens to use gate as a quick way to integrate with all the layers of Laravel. This really is about showing and hiding features for a number of reasons.

As you saw previously, the workflow is pretty easy. Using migrations, we can push features from staging to production; and by having the UI, a QA person can then manage these features as needed.

One situation for us is the team if I am on programs, on production, or the mainline branch. This means that at any moment, a hotfix will be needed; and at the same time, a feature will be in progress. Feature flags allows us to code in such a way that we do not have to worry about this.

▶ Martin Fowler at `http://martinfowler.com/articles/feature-toggles.html`

▶ Feature flags in Laravel at `https://alfrednutile.info/posts/175`

Implementing Socialite to allow users to login with Facebook

Keep the track of passwords is not fun. In this section, we are going to make the app allow the user to login using Facebook! Thanks to Socialite this is super easy.

Getting ready

A fresh install of Laravel will do as I am going to work it into my existing comic book app.

How to do it...

1. Install the Socialite library. Make sure you read its docs for the steps needed to get the setup at `https://github.com/laravel/socialite`.

2. Set up `config/services.php` to add Facebook:

```
'facebook' => [
    'client_id'     => env('FB_CLIENT_ID'),
    'client_secret' => env('FB_CLIENT_SECRET'),
    'redirect'      => env('APP_URL') . '/facebook/callback',
],
```

Adding ENV settings

3. Make a controller:

```
>php artisan make:controller FacebookAuthController
```

4. Set up the controller to do some work:

```
use ...;

class FacebookAuthController extends Controller
{

    private $providerUser;

    public function redirect()
    {
        return Socialite::driver('facebook')->redirect();
    }

    public function callback()
    {
        $this->providerUser = Socialite::driver('facebook')->user();

        try
        {
            if($user = User::where('email', $this->providerUser->getEmail())->first()) {
                Auth::login($user);
                return Redirect::to('/')->with("message", "Thanks for setting up Facebook!");
            } else {
                $user = $this->createUserAndProfile();
                Auth::login($user);

                return Redirect::to('/')->with("message", "Thanks for setting up Facebook!");
            }


        } catch (\Exception $e) {
            return Redirect::to('login')->withError("We could not log your in");
        }
    }

    private function createUserAndProfile()
    {
        $user = new User();

        $user->email        = $this->providerUser->getEmail();
        $user->name         = $this->providerUser->getName();
        $user->password     = bcrypt(str_random(32));
        $user->save();

        $profile = new Profile();
        $profile->favorite_comic_character = 'Spider-man';
        $profile->user_id = $user->id;
        $profile->save();
```

5. Get your key from Facebook at `https://developers.facebook.com/`. They have made this fairly very easy. In the end, I ended up with this dash:

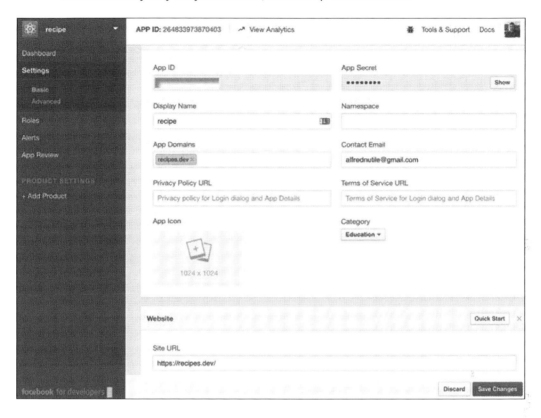

6. Now, plug in app ID and app secret into your `.env` file, since we will use this in `config/service.php`:

Adding settings to .env

7. Let's update the `app/Http/routes.php` route to give us the two routes that we need:

```
Route::group(['middleware' => ['web']], function () {

    Route::auth();

    Route::get('/facebook/redirect', 'FacebookAuthController@redirect');

    Route::get('/facebook/callback', 'FacebookAuthController@callback');
```

8. Update the login form at `resources/views/auth/login.blade.php` and we are done:

```
<div class="form-group">
    <div class="col-md-8 col-md-offset-4">
        <button type="submit" class="btn btn-primary">
            <i class="fa fa-btn fa-sign-in"></i>Login
        </button>
        <a class="btn btn-success" href="/facebook/redirect">
            <i class="fa fa-facebook"></i> Facebook Login</a>
        <a class="btn btn-link" href="{{ url('/password/reset') }}">
            Forgot Your Password?</a>
    </div>
</div>
```

How it works...

Wow! What used to be quite intimidating just became super easy and unified for GitHub, Twitter, and other providers.

Let's explore some code real quick now.

First, if we look at the controller that we made, we will see that the Socialite Facade is being used:

```
public function callback()
{
    $this->providerUser = Socialite::driver('facebook')->user();
```

The driver eventually ends up at `vendor/laravel/socialite/src/Two/` `FacebookProvider.php`, which handles some of the other requests back to their API for you. Here, it uses Guzzle to make a request:

```
*/
public function getAccessToken($code)
{
    $response = $this->getHttpClient()->get($this->getTokenUrl(), [
        'query' => $this->getTokenFields($code),
    ]);

    return $this->parseAccessToken($response->getBody());
}

/**
 * {@inheritdoc}
```

So our controller, which is for Facebook and our routes that I also prefixed for Facebook, allows us to later on plug in Twitter and other login tools.

Also note that I used `.env` for this! This really is the key since this is local, and as you see in the Facebook settings that I need to tell it about the URL that this is for. When I go to production, I will need a different URL.

Of course, our button is just a link to our own route to trigger this process, which again plugs back into the provider to make all of this happen:

```
/**
 * Redirect the user of the application to the provider's au
 *
 * @return \Symfony\Component\HttpFoundation\RedirectRespons
 */
public function redirect()
{
    $state = null;

    if ($this->usesState()) {
        $this->request->getSession()->set('state', $state =
    }

    return new RedirectResponse($this->getAuthUrl($state));
}
```

See also

▸ Laravel 5.2 Socialite Facebook login: It goes into detail on Facebook: `http://blog.damirmiladinov.com/laravel/laravel-5.2-socialite-facebook-login.html`

▸ Laracast: Socialite `https://laracasts.com/series/whats-new-in-laravel-5/episodes/9`

Adding custom middleware to protect user admin area

In this section, I am going to use middleware to protect an admin area. We will build this area as our user admin area later, but for now I just want to show how to implement middleware that makes sure that the user is the admin.

Getting ready

Base install of Laravel with users imported.

How to do it...

1. First, I am going to add a new field to the user table to set some users as admins:

```
> php artisan make:migration alter_user_table_add_is_admin
```

2. I will edit the `database/migrations/2016_05_21_132909_alter_user_table_add_is_admin.php` file so that it looks as follows:

```php
class AlterUserTableAddIsAdmin extends Migration
{
    public function up()
    {
        Schema::table('users', function (Blueprint $table) {
            $table->boolean('is_admin')->default(0);
        });
    }
    /**
     * Reverse the migrations.
     *
     * @return void
     */
    public function down()
    {
        Schema::table('users', function (Blueprint $table) {
            if (Schema::hasColumns('users', ['is_admin'])) {
                $table->dropColumn('is_admin');
            }
        });
    }
}
```

Migration

3. Then, I will make middleware to consider this:

```
> php artisan make:middleware IsAdminMiddleWare
```

4. I will then edit the `app/Http/Middleware/IsAdminMiddleWare.php` file, so it looks like this:

```php
class IsAdminMiddleWare
{
    /**
     * Handle an incoming request.
     *
     * @param  \Illuminate\Http\Request  $request
     * @param  \Closure  $next
     * @return mixed
     */
    public function handle($request, Closure $next)
    {
        if(Auth::guest() || !Auth::user()->isAdmin())
            return redirect('/', 301)->with('message', 'You need to be admin to see this page.')

        return $next($request);
    }
}
```

5. Then, I will update `app/Http/Kernel.php` to include the new `is_admin` middleware:

```
 * @var array
 */
protected $routeMiddleware = [
    'auth' => \App\Http\Middleware\Authenticate::class,
    'auth.basic' => \Illuminate\Auth\Middleware\AuthenticateWithBasicAuth::cla
    'guest' => \App\Http\Middleware\RedirectIfAuthenticated::class,
    'throttle' => \Illuminate\Routing\Middleware\ThrottleRequests::class,
    'is_admin' => \App\Http\Middleware\IsAdminMiddleWare::class,
];
}
```

6. Then, I will make the route for this admin area, which, right now, will not return much; but later on it will return the admin area of the site:

```
Route::group(['middleware' => ['web']], function () {

    Route::auth();

    Route::group(['middleware' => ['is_admin']], function () {
        Route::get('/admin/users', function () {
            return "You are here";
        })->name('admin.users');
    };
```

7. Then, I will test this as two users using PHPUnit. First, make the following test:

```
> php artisan make:test IsAdminTest
```

8. Then, update this file to start the testing and to prove that your route works:

```
/**
 * @test
 */
public function user_should_be_rejected()
{
    $user = factory(\App\User::class)->create();

    $this->be($user);

    $this->call('GET', '/admin/users');

    $this->assertResponseStatus(301);

    $this->visit('/admin/users')->see("You need to be admin to see this page.")
}
}
```

9. The test will fail because we did not add the `isAdmin` method to the user model called `app/User.php`:

```php
public function isAdmin()
{
    return $this->is_admin == 1;
}
```

10. Now, it will work:

```
vagrant@homestead:~/Code/recipes$ phpunit --filter=user_should_be_rejected
PHPUnit 4.8.25 by Sebastian Bergmann and contributors.

.

Time: 10.03 seconds, Memory: 18.00MB

OK (1 test, 4 assertions)
vagrant@homestead:~/Code/recipes$
```

11. Then, we will try it as an admin:

```php
/**
 * @test
 */
public function user_should_not_be_rejected()
{
    $user = factory(\App\User::class)->create(
        ['is_admin' => 1]
    );

    $this->be($user);

    $this->call('GET', '/admin/users');

    $this->assertResponseStatus(200);

    $this->visit('/admin/users')->see("You are here");
}
```

12. Now you will see that this passes too:

```
vagrant@homestead:~/Code/recipes$ phpunit --filter=user_should_not_be_rejected
PHPUnit 4.8.25 by Sebastian Bergmann and contributors.

.

Time: 4.31 seconds, Memory: 16.00MB

OK (1 test, 3 assertions)
vagrant@homestead:~/Code/recipes$
```

How it works...

Middleware is really worth understanding. You can use it before and after users access a route. This can help you trigger events, gather data about traffic on your site, and more. Keep in mind that you can stack more than one of these for a group of routes.

In this case, I added the `is_admin` field, and now I can set users as the state. Notice that I did not change the model to be fillable, since we really want to protect this field from mass assignment.

Thanks to Artisan, I can quickly generate the middleware file for this, and then add a quick check for the user. Note that I put `isAdmin` on the model called `User`. I just like how the logic about the user is in one place—the user model.

Finally, instead of going to the browser and reloading the page over and over until I get it right, I open up PHPUnit and make two tests that do it all for me, now and for each build! It is nice to know that my routes are protected from unauthorized access throughout the life of this project!

Read up on this; it really is an amazing feature in Laravel, PHP, and other frameworks.

See also

▸   Laravel docs: middleware: `https://laravel.com/docs/5.2/middleware`
▸   Laracast: HTTP middleware: `https://laracasts.com/series/intermediate-laravel/episodes/7`

Using Laravel to set up a subscription site

So, you want to take memberships! I will show you how to add a subscription service to our site. We will use Stripe to take subscriptions and use Laravel's Cashier to make it rather easy. This will go into more template and Stripe details rather than Laravel docs.

Getting ready

The base install is fine. Also, make sure that you migrate your users so that we have this in place too.

How to do it...

1. First, read the docs on Laravel at `https://laravel.com/docs/master/billing` and then follow along.

2. Now, install the library in line with `https://github.com/laravel/cashier` and the main docs.

3. I will set up my `.env` file to look like this:

```
STRIPE_PUBLIC=pk_test_fkjZujHyW1JsmyqGSx4Foo
STRIPE_SECRET=sk_test_xneZnRblxQIUn5ChcxgBar
```

Make sure the keys are just like they are in the docs and making sure I put public key in the right place, which is prefixed by `pk` and secret key by `sk`.

4. Then, I update `config/services.php`, which is needed to match the preceding keys:

```
'stripe' => [
    'model'  => App\User::class,
    'key'    => env('STRIPE_PUBLIC'),
    'secret' => env('STRIPE_SECRET'),
],
```

5. Then, I set up my routes to handle the traffic while I keep in mind that this is inside the default `Route::group ['middleware' => ['web']]` area:

```php
Route::group(['prefix' => 'subscribe'], function() {
    Route::get('/', 'SubscribeController@getLevelsPage')
        ->name('user.membership.signup');

    Route::post('comicslevel1', 'SubscribeController@postLevel1')
        ->name('user.membership.level1');

    Route::post('comicslevel2', 'SubscribeController@postLevel2')
        ->name('user.membership.level2');
});
```

6. To prevent token mismatch, I had to update this `app/Http/Middleware/VerifyCsrfToken.php` file:

```php
class VerifyCsrfToken extends BaseVerifier
{
    /**
     * The URIs that should be excluded from CSRF verification.
     *
     * @var array
     */
    protected $except = [
        'subscribe',
        'subscribe/*',
        'stripe/*'
    ];

    public function handle($request, Closure $next)
    {
        Log::info("Looking for token");

        if (
            $this->isReading($request) ||
            $this->runningUnitTests() ||
            $this->shouldPassThrough($request) ||
            $this->tokensMatch($request)
        ) {
            Log::info("Looking for token here 1");
            return $this->addCookieToResponse($request, $next($request));
        }

        throw new TokenMismatchException;
    }
}
```

7. Now we put our simple `app/Http/Controllers/SubscribeController.php` file in place:

```php
class SubscribeController extends Controller
{
    /**
     * @var SubscribeRepository
     */
    private $subscribeRepository;

    public function __construct(SubscribeRepository $subscribeRepository)
    {
        $this->subscribeRepository = $subscribeRepository;
    }

    public function getLevelsPage()
    {
        $public_key = env('STRIPE_PUBLIC');
        return view('stripe.subscribe', compact('public_key'));
    }

    public function postLevel1()
    {
        $input = Input::all();

        if(empty($input['stripeToken']))
            return Redirect::back();

        $user = $this->subscribeRepository->registerUser($input, Plans::$LEVEL1);

        Auth::login($user);

        return Redirect::to('profile')->with("message", "Thanks!");
    }

    public function postLevel2()
    {
        $input = Input::all();

        if(empty($input['stripeToken']))
            return Redirect::back();

        $user = $this->subscribeRepository->registerUser($input, Plans::$LEVEL2);

        Auth::login($user);

        return Redirect::to('profile')->with("message", "Thanks!");
    }
```

8. I will put a lot of the logic inside a repository class called `app/Repositories/SubscribeRepository.php`:

```php
class SubscribeRepository
{
    public function registerUser($input, $level, $charge = false)
    {
        try {
            if($user = $this->existingUser($input, $level, $charge)) {
                return $user;
            } else {
                $user = $this->createNewCustomer($input, $level, $charge);
                return $user;
            }
        } catch (\Exception $e) {
            throw new \Exception(
                sprintf("Error subscribing user %s %s %d", $e->getMessage(), $e->getFile(), $e->getLine()));
        }
    }

    private function existingUser($input, $level, $charge)
    {
        /** @var (App\User $user */
        if($user = User::where("email", $input['stripeEmail'])->first()) {
            if($user->subscribed()) {
                $user = $this->chargeOrSwap($user, $charge, $level);
            } else {
                $user = $this->chargeOrSubscribe($user, $charge, $level, $input);
            }
            return $user;
        }
        return false;
    }

    private function createNewCustomer($input, $level, $charge)
    {
        $user = User::create(
            [
                'email' => $input['stripeEmail'],
                'password' => Hash::make(Str::random())
            ]
        );

        $user = $this->chargeOrSubscribe($user, $charge, $level, 'input');

        return $user;
    }

    private function chargeOrSubscribe($user, $charge, $level, $input)
    {
        if($charge) {
            $user->charge($level);
        } else {
            $subscription = $user->newSubscription($level, $level);
            $subscription->create($input['stripeToken']);
        }
        return $user;
```

9. Of course, a number of changes and additions to the view files are also required:

    ❑ `resources/views/stripe/subscribe.blade.php`:

```
@extends('layout')

@section('header')
    <div class="page-header">
        <h1><i class="fa fa-money"></i> Sign up for membership</h1>
    </div>
@endsection


@section('content')

    <div role="tabpanel">


        <!-- Tab panes -->
        <div class="tab-content">
            <div role="tabpanel" class="tab-pane active" id="monthly">
                @include('stripe.monthly')
            </div>
        </div>

    </div>


@endsection
```

Monthly Blade

    ❑ Then, `resources/views/stripe/monthly.blade.php`:

```
<div class="pricing-tables">

    <div class="row">
        <div class="col-sm-4 col-md-4">
            @include('stripe.level2')
        </div>


        <div class="col-sm-4 col-md-4 ">
            @include('stripe.level1')
        </div>


        <div class="col-sm-4 col-md-4    ">
            @include('stripe.fan')

        </div>

    </div> <!-- row-->

</div> <!-- pricing-tables -->
```

❑ Then, `resources/views/stripe/level1.blade.php`; all the levels look like this and I will cover the #1 and #2 details in the *How it works...* section of this recipe; thus, just use the same idea for `stripe.level1` and `stripe.fan`:

```
<div class="plan">

    <div class="head">
        <h2>Level 1</h2>

    </div>

    <ul class="item-list">
        <li>Keep the site going</li>
        <li>Get our Newsletter</li>
        <li> </li>
    </ul>

    <div class="price">
        <h3><span class="symbol">$</span>5</h3>
        <h4>per month</h4>
    </div>

    <form action="/subscribe/comicslevel1" method="POST">
        <script
            src="https://checkout.stripe.com/checkout.js" class="stripe-button"
            data-key="{{ $public_key }}"
            data-amount="500"
            data-name="Comics Level 1"
            data-description="Comics Level 1 ($5.00)"
            data-image="/128x128.png">
        </script>
    </form>

</div>
```

10. Here is what my dash looks like for Stripe. Note that **Testing** mode is on:

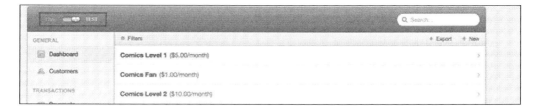

11. This is what a plan will look like. Note the ID matches what I have in the Blade template files:

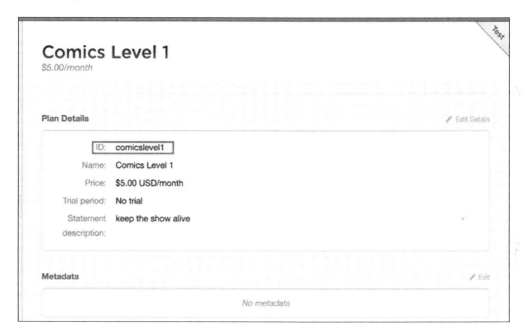

12. As per the docs my migration file `database/migrations/2016_05_21_153145_create_cashier_migrations.php` is in place:

```
>php artisan make:migration create_cashier_migrations
```

```php
    public function up()
    {
        Schema::table('users', function ($table) {
            $table->string('stripe_id')->nullable();
            $table->string('card_brand')->nullable();
            $table->string('card_last_four')->nullable();
            $table->timestamp('trial_ends_at')->nullable();
        });

        Schema::create('subscriptions', function ($table) {
            $table->increments('id');
            $table->integer('user_id');
            $table->string('name');
            $table->string('stripe_id');
            $table->string('stripe_plan');
            $table->integer('quantity');
            $table->timestamp('trial_ends_at')->nullable();
            $table->timestamp('ends_at')->nullable();
            $table->timestamps();
        });
    }

    /**
     * Reverse the migrations.
     *
     * @return void
     */
    public function down()
    {
        Schema::table('users', function (Blueprint $table) {

            $columns = [
                'trial_ends_at',
                'card_brand',
                'card_last_four',
                'stripe_id'
            ];

            if (Schema::hasColumns('users', $columns)) {
                $table->dropColumn($columns);
            }
        });

        Schema::drop('subscriptions');
    }
```

13. Your **Subscription** page will look like this with a little help from this theme at `https://wrapbootstrap.com/theme/flat-pricing-table-WB0D37764`, but you can go at it without the theme if you want:

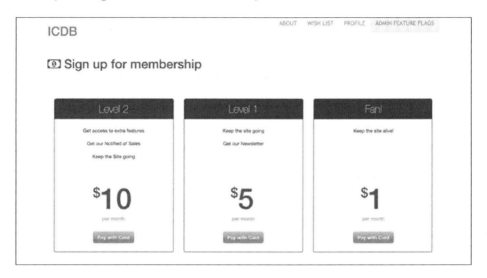

14. When users pay, they will see this screen, as provided by Stripe and the JS file that you saw me referencing in the preceding Blade files. For now, you can fill it in with a dummy credit card:

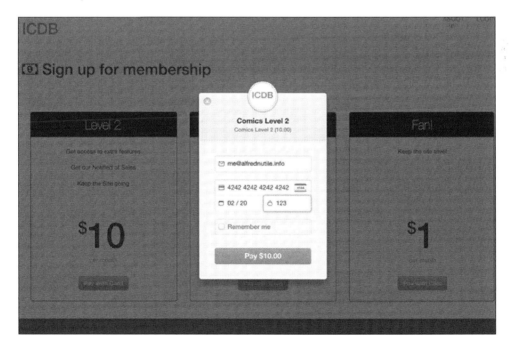

15. All things are in place! When you subscribe, you will get this:

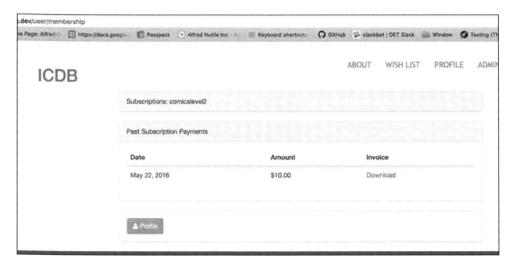

How it works...

Okay, let's go over all of this slowly now. The `.env` file is the key here, as you test this frequently before going live with your Stripe Test settings. And Live has different keys, so using the `service.php` file to plug all of this in makes it easy to go back and forth. The migrations then gets us the fields that we need to track the user relationships to the subscriptions. So far, all this is standard stuff.

Then, there are the routes. We visit the main one that has all the subscription blocks, but each one of the routes is a form. And they are set to POST. Note that they include the JS file that lives on Stripes servers. So, after this is done and the information based on the *data* inside the `script` tag is submitted, they will POST the results back to these endpoints. Pretty cool how they handle a lot of this for us. Now, taking care of the money part, the forms and sending us back a token so we have *nothing* to worry about on our site for credit card information.

These controller and repository classes then have to do several things. First, we figure out whether this is a new user or not and make them or find them, and then, either way, we then authenticate them. Once this is done, we can deal with their subscription. As per the Laravel docs, we added Billable to our user model:

```
use Laravel\Cashier\Billable;

class User extends Authenticatable
{

    use Billable;
    /**
     * The attributes that are mass assignable.
     *
     * @var array
     */
    protected $fillable = [
        'name', 'email', 'password',
    ];
```

With this in place, we get the relations and interactive methods around this model. This is why I can ask for things such as `newSubscription` in `app/Repositories/SubscribeRepository.php`.

After this, I made a simple page for the users to see their invoices and download them, as per the docs on Laravel. Soon, I will show you how to edit a subscription.

At this point, you can use gate to hide and show areas and features on the site in line with the docs. I will not use feature flags because they are used more for deployment needs. But you can, for example, only allow users who are fans or higher to add Favorites.

Once again Laravel makes things amazingly easy; it also increases your choices as it supports Braintree as an almost drop as an alternative to Stripe.

See also

- Laravel docs: Cashier: `https://laravel.com/docs/master/billing`
- Stripe Testing docs: `https://stripe.com/docs/testing`
- Laracast: subscriptions with Stripe: `https://laracasts.com/lessons/painless-subscriptions-with-laravel-and-stripe`

Creating an interface for the user to manage subscriptions

Alright, the preceding recipe made it possible for people to subscribe, but what happens when they want to change the plan or cancel it!

I will cover making an area where they can update or swap out their plan. You can take this much further at the UI level. I am keeping it very simple.

Getting ready

See the preceding recipes, as you really need to have the cashier set up to get this far.

How to do it...

1. I will make a controller to keep our logic in one controller:

   ```
   > php artisan make:controller SubscriptionSwapController
   ```

   ```php
   class SubscriptionSwapController extends Controller
   {

       public function swap(Request $request, SubscribeRepository $repository)
       {
           try {
               $repository->swap($request->input('current'), false);
               return redirect()->route('user.membership.show')->with('message', "Membership Swapped");
           } catch (\Exception $e)
           {
               return redirect()->route('user.membership.show')->withErrors("Could not swap membership");
           }
       }
   }
   ```

2. Then, I will make the route for this controller:

   ```php
   Route::post('/user/membership', 'SubscriptionSwapController@swap')
       ->name('user.membership.swap');
   ```

3. Now, to add some logic to the repository class called `app/Repositories/SubscribeRepository.php`, the controller uses:

```php
public function swap($current, $new_plan = false)
{

    if($new_plan == false) {
        $new_plan = $this->getNewPlanFromCurrent($current);
    }

    $user = Auth::user();

    /** @var \App\User $user */
    $subscription = $user->subscription($current);

    return $subscription->swap($new_plan);
}


public function getNewPlanFromCurrent($current)
{
    if($current == Plans::$LEVEL1) {
        return Plans::$LEVEL2;
    }

    return Plans::$LEVEL1;
}
```

4. Update the previous view for `resources/views/stripe/status.blade.php`:

```html
<div class="row">
    <div class="col-lg-10 col-lg-offset-1">
        <div class="panel panel-default">
            <div class="panel-heading">
                Subscriptions: {{ \App\Plans::returnDisplayName($subscription['stripe_plan']) }}
                <form action="{{ route('user.membership.swap') }}" method="POST" style="..."
                    onsubmit="if(confirm('Are you sure you want to change your level?')) { return tr
                    <input type="hidden" name="current" value="{{ $subscription['stripe_plan'] }}">
                    <input type="hidden" name="_token" value="{{ csrf_token() }}">
                    <button type="submit" class="btn btn-xs btn-info"><i class="fa fa-thumbs-up"></i>
                         Update
                    </button>
                </form>
```

5. Now, the UI will look like this at `/user/membership`:

6. When you press the button:

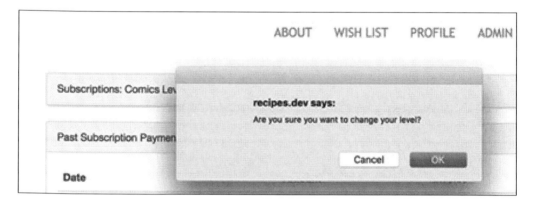

7. That's it! It will swap out memberships for you and make a new invoice.

How it works...

Like I said at the start, this is one of the many ways to do this. In this case, I focused on two levels. You might have more. You may even want the user to choose a level. In this case, I had them just POST to an endpoint and make a choice from there based on what they have now.

So, the Blade file happens to have a form that hides a value to pass into the controller. I could even get this from the user's model.

Once in there, the repository has a method to see what the level is now and grab the other level. Again, this is very simple as you can take this as far as you want. For example, make a select list of all the levels for them to choose, and then POST right back to the same endpoint.

Finally, the user gets redirected back to the page and the swap is done!

Creating an admin interface for subscriptions

In this section, I will cover making a place for an admin user to come in and see reports about members. This will need some seed data, as I will attempt to show the membership statuses in one place.

We will aim for something as follows:

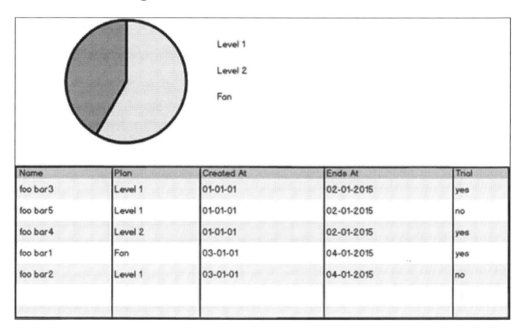

Name	Plan	Created At	Ends At	Trial
foo bar3	Level 1	01-01-01	02-01-2015	yes
foo bar5	Level 1	01-01-01	02-01-2015	no
foo bar4	Level 2	01-01-01	02-01-2015	yes
foo bar1	Fan	03-01-01	04-01-2015	yes
foo bar2	Level 1	03-01-01	04-01-2015	no

Getting ready

If you have not followed this far, then you will need at least a base Laravel installed with the cashier and auth setups.

How to do it...

1. Set up a route for the admin dashboard:

```
Route::get('/admin/memberships', 'AdminMembershipsDashboardController@get');
```

2. Make a controller for the route:

   ```
   >php artisan make:controller AdminMembershipsDashboardController
   ```

3. Let's protect the `app/Http/Controllers/`
   `AdminMembershipsDashboardController.php` controller:

   ```php
   class AdminMembershipsDashboardController extends Cont
   {
       public function __construct()
       {
           $this->middleware('isAdmin');
       }

       public function get(Request $request)
       {
           //
       }
   }
   ```

4. Now, we need to add middleware to check whether this user is an admin. I already added is_admin as a boolean field on the users table; see *Chapter 5, Working with Data*; we also created middleware using *Chapter 7, Authentication, Security and Subscriptions* to protect the user admin area, so we know this is protected.

5. Seed some users with subscriptions, past members, trials and so on: `database/seeds/UserTableSeeder.php`. I covered seeding in *Chapter 5, Working with Data* so you can see how your app looks:

```
factory(\App\User::class, 7)->create()->each(function($u) {
    factory(\Laravel\Cashier\Subscription::class)->create(
        ['name' => "Level 1", "stripe_id" => \App\Plans::$LEVEL1, "user_id" => $u->id]
    );
});

factory(\App\User::class, 7)->create()->each(function($u) {
    factory(\Laravel\Cashier\Subscription::class)->create(
        ['name' => "Fan", 'stripe_id' => \App\Plans::$FAN, 'user_id' => $u->id]
    );
});

factory(\App\User::class, 2)->create()->each(function($u) {
    factory(\Laravel\Cashier\Subscription::class)->create(
        [
            'name' => "Level 2",
            'user_id' => $u->id,
            'stripe_id' => \App\Plans::$LEVEL2,
            'trial_ends_at' => \Carbon\Carbon::now()->day(rand(4,10))
        ]
    );
});

factory(\App\User::class, 5)->create()->each(function($u) {
    factory(\Laravel\Cashier\Subscription::class)->create(
        ['name' => "Level 2", 'stripe_id' => \App\Plans::$LEVEL2, 'user_id' => $u->id]
    );
});
```

6. The factory that I am using looks like `database/factories/ModelFactory.php`:

```
$factory->define(Laravel\Cashier\Subscription::class, function (Faker\Generator $faker) {
    return [
        'name' => \App\Plans::$LEVEL1,
        'stripe_id' => \App\Plans::$LEVEL1,
        'stripe_plan' => str_random(16),
        'quantity' => 1,
        'ends_at' => null,
        'user_id' => function () {
            return factory(App\User::class)->create()->id;
        }
    ];
});
```

7. Let's install the chart library that we will use:

    > **bower install angular-google-chart#0.1.0 –save**

8. Place it into our AngularJS app file; first, copy it into our `assets/vendor` folder:

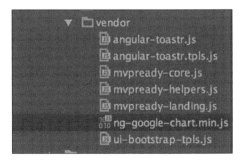

9. Then, run `gulp` to pull it in and then `gulp watch`:

   ```
   >gulp scripts
   >gulp watch
   ```

10. Then, we will make the Blade view called `resources/views/admin/subscriptions.blade.php`:

```blade
@extends('layout')

@section('header')
    <div class="page-header clearfix">
        <h1><i class="fa fa-group"></i> Admin Memberships</h1>
    </div>
@endsection

@section('content')
    <div ng-controller="ChartController as vm">
        <div google-chart chart="vm.myChartObject" style="..."></div>

        @if($users->count())
            <table class="table table-condensed table-striped">
                <thead>
                <tr>
                    <th>ID</th>
                    <th>Name</th>
                    <th>Email</th>
                    <th>Plan</th>
                    <th>Created At</th>
                    <th>Ends At</th>
                    <th>Trail</th>
                </tr>
                </thead>

                <tbody>
                @foreach($users as $user)
                    <tr>
                        <td>{{$user->id}}</td>
                        <td>{{$user->name}}</td>
                        <td>{{$user->email}}</td>
                        <td>{{$user->subscriptions->first()->name}}</td>
                        <td>{{$user->subscriptions->first()->created_at->format('M d Y')}}</td>
                        <td>
                            @if($user->subscriptions->first()->ends_at)
                                {{ $user->subscriptions->first()->ends_at->format('M d Y') }}
                            @endif
                        </td>
                        <td>
                            @if($user->subscriptions->first()->trial_ends_at)
                                {{ $user->subscriptions->first()->trial_ends_at->format('M d Y') }}
                            @endif
                        </td>
                    </tr>
                @endforeach
                </tbody>
            </table>
        @else
            <h3 class="text-center">No Subscriptions!</h3>
        @endif
    </div>
@endsection
```

11. Then, the Laravel controller:

```php
<?php

namespace App\Http\Controllers;

use App\Plans;
use App\User;
use Illuminate\Http\Request;

use App\Http\Requests;
use Laravel\Cashier\Subscription;

class AdminMembershipsDashboardController extends Controller
{
    public function __construct()
    {
        $this->middleware('is_admin');
    }

    public function get(Request $request)
    {
        $users = User::with('subscriptions')->has('subscriptions')->get();

        $level1 = Subscription::where('stripe_id', Plans::$LEVEL1)->count();
        $level2 = Subscription::where('stripe_id', Plans::$LEVEL2)->count();
        $fan    = Subscription::where('stripe_id', Plans::$FAN)->count();

        $levels = [

            'level1' => ['name' => "Level 1", 'total' => $level1],
            'level2' => ['name' => "Level 2", 'total' => $level2],
            'fan'    => ['name' => "Fan", 'total' => $fan],

        ];

        \JavaScript::put([
            'levels' => $levels
        ]);

        return view('admin.subscriptions', compact('users'));
    }
}
```

12. Now, the AngularJS controller called `resources/assets/js/custom/app.js`:

```javascript
(function(){
    'use strict';

    angular.module('app', ['ui.bootstrap', 'ngAnimate', 'toastr', 'googlechart']);

    ChartController.$inject = ['$window'];

    function ChartController($window) {
        var vm = this;
        vm.myChartObject = {};


        activate();

        function activate()
        {
            myChartObject();
        }

        function myChartObject()
        {

            var levels = $window.levels;

            vm.myChartObject = {};

            vm.myChartObject.type = "PieChart";

            vm.myChartObject.data = {"cols": [
                {id: "t", label: "Name", type: "string"},
                {id: "s", label: "Total", type: "number"}
            ], "rows": [
                {c: [
                    {v: levels.level1.name},
                    {v: levels.level1.total}
                ]},
                {c: [
                    {v: levels.level2.name},
                    {v: levels.level2.total}
                ]},
                {c: [
                    {v: levels.fan.name},
                    {v: levels.fan.total}
                ]}
            ]};

            vm.myChartObject.options = {
                'title': 'Memberships'
            };
        }
    }
})
```

13. This is what you get:

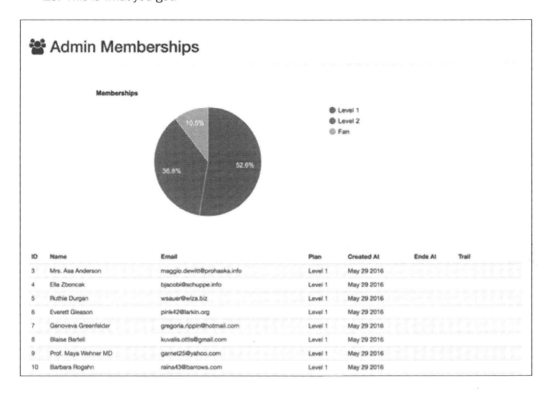

👥 Admin Memberships

ID	Name	Email	Plan	Created At	Ends At	Trail
3	Mrs. Asa Anderson	maggio.dewitt@prohaska.info	Level 1	May 29 2016		
4	Ella Zboncak	bjacobi@schuppe.info	Level 1	May 29 2016		
5	Ruthie Durgan	wsauer@wiza.biz	Level 1	May 29 2016		
6	Everett Gleason	pink42@larkin.org	Level 1	May 29 2016		
7	Genoveva Greenfelder	gregoria.rippin@hotmail.com	Level 1	May 29 2016		
8	Blaise Bartell	kuvalis.ottis@gmail.com	Level 1	May 29 2016		
9	Prof. Maya Wehner MD	garnet25@yahoo.com	Level 1	May 29 2016		
10	Barbara Rogahn	raina43@barrows.com	Level 1	May 29 2016		

How it works...

This is a really simple example, but you can see how you can take it much further to include information you need to know about how your subscriptions are doing. And if you look at *Chapter 6, Adding Angular to Your App*, you will see many of the details involved in adding this type of chart to your page.

Note the seeding file, the docs would have suggested me to do this part differently:

```
/**
 * Run the database seeds.
 *
 * @return void
 */
public function run()
{
    factory(App\User::class, 50)->create()->each(function($u) {
        $u->posts()->save(factory(App\Post::class)->make());
    });
}
```

I went with this due to a null issue on save, so I went with the seeding code as seen in the *How to do it...* section.

As far as the charting goes, there are many out there; this one just happens to keep it simple. But basically, you can see how I formatted it in the Laravel controller, leaving as little work as possible for me to do in JavaScript or AngularJS. I try to keep my logic in the backend, giving the frontend as close to possible as what it needs for data, and let the frontend just iterate over the data. This keeps the business logic from spreading out into two places whenever possible.

8

Testing and Debugging Your Application

In this chapter, we will cover the following topics:

- ▶ Generating test
- ▶ Using tests to think through your code **TDT** (**Test Driven Thinking**)
- ▶ Using VCR for API testing
- ▶ Getting your code onto GitHub
- ▶ Using Travis to run tests with every push
- ▶ Launching Gulp watch into your workflow
- ▶ Using Mockery to test your controllers
- ▶ Troubleshooting your application

Introduction

It's time for testing. For me, this does not mean TDD and testing every bit of code, but sometimes it is just a tool to help me think through some ideas, can quickly verify something is working as I hoped for. So, the recipes in this section will cover the concepts of what to test, how to get started, mocking, and more.

Generating tests

We need to make a test to start testing. And once again, Laravel makes this super easy.

Getting ready

SSH into Homestead using the command `homestead ssh` and cd into the recipe directory.

 I actually wrote this Artisan command for Laravel in September 2015. Inspired by all the easy workflows I get out of Artisan, I was surprised this one was not there. And I am not bringing this up just to show off, but just to show how you can add your ideas to this framework. Of course, some ideas get rejected, and this is fine, so go make a library to then use in Laravel, but keep trying! The commit is at `https://github.com/laravel/framework/pull/10170`.

How to do it...

1. Type the following:

    ```
    >php artisan make:test ResultsRepositoryTest
    ```

2. That's it!

How it works...

This is not much of a recipe! But let's dig into some of its aspects.

Why did I call it `ResultsRepositoryTest`? It might get tempting to just stick all your tests in one file but as your app grows, the file will become too hard to read. So, by breaking your tests into files named after the class they are testing, you start to create order for your application for now and when it grows.

Second, this generated a file to get you going, so let's look at it:

```php
<?php

use Illuminate\Foundation\Testing\WithoutMiddleware;
use Illuminate\Foundation\Testing\DatabaseMigrations;
use Illuminate\Foundation\Testing\DatabaseTransactions;

class ResultsRepositoryTest extends TestCase
{
    /**
     * A basic test example.
     *
     * @return void
     */
    public function testExample()
    {
        $this->assertTrue(true);
    }
}
```

Right away, we have a method that is an example of a test. Run the following:

```
>phpunit --filter=testExample
```

Then, this would run just this method:

```
> phpunit --testdox-text tests/ResultsRepositoryTest.php
```

You will get this:

```
vagrant@homestead:~/Code/levnetserver$ phpunit --testdox-text tests/ResultsRepositoryTest.php
Example
 [x] Basic example

ResultsRepository
 [x] Example

PHPUnit 4.8.24 by Sebastian Bergmann and contributors.

.

Time: 3.63 seconds, Memory: 10.00Mb

OK (1 test, 2 assertions)
vagrant@homestead:~/Code/levnetserver$ 
```

Now, this converts the `camelCase` method into a list of features being tested and the class that they belong to.

This is really nice.

So, in 6 months from now, when you open up this application and then the `ResultsRepository` class, and if you cannot remember for the life of you what this call does and how it works, find the test, read it, run it, and, hopefully, you will get a sense of what is going on.

There's more...

You can, of course, set up your machine for Nginx, PHP, MySQL, and all the rest, but there are a lot of reasons why the previous is best. On a team or alone, having your environment contained like this makes upgrading your machine, going from desktop to laptop, pushing code to production, having up-to-date libraries for new apps and older libraries for legacy apps, and more all so much easier.

See also

- ▶ **Laravel**: `https://laravel.com/docs/5.2/homestead`
- ▶ **Vagrant**: `https://www.vagrantup.com/`
- ▶ **VirtualBox**: `https://www.virtualbox.org/wiki/Downloads`

Using tests to think through your code TDT (Test Driven Thinking)

In this section, we are just going to think about a small chunk of code using tests. It is not TDD in that I am testing Red, Green, and Refactor. It just uses unit tests to build, think, and iterate over simple or complex ideas. If you find yourself reloading a browser to see if something is working right, then it is a good sign. You can just be writing a test. Even if you end up not keeping the test, it will get you to the final code quicker.

Getting ready

SSH into Homestead using the command `homestead ssh` and cd into the recipe directory and let's get testing. Also, we are going to use the client that we made to query the Marvel Comics API. So, you will need an API Key and a Token from them at `https://developer.marvel.com/account`.

How to do it...

1. First, we need to add the key and secret to your `.env` file:

```
MARVEL_API_KEY=foo
MARVEL_API_SECRET=bar
```

2. Then, we will make a test around this setup:

   `>php artisan make:test MarvelApiClientTest`

3. First, let's just write in the test what we are trying to do. Aim low:

```
use ...

class MarvelApiClientTest extends TestCase
{
    /**
     * @test
     */
    public function test_first_setup()
    {
        //1 I need to set Guzzle to pass my key and secret with each request to Marvel
        //2 I then need a method (getAllComicsPaginated) and see if I can connect
        //3 Then I need to move this into a Provider
        //4 Finally I need to make a Service around these interactions with Marvel

    }
}
```

Figure 1 Stubbed out test with goals

4. In this file, we will do our first attempt at hitting the API, then we will move it into a cleaner approach as seen here:

```
> phpunit --filter=test_first_setup
```

```php
class MarvelApiClientTest extends TestCase
{
    /**
     * @test
     */
    public function test_first_setup()
    {
        //1 I need to set Guzzle to pass my key and secret with each request to Marvel
        //2 I then need a method (getAllComicsPaginated) and see if I can connect
        //3 Then I need to move this into a Provider
        //4 Finally I need to make a Service around these interactions with Marvel

        $config = [
            'base_uri'          => env('MARVEL_API_BASE_URL'),
            'timeout'           => 0,
            'allow_redirects'   => false,
            'verify'            => false,
            'headers'           => [
                'Content-Type'  => 'application/json'
            ]
        ];

        $client = new Client($config);

        $ts = \Carbon\Carbon::now();

        $query = [
            'ts'        => $ts->timestamp,
            'hash'      => md5($ts->timestamp . env('MARVEL_API_SECRET') . env('MARVEL_API_KEY')),
            'apikey'    => env('MARVEL_API_KEY')
        ];

        $results = $client->request('GET', 'comics', ['query' => $query]);

        $this->assertEquals(200, $results->getStatusCode());

    }
}
```

```
vagrant@homestead:~/Code/recipes$ phpunit --filter=test_first_setup
PHPUnit 4.8.24 by Sebastian Bergmann and contributors.

.

Time: 3.84 seconds, Memory: 15.00Mb

OK (1 test, 1 assertion)
vagrant@homestead:~/Code/recipes$
```

5. Now, let's move it into a provider to clean up this request:

    ```
    > php artisan make:provider MarvelApiClient
    ```

6. In this file, we need to start moving in the work that we did in
    `GuzzleClientProvider.php` so that it looks like this:

```php
<?php

namespace App\Providers;

use ...

class MarvelApiClient extends ServiceProvider
{
    /**
     * Bootstrap the application services.
     *
     * @return void
     */
    public function boot()
    {
        $this->app->bind(\App\Interfaces\ComicClientInterface::class, function() {
            $config = [
                'base_uri'          => env('MARVEL_API_BASE_URL'),
                'timeout'           => 0,
                'allow_redirects'   => false,
                'verify'            => false,
                'headers'           => [
                    'Content-Type'  => 'application/json'
                ]
            ];

            $client = new Client($config);
            $key = env('MARVEL_API_KEY');
            $secret = env('MARVEL_API_SECRET');
            $client =  new MarvelApi($key, $secret, $client);
            $client->setApiVersion(env('MARVEL_API_VERSION'));
            return $client;
        });

    }

    /**
     * Register the application services.
     *
     * @return void
     */
    public function register()
    {
```

7. Then, let's make a plan interface file in the Interfaces folder:

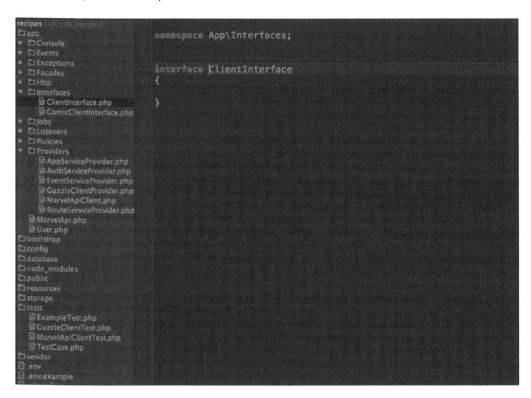

8. Now, make a file to start our `Marvel API Comic` class in the `app` folder called `MarvelApi.php`:

```php
<?php

namespace App;

use App\Interfaces\ComicClientInterface;
use Carbon\Carbon;
use GuzzleHttp\Client;

class MarvelApi implements ComicClientInterface
{
    protected $key = false;
    protected $secret = false;
    protected $base_url = false;
    protected $api_version = '/v1/public';

    /**
     * @var Client
     */
    protected $client = null;

    public function __construct($key, $secret, Client $client)
    {
        $this->key = $key;
        $this->secret = $secret;
        $this->client = $client;
    }

    public function comics($title = false)
    {
        $query = ['query' => $this->makeAuth()];

        if($title)
        {
            $query['query'] = array_merge($query['query'], ['titleStartsWith' => $title]);
        }

        $results = $this->client->request('GET', $this->getApiVersion() . '/comics', $query);

        return json_decode($results->getBody());
    }

    protected function makeAuth()
    {
        $ts = Carbon::now();
        $hash = md5($ts->timestamp . $this->secret . $this->key);
        return ['apikey' => $this->key, 'ts' => $ts->timestamp, 'hash' => $hash];
    }
}
```

9. Add your provider to the `config/app.php` file:

```
▶ ☐ Jobs                         /*
▶ ☐ Listeners                     * Application Service Providers...
▶ ☐ Policies                      */
▶ ☐ Providers                    App\Providers\AppServiceProvider::class,
   ☐ MarvelApi.php               App\Providers\AuthServiceProvider::class,
   ☐ User.php                    App\Providers\EventServiceProvider::class,
▶ ☐ bootstrap                    App\Providers\RouteServiceProvider::class,
▼ ☐ config                       App\Providers\GuzzleClientProvider::class,
   ☐ app.php
   ☐ auth.php                    App\Providers\MarvelApiClient::class
   ☐ broadcasting.php
   ☐ cache.php              •
   ☐ compile.php
   ☐ database.php               ],
   ☐ filesystems.php
```

10. Let's update the `.env` file with all new settings for this:

```
MARVEL_API_KEY=foo
MARVEL_API_SECRET=bar
MARVEL_API_BASE_URL=https://gateway.marvel.com
MARVEL_API_VERSION=/v1/public
```

11. Finally, let's show this working in our test:

```php
<?php

use GuzzleHttp\Client;
use Illuminate\Foundation\Testing\WithoutMiddleware;
use Illuminate\Foundation\Testing\DatabaseMigrations;
use Illuminate\Foundation\Testing\DatabaseTransactions;
use Illuminate\Support\Facades\App;

class MarvelApiClientTest extends TestCase
{
    /**
     * @test
     */
    public function test_first_setup()
    {
        //1 I need to set Guzzle to pass my key and secret with each request to Marvel
        //2 I then need a method (getAllComicsPaginated) and see if I can connect
        //3 Then I need to move this into a Provider
        //4 Finally I need to make a Service around these interactions with Marvel

        $client = App::make(\App\Interfaces\ComicClientInterface::class);

        $results = $client->comics();

        $this->assertEquals(200, $results['code']);

    }
}
```

How it works...

This was a lot of work! Let's go over why and what took place.

First, I set up my `.env` file to have some configuration information. One reason is that this is secret information, and I do not want it to be on GitHub once I upload the code. But this type of information might change depending on who is using the library (if we make this a library later) and what version of the API we are using, for example, Marvel Production versus a Marvel Dev API. Some APIs offer the feature that does not allow you to hit the real API during testing or the production data while not doing production work.

Then, we make our test; pretty clear and simple there. I just stub out an idea I have or a nontechnical set of goals to get to where I need to get to make this work.

From here, I start coding. But I still keep it simple. Later, I can break it into more classes, but right now, I just want to keep it is a simple as possible. We instantiate Guzzle just as we did in *Chapter 2, Using Composer Packages*. We pass in the secret, key, and the odd hash they have. Personally, I have never seen this before. You will also see another use of `env` for `MARVEL_API_BASE_URL`. I can move this later to a `config` file, but for now, I will put it into `.env` and call it here. Also, why not just hardcode this might be what you are thinking, and that is fine, I just tend to not do this, so I can easily replace this as needed during testing and what not. Now we are ready to test the Client.

And it works!

OK, now it is time to clean up. I do not want a huge effort every time I want to call Marvel, so let's start to centralize our use of `MarvelClient` that we are building. To start with, I make another provider. These are super helpful for instantiating classes ahead of time for easy use and injection.

 You can read a lot about this at `https://laravel.com/docs/5.2/providers`. Keep in mind Dependency Injection is a really simple concept and is core to writing applications in Object Oriented PHP.

Then, we move a lot of code from the test into this file. Binding our `Abstract Class` the interface to the `Concrete` implementation of our class. Why? Well, in some ways, we are making it easy to use this class in different parts of our application; in other ways, we are prepping our app to later on have a DC Comics or Comixology API Client that we can talk to in the same manner as Marvel.

Lastly, we start to build up a class that uses the interface with some common methods that our DC Client can use later. I will now start to grow out the Client, so it looks more like the class here:

```php
<?php

namespace App\Interfaces;

interface ComicClientInterface
{
    public function comics($title = false);

}
```

Now we have an interface that we can use later on when we decide to also talk to the DC API.

Most importantly, all of this came from taking my time, outlining some goals, and then working slowly to that goal using a `phpunit` test.

See also

  ▸ **Marvel API Docs**: `http://developer.marvel.com/docs`

  ▸ **More Testing Help**: `https://laracasts.com/series/the-lifecycle-of-a-new-feature`

Getting your code onto GitHub

This next recipe will help you use this amazing tool called Git and a company called GitHub that has wrapped this technology with a service. Whether you are working alone or with others, it is important to work using version control systems, such as Git. You have automatic backup of your work by putting it on GitHub; you have version control so that you can go back in time if you need to find some old code; and you can easily work with others on your application.

Getting ready

Okay, so you will need a GitHub account, but the good news it is free, and it is a good place to show off the work you are doing. Once you have the account set up, make sure you have it installed on your PC/Mac; I will provide some links going forward.

How to do it...

1. Let's first make the new repo on GitHub:

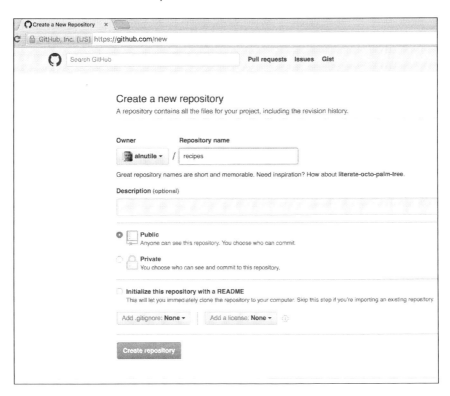

2. Now, go to your command line on your Mac as follows:

```
> cd ~/Code/recipes
> git init
> git remote add origin git@github.com:alnutile/recipes.git
> git add --all
> git commit -m "my first push of app"
> git push origin master
```

3. Update your `.gitingore`:

```
/vendor
/node_modules
/public/storage
Homestead.yaml
Homestead.json
.env
.idea
```

4. Now, clean out the accidental inclusion of the `.idea` folder that PHPStorm made:

```
> git rm -rf --cache .idea
> git commit -m "clean up"
> git push origin master
```

How it works...

Even though this is not Laravel specific, it really is key to working with Laravel and in modern PHP. You also have a graph showing how busy you are coding!

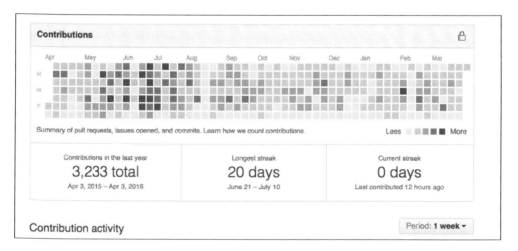

This really does help when you are looking for work as a freelancer or full-timer.

You also have a place to see past versions of your code, and you can share your project with other developers.

Also note that in step 4, I accidentally put my .idea folder in my application into Git that PHPStorm created. But this is odd. If another developer comes on, I would be overwriting his folder for no good reason. So, I take a moment to rm or remove the folder with recursive and force, for example, -rf, and then using --cache, I'd tell Git to not remove the folder from my computer, but just take it out of its database.

Also, I am doing this work on Mac, not in Homestead. You can do it in Homestead, but I have seen Vagrant to be a bit slower on file-intensive work, such as Git; and also, you need to configure Git so that when you push to GitHub, it shows your GitHub username, so you are really getting credit for your work.

See also

- GitHub has a Graphical Tool is at—https://desktop.github.com/
- The Git for Windows command-line tool is at—https://git-for-windows.github.io/
- Installing on Mac—https://git-scm.com/book/en/v2/Getting-Started-Installing-Git#Installing-on-Mac
- Of course, Laracasts for more info on Git—https://laracasts.com/series/git-me-some-version-control

Using VCR for API testing

Alright, we are now making calls with Guzzle to a real API (see the section *Using Tests to Think Through Your Code TDT (Test Driven Thinking)* earlier in this chapter). But they are going to get pretty annoyed with us if we are hitting their API for all our tests. Also, it is going to slow down our tests. Right now, the speed difference is nominal since there is only one request, but once there are more, the time will really add up. So, to prevent this, we begin to use VCR to create fixtures of our HTTP requests and responses so that the next time we call them, they are delivered to us instead.

Getting ready

This one is a bit tricky on the installation. I will cover the installation in the upcoming steps, and then go into detail in the *How it Works...* section. Also, this is one of the recipes that I will be doing from inside Homestead, so begin with homestead ssh into your box.

How to do it...

1. Install SOAP for PHP:

```
> sudo apt-get install php-soap
```

2. Then, we can go on and install PHP VCR per their website:

```
>composer require --dev php-vcr/phpunit-testlistener-vcr
```

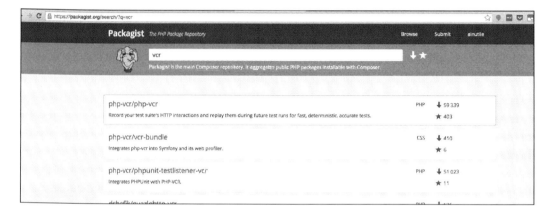

3. Now, we need to set up our `phpunit.xml` in the root of the Laravel application:

```
<filter>
    <whitelist>
        <directory suffix=".php">app/</directory>
    </whitelist>
</filter>
<listeners>
    <listener class="PHPUnit_Util_Log_VCR" file="vendor/php-vcr/phpunit-
</listeners>
<php>
    <env name="APP_ENV" value="testing"/>
    <env name="CACHE_DRIVER" value="array"/>
    <env name="SESSION_DRIVER" value="array"/>
    <env name="QUEUE_DRIVER" value="sync"/>
</php>
</phpunit>
```

Figure 2 phpunit.xml

```
<listeners>
        <listener class="PHPUnit_Util_Log_VCR" file="vendor/php-
vcr/phpunit-testlistener-vcr/PHPUnit/Util/Log/VCR.php" />
</listeners>
```

4. Lastly, we will modify our test to have the needed `@vcr fixture_name` annotation:

5. In this test you, will see a new method called `setTimeStamp`, so let's go and add it to the `MarvelApi.php` class. I will explain why in the *How it Works...* section:

   1. Add it to the bottom of the file:

```
private function getTimeStamp()
{
    if(!$this->ts)
        $this->setTimeStamp();

    return $this->ts;
}

public function setTimeStamp($ts = null)
{
    if(!$ts)
        $ts = Carbon::now()->timestamp;

    $this->ts = $ts;

    return $this;

}
}
```

2. Then add it at the top of the file:

```
class MarvelApi implements ComicClientInterface
{
    protected $key = false;
    protected $secret = false;
    protected $base_url = false;
    protected $ts = null;
    protected $api_version = '/v1/public';

    /**
```

3. Lastly, update the `makeAuth` method:

```
protected function makeAuth()
{
    $hash = md5($this->getTimeStamp() . $this->secret . $this->key);
    return ['apikey' => $this->key, 'ts' => $this->getTimeStamp(), 'hash' => $hash];
}
```

6. Make a folder called `tests/fixtures`.

7. Place an empty file in this folder called `.gitkeep`:

   `>touch tests/fixtures/.gitkeep`

8. Then, we can run the test as we did before:

   `>phpunit tests/MarvelApiClientTest.php`

9. Look in the `tests/fixtures` folder and you will see a file called `stub_comics_request`, which is full of information; I will explain about it shortly.

   Turn off the Wifi/Ethernet on your PC/Mac, and run the test again! It will pass even though there is no Internet!

How it works...

Overall, once this is installed, VCR really comes down to the annotation on the test. You can see in the following screenshot how the annotation called `@vcr stub_comics_request` later becomes the fixture, or as they call it—the cassette—that is used to replay the request and responses from the API:

```
recipes (~/Code/recipes)
▼ □ app
   ► □ Console
   ► □ Events
   ► □ Exceptions
   ► □ Facades
   ► □ Http
   ► □ Interfaces
   ► □ Jobs
   ► □ Listeners
   ► □ Policies
   ► □ Providers
     📄 MarvelApi.php
     📄 User.php
   ► □ bootstrap
   ► □ config
   ► □ database
   ► □ public
   ► □ resources
   ► □ storage
   ▼ □ tests
      ▼ □ fixtures
         📄 gitkeep
         📄 stub_comics_request
      📄 ExampleTest.php
      📄 GuzzleClientTest.php
      📄 MarvelApiClientTest.php
      📄 TestCase.php
   ► □ vendor
     📄 .env
     📄 .env.example
     📄 gitattributes
```

```php
use ...

class MarvelApiClientTest extends TestCase
{
    /**
     * @test
     * @vcr stub_comics_request
     */
    public function test_first_setup()
    {
        //1 I need to set Guzzle to pass my key and secret w
        //2 I then need a method (getAllComicsPaginated) and
        //3 Then I need to move this into a Provider
        //4 Finally I need to make a Service around these in

        $client = App::make(\App\Interfaces\ComicClientInter

        $ts = '1459629709';
        $results = $client->setTimeStamp($ts)->comics();

        $this->assertEquals(200, $results['code']);
    }
}
```

There was a lot of setup for the first use. For one, you will see I used the PHPUnit-focused library to get VCR set up `php-vcr/phpunit-testlistener-vcr`. Then, I had to go into the `phpunit.xml` file to add the Listener that hooks into the system. Notice that while you are in there, this file also has ENV settings and more!

Then, there was one more thing I had to do, which is really not about VCR in so much as about the Marvel API. They wanted a timestamp and hash with each request. But in doing this, each request was different. Since VCR uses the request I make to find the matching request in the `stub_comics_request` file, it never finds it but keeps building more and more requests into this file. Then, I made a setter so that my tests can easily set the timestamp to a static number. It's not something I need to do with most other APIs this is used on.

Then, I ran the test, and it made the fixture file; and, finally, I turned off the Ethernet on my Mac to see if it really worked and it did. I can remove the fixture to make it update if needed.

If you open this file, you will see a YAML-based file that has different Key/Values around the Request and Response cycle; pretty interesting stuff really.

Now you can run your tests, or more importantly, iterate through building your App more quickly because if you have follow my TDT in the previous section, you can quickly iterate over ideas without hitting their API.

See also

▸ **More about VCR**: `http://php-vcr.github.io/`

▸ **Laracast and VCR**: `https://laracasts.com/lessons/testing-http-requests`

Using Travis to run tests with every push

So, we have a test as seen in the first section of this chapter. And as we move on with our work, we want all of our tests to run before and after we push our code. Before pushing is *easy*; you run them, or as you will see later on, we set up Gulp to do that for us. But for now, we will get all the tests to run after we push to GitHub, thanks to Travis CI at `https://travis-ci.org/`:

So, in this section, we will set our App so that when we push to GitHub, we trigger a test on Travis. By the time we are done, we will have a `badge` on our repo showing the status of our project as well:

Getting ready

I will walk through the steps, but to begin with, sign into `https://travis-ci.org/` using your GitHub account. So, first log in to GitHub, then when you visit Travis, you will see **Sign in with GitHub** on the top right.

The rest of the work I will take step by step.

How to do it...

1. First, we will make the `.travis.xml` file in the root of our application. For now, ours will look like this. I will explain it later on:

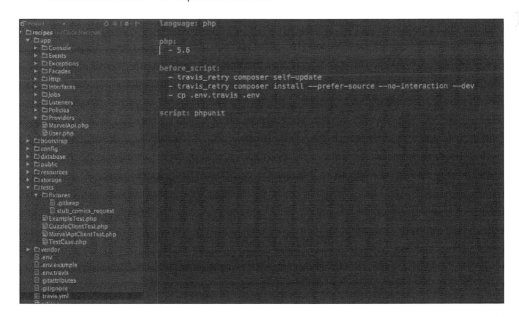

2. Then, copy the `.env` file to `.env.travis`, leaving all the values in place.

> This is a huge security risk in that you are handing out your Marvel API! I will cover this shortly.

3. Then, we will also update our `phpunit.xml` file, so it looks like the image here. I will cover why we are doing this and `.env.travis` in the *How it works...* section:

```
    <listeners>
        <listener class="PHPUnit_Util_Log_VCR" file="vendor/php-vcr/phpunit-testlistener-v
    </listeners>
    <php>
        <env name="APP_ENV" value="testing"/>
        <env name="CACHE_DRIVER" value="array"/>
        <env name="SESSION_DRIVER" value="array"/>
        <env name="QUEUE_DRIVER" value="sync"/>
        <env name="APP_KEY" value="sync"/>
        <env name="ADMIN_PASSWORD" value="Xidkr59zYNuPVKWqHLiMwppEgK3Effoo"/>
        <env name="API_CLIENT_URL" value="https://en.wikipedia.org/"/>
        <env name="MARVEL_API_VERSION" value="/v1/public"/>
        <env name="MARVEL_API_BASE_URL" value="https://gateway.marvel.com"/>
        <env name="MARVEL_API_KEY" value="eeaef8ccb27b7aa1e20c80bd2f0d78a5"/>
        <env name="MARVEL_API_SECRET" value="7ba1bfda7586b8392174ae93471383ff549a6be1"/>
    </php>
</phpunit>
```

4. Set your GitHub repo to send Travis a webhook with each push:

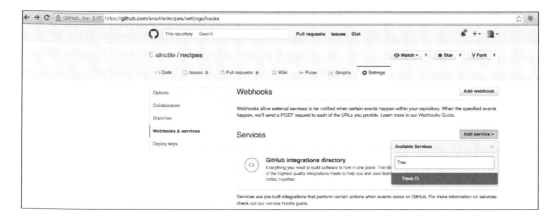

5. Then, go to your Travis profile at `https://travis-ci.org/profile/alnutile`; **alnutile** is my my GitHub account name. Now turn on this repo:

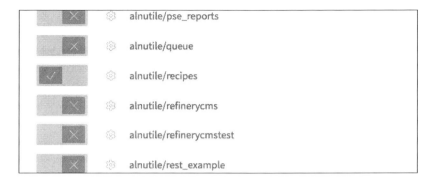

6. Now, let's push the code to master and watch the build happen. You will end up at `https://travis-ci.org/alnutile/recipes`, seeing a build happening; and if you click into the build, you will see this cool progress page:

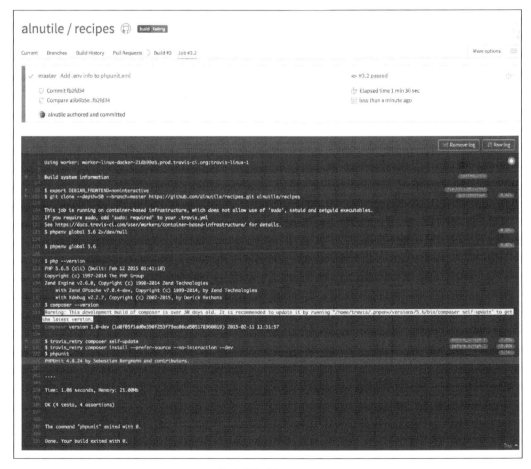

TravisCI build progress

7. Let's now add the badge to `readme.md` so that when we go to the repo, we see our `master` branch passing:

    1. Edit `readme.md`

    2. Clear out all the default Laravel `readme.md`

    3. Add `# Recipes` at the top of it; this is an `H1` in **Markdown**

    4. Then under this, insert the following all in one line:

       ```
       [![Build Status](https://travis-ci.org/alnutile/recipes.
       svg?branch=master)](https://travis-ci.org/alnutile/recipes)
       ```

    You can get the by clicking on the `badge` on Travis:

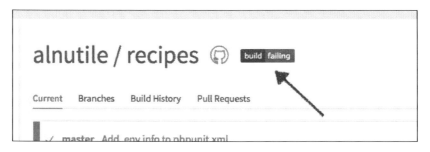

8. Then, choose **Markdown** in the modal:

9. Instead of pushing and running a test, since we did not change anything, we will push our work up using this command.

10. Then we will see the following when we visit our GitHub page:

Not a great `readme.md` file, but we can at least show others we have a passing code base.

How it works...

Let's walk through the details of setting up Travis CI. It first begins with amazing APIs and Webhooks happening between Travis CI and GitHub. It is really inspiring how tools from different companies can work together.

Then, using the `.travis.yml` file, we can use the YAML `https://en.wikipedia.org/wiki/YAML` syntax to define some basic settings and steps to set up our app on their servers. It's just amazing how such a complex task is abstracted out to the `yml` file!

You can also see that I made the `.env.travis.yml` file. We could have done this with the ENV settings. We could have used the `.travis.yml` setup feature to copy this over, and we would have been done with it. But I decided that I'd rather stick all of this in the `phpunit.xml` file. Then, I would have got to use those settings both locally and on Travis CI. Note that I like to setup up the `DB_DATABASE` in there as well to be `app_name_testing`. `App_Name` being replaced with the name of my application.

Once we set up GitHub to send Webhooks to Travis CI and Travis CI to listen to them, we are done! They take care of all the heavy lifting and running our tests, reporting pass or fail; and later on, we will see how to stop deployments on a fail.

You previously saw how I also used my Marvel secrets in the code that I pushed to GitHub. This is a huge no.

The trick here is that I need to keep VCR happy, and all of its fixtures are based around them. And then, I went to Marvel to get a new API Secret.

One last comment is my last push that I used `[ci skip]` in my git push. Sometimes, you are just doing an update to a readme file or something small like that, and you really do not need to run a test. Be careful about this; better safe than sorry. But on the other hand, it is nice to save Travis CI some resources.

See also

 ▸ **Travis CI**: `https://travis-ci.org/`
 ▸ **Laracasts**: `https://laracasts.com/lessons/continuous-integration-with-travis`

Launching Gulp watch into your workflow

As we saw previously, it is super handy to have Travis CI running tests as you push to GitHub. But it is actually pretty slow to wait so long to see whether your tests are passing; better to run it locally before you push. But who can remember to do this? Well, with Gulp, we will see no need to remember it, just run it!

Getting ready

SSH into Homestead using the command `homestead ssh` and cd into the recipe directory. Then, let's get going.

How to do it...

1. Take a moment to run `npm install` from within the `app` directory.

    This will take a few minutes! Go get some coffee and welcome to NPM!

2. While this is running or after it is done, edit `gulpfile.js`, and make it look as follows:

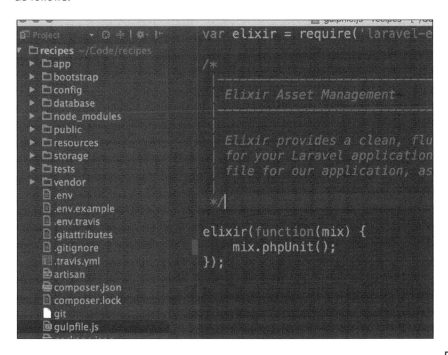

3. Then, run `gulp watch`.

4. Start editing it:

1. Edit `MarvelApiClientTest.php`, and add an example unit test:

Simple test to show gulp working

2. Then, you will see something like this at your command line:

3. Then, go edit `app/MarvelApi.php`, and click on save. Go check out the console, and you will see the same type of output!

How it works...

Pretty amazing. What used to take many steps to set up, Laravel and Elixir introduced in 5.x made this a breeze.

If you dig deeper into the libraries you pulled in when running `npm install`, you will see how Elixir brings a lot of this together `node_modules/laravel-elixir/Config.js`. Of course, you would not edit this file, but it is cool to dig in and see how this library was put together to do a lot of the common workflows that we all need in our day-to-day work, not just for JavaScript and CSS but also testing.

See also

- ▶ **Laravel Docs**: `https://laravel.com/docs/5.2/elixir`
- ▶ **Laracasts Gulp TDD**: `https://laracasts.com/series/painless-builds-with-laravel-elixir/episodes/7`

Using mockery to test your controllers

We will cover a feature in Laravel to test your controllers. In doing so, I will show how to swap out the injected methods so that when your controller tries to inject the method, it will get your mock instead.

Getting ready

Since Mockery is already part of Laravel, we are ready to go! Just start `gulp watch` as we talked about earlier in this chapter if you want to tests to just happen as you write.

How to do it...

1. Make a Controller:

   ```
   >php artisan make:controller SearchComics
   ```

2. Now, let's go set up the Controller called `app/Http/Controllers/SearchComics.php` for our request.

When you are done, your Controller will look like this:

```php
<?php

namespace App\Http\Controllers;

use App\Interfaces\ComicClientInterface;
use App\MarvelApi;
use Illuminate\Http\Request;
use Illuminate\Support\Facades\File;
use Illuminate\Support\Facades\Response;

class SearchComics extends Controller
{
    /**
     * @var MarvelApi
     */
    private $clientInterface;

    public function __construct(ComicClientInterface $clientInterface)
    {
        $this->clientInterface = $clientInterface;
    }

    public function searchComicsByName(Request $request)
    {
        try
        {
            $name = $request->input('name');
            $results = $this->clientInterface->comics($name);

            //File::put(base_path('tests/fixtures/search_no_name.json'),
            //  json_encode($results, JSON_PRETTY_PRINT));
            return Response::json(['data' => $results['data'], 'message' => "Success Getting
        }
        catch (\Exception $e)
        {
            return Response::json(
                ['data' => [], 'message' => sprintf("Error Getting Comics %s", $e->getMessage()
        }
    }
}
```

 Note that `@var MarvelApi` is a nice feature in most IDEs.
Even though it is an interface, I can tell it what concrete class it is
representing, and then I can click into this class and explore it.

3. And our Route (notice we are taking over the home `route` /):

```php
<?php

/*...*/


/*
|
| Application Routes
|
|
| This route group applies the "web" middleware group to
| it contains. The "web" middleware group is defined in
| kernel and includes session state, CSRF protection, an
|
*/

Route::group(['middleware' => ['web']], function () {



});

Route::get('/', ['as' => 'search',
        'uses' => 'SearchComics@searchComicsByName']);
```

Setting our search route

4. Make a test for the controller:

```
> php artisan make:test SearchControllerTest
```

5. Then, we will set up the Test class called `tests/SearchControllerTest.php` like this:

```php
<?php

use Illuminate\Support\Facades\File;
use Mockery as m;

class SearchControllerTest extends TestCase
{
    public function test_search_comics_no_name()
    {
        //Arrange
        $mock = m::mock('App\Interfaces\ComicClientInterface');
        $fixture = File::get(base_path('tests/fixtures/search_no_name.json'));
        $mock->shouldReceive('comics')->andReturn(json_decode($fixture, true));
        $mock->shouldReceive('getStatusCode')->andReturn(200);
        $mock->shouldReceive('getContent')->andReturn($fixture);
        $this->app->instance('App\Interfaces\ComicClientInterface', $mock);

        //Act
        $results = $this->call('GET', '/');

        //Assert
        $this->assertEquals(200, $results->getStatusCode());
        $content = json_decode($results->getContent(), true);
        $this->assertEquals(20, $content['data']['count']);
    }

    public function tearDown()
    {
        parent::tearDown();
        m::close();
    }
}
```

6. Then, we run the test to see this:

```
vagrant@homestead:~/Code/recipes$ phpunit --filter=search_comics_no_name
PHPUnit 4.8.24 by Sebastian Bergmann and contributors.

.

Time: 3.74 seconds, Memory: 12.00Mb

OK (1 test, 2 assertions)
```

7. Let's change the fixture for a moment to be `count: 21` and see what happens when we run the test:

   1. Edit `tests/fixtures/search_no_name.json` so that it looks like this:

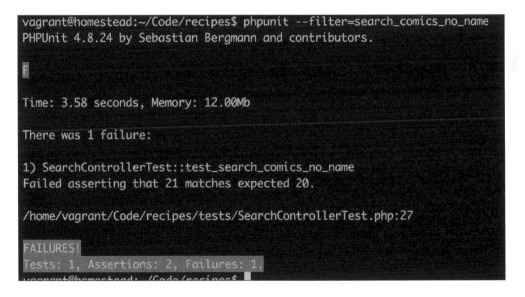

   2. Then, run the test:

```
vagrant@homestead:~/Code/recipes$ phpunit --filter=search_comics_no_name
PHPUnit 4.8.24 by Sebastian Bergmann and contributors.

F

Time: 3.58 seconds, Memory: 12.00Mb

There was 1 failure:

1) SearchControllerTest::test_search_comics_no_name
Failed asserting that 21 matches expected 20.

/home/vagrant/Code/recipes/tests/SearchControllerTest.php:27

FAILURES!
Tests: 1, Assertions: 2, Failures: 1.
vagrant@homestead:~/Code/recipes$
```

8. Okay, so now we know it is working!

How it works...

Now, I will explain in more detail how I was able to swap out our mocked class for the client, and then, even better, I was able to return the fixture data.

First, let me say that we could have done this with VCR, since this class exists and makes an HTTP request. But this is rare. Typically, you are mocking a class for other reasons; as in it does not exist, or you do not want to test the class, but how your class handles its incoming message and so forth. But one thing is that I actually like to make fixture like this, since it gives me a bit more control than VCR, so we can consider this an alternative way to not hit the API. And you will see in the controller, which I will remove, the line where I make the fixture, as I hit the real API from my tests:

```
//File::put(base_path('tests/fixtures/search_no_name.json'),
//    json_encode($results, JSON_PRETTY_PRINT));
```

You can see how easily I can make this using my test class:

```php
<?php

use Illuminate\Support\Facades\File;
use Mockery as m;

class SearchControllerTest extends TestCase
{
    public function test_search_comics_no_name()
    {
        //Arrange
        //$mock = m::mock('App\Interfaces\ComicClientInterface');
        //$fixture = File::get(base_path('tests/fixtures/search_no_name.json'));
        //$mock->shouldReceive('comics')->andReturn(json_decode($fixture, true));
        //$mock->shouldReceive('getStatusCode')->andReturn(200);
        //$mock->shouldReceive('getContent')->andReturn($fixture);
        //$this->app->instance('App\Interfaces\ComicClientInterface', $mock);

        //Act
        $results = $this->call('GET', '/');

        //Assert
        $this->assertEquals(200, $results->getStatusCode());
        $content = json_decode($results->getContent(), true);
        $this->assertEquals(20, $content['data']['count']);
    }

    public function tearDown()
    {
        parent::tearDown();
        m::close();
    }
}
```

Just by pounding out these lines, I can make the fixture.

Now back to the main point: the Controller is injecting the `App\Interfaces\ComicClientInterface` class in `__constructor`. And we registered this earlier in a Provider. But you can do this with any class. Laravel will use the Reflection API to get this class and any classes it depends on to instantiate them!

The trick here is that this is an interface, and an interface cannot be instantiated; but we bound the instance here:

```php
<?php

namespace App\Providers;

use ...

class MarvelApiClient extends ServiceProvider
{
    /**
     * Bootstrap the application services.
     *
     * @return void
     */
    public function boot()
    {
        $this->app->bind(\App\Interfaces\ComicClientInterface::class, function() {
            $config = [
                'base_uri'        => env('MARVEL_API_BASE_URL'),
                'timeout'         => 0,
                'allow_redirects' => false,
                'verify'          => false,
                'headers'         => [
                    'Content-Type' => 'application/json'
                ]
            ];

            $client = new Client($config);
            $key = env('MARVEL_API_KEY');
            $secret = env('MARVEL_API_SECRET');
            $client = new MarvelApi($key, $secret, $client);
            $client->setApiVersion(env('MARVEL_API_VERSION'));
            return $client;
```

So, the DIS knows that when we ask for this interface, we really want our callback.

You can think of it as an array in the scope of the `$app` object; and as it iterates over the keys and finds `\App\Interfaces\ComicClientInterface`, we swap it out in the test with our mock! Lastly, we take the fixture and change the count from 20 to 21 to prove that it is working.

One big deal when using Mockery is to make sure to `tearDown` the method when you are done testing it. Else, its state is saved throughout all the tests in the class, causing many possible issues.

See also

▸ **Laracasts and Mock That**
Thang: https://laracasts.com/lessons/mock-that-thang

Troubleshooting your application

In this tip, I am not going to suggest Xdebug or some browser plugin to watch all the methods being called. I am just going to cover some basic things you can do to approach any issue. I will cover a few common troubleshooting situations and how to deal with them.

Getting ready

Not much to do here; feel free to follow along by writing the code that will break, and then we have to fix it.

How to do it...

1. You go to a page in your browser only to see a breaking site:

If I did not have `debug=true` in `.env`, then I would only see the *Whoops* message. Keep in mind you do not want to keep this as true on publically accessible sites, because it leaks out possible information about your application that can be a huge security risk. But locally it rocks.

Also, unlike the preceding message where I just happen to have imported the wrong Response class, it should have been `Illuminate\Support\Facades\Response`. Sometimes, especially in Views, the message may not be so clear. So, here are some attack points for finding the problem:

2. Work from the request into the response. Just think about it one step at a time:

   ❏ The request comes in through the browser

   ❏ The route takes the request

   ❏ The route may have middleware before and after the request

   ❏ The controller takes it from the route unless it is just a callback

   ❏ And then from the controller to whatever you have going on there. View, Repository class, Model

Get into each of these areas in order with your secret weapon called dd; yup, I am a dd guy. I have rarely ever had a problem I cannot solve in a short amount of time with dd.

3. Tail Laravel's log:

   ```
   >tail -f storage/logs/laravel.log
   ```

4. Tail Nginx or Apache's log:

   ```
   >sudo tail -f /var/log/nginx/error.log
   ```

   You need to find out where your log is going to find the configuration file for your site, and see if it is logging into an area specific to the application.

   But in most cases, the server level is not the problem if you are using Homestead or standard configurations on your servers.

5. Command-line problems still have the same mindset called *Request into the Response*. Follow it through each method that plays a part in the process. Use dd by typing `dd('here')` in the method before and after it does its work to know you made it this far.

6. Testing plays a part in this too. You can use a unit test to replicate the incoming Request that is causing this problem and more easily iterate through the issue.

Request into the *Response* kind of reminds me of when I worked as a computer technician back in the Windows 95 days. A lead technician said to me, *It comes down to two things, Hardware or Software.* It was both a no *duh* moment, but at the same time, it helped me a lot to break down my thinking about problems in this space.

How it works...

The key to the previous issue is to simplify and do not assume. Take it one thing at a time from start to finish; there's no reason to jump ahead unless you have some knowledge of the system and know for sure that it is not some middleware, for example.

All of this is possible because Laravel is written in a way, in my opinion, that makes it easy to follow the code from request to response. Find a good IDE or plugin that allows you to click and explore. Maybe you will put dd('here') inside a method that is part of Laravel or some external libraries code. And this is fine; you can then remove it, but it helps you to follow the request as it gets made into a response.

9

Adding Advanced
Features to Your App

In this chapter, we will cover the following topics:

- ▸ Building an Artisan command
- ▸ Creating scheduler to notify users of new comics
- ▸ Setting up e-mail notices
- ▸ Adding clean URLs for the users profile page
- ▸ Using pusher for live notifications
- ▸ Adding a blog area to update users on new features

Introduction

In this chapter, I will tackle some common needs of application building that are a bit more difficult than the rest. We will see how cool it is to have Artisan commands, and we will understand how to use them. We will also cover setting up notification e-mails so that we can notify users when new comics come in and more.

Building an Artisan command

First, we will build an Artisan command. This is my favorite feature of Laravel. It is a nice wrapper around the Symfony console, making it easy to make commands. Commands are a key solution to long-running background processes or to those commands which you need to maintain your site and more.

For example, many projects that I am working on use this for creating Oauth tokens, stub data for a complex data set, and more; it is also used to run code optimizations using tools such as php-cs-fixer.

Here, we will build a command to search for the latest comics of user favorites that we will use later for scheduled commands.

Getting ready

A fresh install of Laravel is fine. I am still working inside the context of the comic book app. Also, note that this will assume you have a user in `UserTableSeeder`, as I did in *Chapter 5, Working with Data*.

How to do it...

1. Make some seed data for the user to run the following:

   ```
   >php artisan make:seeder FavoritesSeeder
   ```

2. Then, add this file to `database/seeds/DatabaseSeeder.php`:

```php
class DatabaseSeeder extends Seeder
{
    /**
     * Run the database seeds.
     *
     * @return void
     */
    public function run()
    {
        $this->call(UserTableSeeder::class);
        $this->call(WishListTableSeeder::class);
        $this->call(FavoritesSeeder::class);
    }
}
```

3. Then, put some actual code in this file called `database/seeds/`
   `FavoritesSeeder.php`:

```php
class FavoritesSeeder extends Seeder
{
    /**
     * Run the database seeds.
     *
     * @return void
     */
    public function run()
    {

        /**
         * Setup a comic that is part of a series
         * then I will use this to get the series
         * and notify the user of new ones
         */
        $user_id = \App\User::where('email', 'me@alfrednutile.info')->first()->id;

        $seeder = File::get(base_path('tests/fixtures/star_wars_seeder.json'));

        $seeder = json_decode($seeder, true)[0];

        factory(\App\Favorite::class)->create(
            [
                'user_id' => $user_id,
                'comic'   => $seeder
            ]
        );
    }
}
```

4. Make the `latest_favorites` table `php artisan make:migration`
   `create_latest_favorites_table`, and update the file called `database/`
   `migrations/2016_06_05_122239_create_latest_favorites_table.php`:

```php
class CreateLatestFavoritesTable extends Migration
{
    public function up()
    {
        Schema::create('latest_favorites', function (Blueprint $table) {
            $table->increments('id');
            $table->integer('user_id');
            $table->integer('favorite_id');
            $table->text('comic');
            $table->timestamps();
        });
    }

    /**
     * Reverse the migrations.
     *
     * @return void
     */
    public function down()
    {
        Schema::drop('latest_favorites');
    }
}
```

5. Create the model called `php artisan make:model LatestFavorite` to get `app/LastestFavorite.php` ready:

```php
namespace App;

use Illuminate\Database\Eloquent\Model;

class LatestFavorite extends Model
{

    protected $fillable = [
        'comic'
    ];

    protected $casts = [
        'comic' => 'array'
    ];

    public function favorite()
    {
        return $this->belongsTo(\App\Favorite::class);
    }

    public function user()
    {
        return $this->belongsTo(\App\User::class);
    }

}
```

6. Then, we will make the console command to do the work:

```
>php artisan make:console GetUsersLatestsFavoritesConsole
```

7. Now plug the file called `app/Console/Commands/GetUsersLatestsFavoritesConsole.php` into the kernel called `app/Console/Kernel.php`:

```php
class Kernel extends ConsoleKernel
{
    /**
     * The Artisan commands provided by your application.
     *
     * @var array
     */
    protected $commands = [
        // Commands\Inspire::class,
        Commands\GetFixtureForComic::class,
        Commands\GetUsersLatestsFavoritesConsole::class,
    ];

    /**
     * Define the application's command schedule
```

8. Then, we add some code to this file, so we do the work of getting Favorites. I will explain this more in the *How it works...* section:

```php
<?php

namespace App\Console\Commands;

use ...

class GetUsersLatestsFavoritesConsole extends Command
{
    use \App\SeriesTrait;

    protected $signature = 'comics:getlatestfavs';

    protected $description = 'Get User Faves and Create Lastest notices';

    /**
     * @var MarvelApi
     */
    private $clientInterface;

    public function __construct(ComicClientInterface $clientInterface)
    {
        parent::__construct();
        $this->clientInterface = $clientInterface;
    }

    public function handle()
    {
        $favorites = Favorite::all();
        $count = 0;
        foreach($favorites as $favorite)
        {
            if($series_id = $this->isSeries($favorite->comic))
            {
                $results = $this->clientInterface->seriesStories($series_id);
                if($results && $future = $this->hasFutureSeriesDate($results['data']['results']))
                {
                    foreach($future as $comic)
                    {
                        /**
                         * Let's prevent duplicates
                         */
                        $repeat = LatestFavorite::where('user_id', $favorite->user_id)
                                ->where('favorite_id', $favorite->id)
                                ->where('comic->id', 'LIKE', $comic['id'])->first();

                        if(!$repeat)
                        {
                            LatestFavorite::create([
                                'comic' => $comic, 'user_id' => $favorite->user_id,
                                'favorite_id' => $favorite->id]);

                            $count++;
                        }
                    }
                }
            }
        }
    }
```

9. That's it! I have a command I can run once a day to get people's Favorites.

How it works...

It is pretty easy to make a command, add `php artisan make:console CommandClassName` to `app/Console/Kernel.php`, give it a signature plus your logic, and you are done!

In this example, I will cover a few things to keep an eye on. One is that I give the command a prefix of comic. This way, when you run `'php artisan'`, you'll see the results of your `artisan` command:

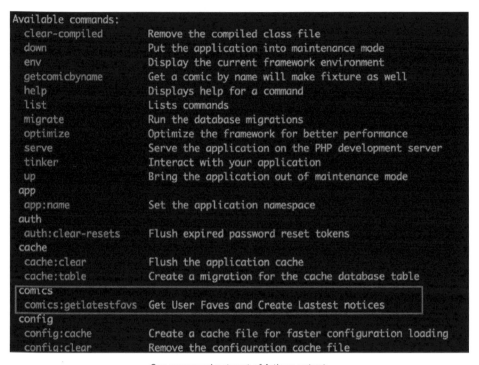

```
Available commands:
  clear-compiled         Remove the compiled class file
  down                   Put the application into maintenance mode
  env                    Display the current framework environment
  getcomicbyname         Get a comic by name will make fixture as well
  help                   Displays help for a command
  list                   Lists commands
  migrate                Run the database migrations
  optimize               Optimize the framework for better performance
  serve                  Serve the application on the PHP development server
  tinker                 Interact with your application
  up                     Bring the application out of maintenance mode
app
  app:name               Set the application namespace
auth
  auth:clear-resets      Flush expired password reset tokens
cache
  cache:clear            Flush the application cache
  cache:table            Create a migration for the cache database table
comics
  comics:getlatestfavs   Get User Faves and Create Lastest notices
config
  config:cache           Create a cache file for faster configuration loading
  config:clear           Remove the configuration cache file
```

Our command not part of Artisan output

This is very helpful in organizing your application commands.

Then, notice how I used the constructor to inject a class into this class. It is just like so many parts of Laravel where I get dependency injection done for me.

Then, also notice that a large amount of this work, just as my controller, happens in another class. Trying to keep the business logic out of the console command, I could even move more out of here around and into `LatestFavoritesRepository`. Basically, we treat it like a controller to keep it slim, but we can also make it easier to test our class outside the command. So, we can just plug the class or classes in when done. Here, I use `\App\SeriesTrait` to test outside this command—see `tests/SeeIfItemIsSeriesAndGetSeriesIdTest.php`.

This makes it easier for us to test the code that can be built while testing, and it is easier to reuse logic.

See also

 ▸ **Laravel docs (learn about arguments and options):** `https://laravel.com/docs/5.2/artisan`

 ▸ Laracasts: Artisan signatures: `https://laracasts.com/series/whats-new-in-laravel-5-1/episodes/6`

Creating scheduler to notify users of new comics

Now is the time for another superpower feature built into Laravel—scheduling! OK, it does not sound that exciting, but the fact that I can set one cron job on my server to do all my tasks makes it a lot easier to move my features from server to server. I will show here one example of how to use it based on the console command that I made previously.

Getting ready

A base install of Laravel is fine. If you follow the preceding recipe, you will have a decent size command to run via this scheduling example.

How to do it...

1. In the previous recipe, we ran `php artisan make:console GetUsersLatestsFavoritesConsole` to get a console command. Then, I added some query work over there to make it do its thing.

2. I then updated the code in `app/Console/Commands/GetUsersLatestsFavoritesConsole.php` to catch any issues and put them in the logs. This way, I can see when things go wrong, since I will not be running this at the command line. I will talk about this more in the *How it works...* section:

```php
public function handle()
{
    try {
        $this->processFavs();
    } catch (\Exception $e)
    {
        $message = sprintf("Error process
        Log::debug($message);
        $this->error($message);
    }
}
```

Adding log debug

3. Then, update the kernel called `app/Console/Kernel.php` to set up the scheduling part of this:

```php
/**
 * Define the application's command schedule.
 *
 * @param  \Illuminate\Console\Scheduling\Schedule  $schedule
 * @return void
 */
protected function schedule(Schedule $schedule)
{
    $schedule
        ->command(\App\Console\Commands\GetUsersLatestsFavoritesConsole::class)
        ->dailyAt('22:00')
        ->sendOutputTo(storage_path('favorites_job.txt'))
        ->emailOutputTo('me@alfrednutile.info');
}
```

4. Then comes the tricky bit of setting up cron at the command line:

```
>crontab -e
```

5. Then the system, if it is your first time, it may ask you what editor you want to use; choose `vim.basic`:

```
vagrant@homestead:~/Code$ crontab -e
no crontab for vagrant - using an empty one

Select an editor.  To change later, run 'select-editor'.
  1. /bin/ed
  2. /bin/nano          <---- easiest
  3. /usr/bin/vim.basic
  4. /usr/bin/vim.tiny

Choose 1-4 [2]: █
```

Because it is `vim`, you will press *I* to go into edit mode.

Then, you add the following to this file:

`* * * * * php /root/of/your/app/artisan schedule:run >> /dev/null 2>&1`

When you are done, press *Esc*, then *Shift + +*, then *W + Q*, and finally *Return*; and you should be out of the cron editor.

6. Now, you are set to have a job that will run at that time.

How it works...

This is pretty simple, and having control of when to run the command is amazing. In this case, I just asked to send it at "22:00" hours. But then, I also made an output file and e-mailed it to my e-mail account! And if there is an exception, I will still get the e-mail.

What is nice here is cron, or the way that we set it up. It will run every minute; and playing off of this, we can then choose from the many scheduler options: yearly, twice daily, monthly, and more. So, we do not need to add any more cron jobs in the obscure, to most users, * * * * * in this format!

As far as setting cron that one time, welcome to the club. The Linux command-line is amazing, but this is one of those commands that uses `vim`, which can seem odd. Also consider "nico" when you see the option list, which is very easy. The good news is that you have now mastered it! Or, at least, you have a sense of how to do this when you need to set up the production server.

 Think about learning Ansible at `http://docs.ansible.com/ansible/cron_module.html` if you need to set up your servers. I cannot say how easy it makes this, including setting up Cron!

Lastly, notice I wrapped my command in a `try...catch` block. Basically, if things go wrong, just as in the controller work I did, I do not want the system to just fail. I want to "catch" it and do something.

In this case, I want to log it, and thanks to the scheduler, send an e-mail there.

See also

> ▶ **Laravel docs (task scheduling):** `https://laravel.com/docs/5.2/scheduling`
>
> ▶ **Wikipedia and cron (take a moment to see how and why this works):** `https://en.wikipedia.org/wiki/Cron`
>
> ▶ **Ansible**:
>
> > ❑ `http://docs.ansible.com/`
> >
> > ❑ `https://serversforhackers.com/an-ansible-tutorial`

Setting up e-mail notices

In this recipe, we are going to use the previous work to trigger an event that will send e-mails. E-mails are a slow process sometimes, so I will put them in a queue. In this case, it will be a database queue since it is just local communication. Once we are done, we will see how to send a "nice" looking e-mail.

Getting ready

A base Laravel install will do. I will be working from the previous work, but you can follow along.

How to do it...

1. First, let's make our queue database tables:

   ```
   > php artisan queue:table && php artisan migrate
   ```

2. Then, let's set this to sync in our `.env` file. Make sure that the `QUEUE_DRIVER` variable in your `.env` file looks like the example here:

   Queue driver setting in .env

3. In the `.enf` file, we will set `MAIL` to log until we are ready:

4. Then, we will make the job:

   ```
   > php artisan make:job SendFavoritesEmail
   ```

5. Let's just add a placeholder there for now, it is `app/Jobs/SendFavoritesEmail.php`:

   ```php
   class SendFavoritesEmail extends Job implements ShouldQueue
   {
       use InteractsWithQueue, SerializesModels;
       /**
        * @var Favorite
        */
       private $favorite;

       /**
        * Create a new job instance.
        *
        * @return void
        */
       public function __construct(Favorite $favorite)
       {
           $this->favorite = $favorite;
       }

       /**
        * Execute the job.
        *
        * @return void
        */
       public function handle()
       {
           Log::info("Fav for user ", $this->favorite->toArray());
       }
   }
   ```

6. Now, our handler will react to the queue, which I will trigger from a console command called `app/Console/Commands/GetUsersLatestsFavoritesConsole.php`, but first, I add the `DispatchesJobs` trait at the top of the class:

```
use \App\SeriesTrait, \Illuminate\Foundation\Bus\DispatchesJobs;
```

7. Then, I dispatch it:

```
$count++;

$this->dispatch(new SendFavoritesEmail($favorite));
```

8. We run it while we tail the logs:

```
>tail -f storage/logs/laravel.log
```

Log output

9. Now, we must update the handler to send a nicer looking e-mail:

```
/**
 * Execute the job.
 *
 * @return void
 */
public function handle(Mailer $mailer)
{

    $comic = (new ComicModel())->setComic($this->favorite->comic);

    $user = $this->favorite->user;

    Mail::send('emails.fav', ['user' => $user, 'comic' => $comic], function ($m) use ($user) {
        $m->from('me@alfrednutile.info', 'ICDB');

        $m->to($user->email, "ICDB User")->subject('New Release in your Favorites Series!');
    });
}
```

10. Let's make our e-mail look nicer; first, I make the template file called `resources/views/e-mails/fav.blade.php`:

```
Hello,

A new release for {{ $comic->title }} see more <a href="{!! $comic->url !!}">here</a>

Description:
{!! $comic->getDescriptionSafe() !!}


From your friendly neighborhood ICDB!
```

11. Now, we can see this e-mail formatting in the log, thanks to `.env` being set to `MAIL_DRIVER =sync`!

Mail output in our log

12. Let's plug in `MailTrap.io` to make sure the e-mail looks nice:

MailTrap Settings

13. Then, set your `.env` file:

```
MAIL_DRIVER=smtp
MAIL_HOST=mailtrap.io
MAIL_PORT=2525
MAIL_USERNAME=bar
MAIL_PASSWORD=foo
MAIL_ENCRYPTION=null
```

14. Let's see how this looks!

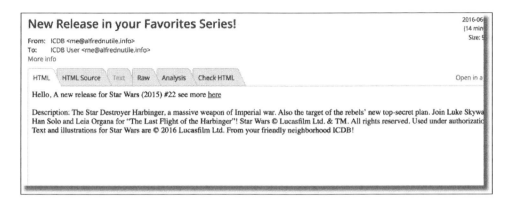

How it works...

Amazing! Laravel makes this so easy that sometimes I feel my job has now become too easy. Let's start off with the `.env` file. I set `QUEUE_DRIVER` to `sync`. This enables all of this to just happen. No need to set up a local queue or anything! But then, I am ready for the real thing when I go live. Same is the case with `MAIL_DRIVER`; there is no need to wait for an e-mail to get at some place to just watch it in the log. This is another boon to the workflow.

Then, for some of the side thinking to this recipe, I make the scheduler find these favorites and send them to the queue. Ideally, I would aggregate this information into one e-mail, adding this to the task list now.

The part of this recipe that you care about is seen in `app/Jobs/SendFavoritesEmail.php` where I call the Mail Facade. Just like a controller sending data to a view, I pass an array of data I want in the e-mail template. In this case, I want "user" and I want "comic". Note that I make a model out of the comic data. This model makes it easier for me to talk about it later on in the e-mail template, by not having tons of logic in different places on how to locate the first URL in the array of comic data. More importantly, and I wish I did a better job at this, data coming from Marvel will be different than the data coming from DC, so by the time I am done, I will want one model to talk to comics and pass the data around my app, but I need to transform these many sources into this one format.

Lastly, there is the Blade file we are all used to by now. In `resources/views/e-mails/fav.blade.php`, I can use the "comic" and "user" array as normal:

```
$user = $this->favorite->user;

Mail::send('emails.fav', ['user'
    $m->from('me@alfrednutile.i
        $m->to($user->email, "ICDB
});
```

Blade path

As seen earlier, I pass this into the façade, such as `View::make`; we are saying use this template and pass it in this array of data, for example, comic and user. The Mail Façade ends up in a closure that I also pass the `$user` information into and the `$m` Façade itself. If we look in the concrete class called `\Illuminate\Mail\Mailer`, we see the `send` method and what it is doing:

```
public function send($view, array $data, $callback)
{
    $this->forceReconnection();

    // First we need to parse the view, which could either be a string or an ar
    // containing both an HTML and plain text versions of the view which should
    // be used when sending an e-mail. We will extract both of them out here.
    list($view, $plain, $raw) = $this->parseView($view);

    $data['message'] = $message = $this->createMessage();

    // Once we have retrieved the view content for the e-mail we will set the b
    // of this message using the HTML type, which will provide a simple wrapper
    // to creating view based emails that are able to receive arrays of data.
    $this->addContent($message, $view, $plain, $raw, $data);

    $this->callMessageBuilder($callback, $message);

    if (isset($this->to['address'])) {
        $message->to($this->to['address'], $this->to['name'], true);
    }

    $message = $message->getSwiftMessage();

    return $this->sendSwiftMessage($message);
}
```

Digging into the code

We can see how the view is used, making a "plain, raw, and view". We see the `to` address and how it is set up. If you look in this class, it even has the `queue` method that the docs talk about at `https://laravel.com/docs/5.2/mail#queueing-mail`. Also, after digging around this class, we can see how, in the end, it is just a wrapper for `SwiftMailer`. It is nice to see how Laravel uses the tools of the community to make all of this happen.

Notice too that if I am unit testing and Behat testing, I do not want to hit MailTrap or real queues; so, I can still set this to `sync` and `log`. For PHPUnit, I would open up `phpunit.xml` and set it in the `<env>` area. If I was using Behat, then `env.behat` would take care of it at the non-JavaScript level only. This gets really tricky in testing at the JavaScript level.

See also

▸ **Mailtrap (fake SMTP server):** `https://mailtrap.io/`

▸ **SwiftMailer (the core library behind e-mail that Laravel wraps around):** `https://github.com/swiftmailer/swiftmailer`

▸ **Laracast**: trapping your e-mail: `https://laracasts.com/lessons/trapping-your-email`

Adding clean URLS for the users profile page

There is nothing like sending a user to `profile/44444-55555-6666-7777` or any page in our application. In this recipe, I will add some slugs to the user profile page.

Slug? Semantic URL

Semantic URLs, also sometimes referred to as clean URLs, RESTful URLs, user-friendly URLs, or search engine-friendly URLs...

Refer to Wikipedia for more information: `https://en.wikipedia.org/wiki/Semantic_URL` and see an example slug in that URL.

Getting ready

A fresh install of Laravel can work for you with a database for making users for whom you can add a Slug.

How to do it...

1. Install the needed library from `https://packagist.org/packages/spatie/laravel-sluggable`:

   `>composer require spatie/laravel-sluggable`

2. Update the database as needed, so we can save this slug for the user model:

```
vagrant@homestead:~/Code/recipes$ php artisan make:migration alter_user_table_add_url
```

3. Now is the time for the code to do the alteration on the table:

```
use ...

class AlterUserTableAddUrl extends Migration
{
    public function up()
    {
        Schema::table('users', function (Blueprint $table) {
            $table->string('url')->nullable();
        });
    }
    /**
     * Reverse the migrations.
     *
     * @return void
     */
    public function down()
    {
        Schema::table('users', function (Blueprint $table) {
            if (Schema::hasColumns('users', ['url'])) {
                $table->dropColumn('url');
            }
        });
    }
}
```

4. Then, run the migration:

   `>php artisan migrate`

5. Update the code in `app/User.php` as per the package docs:

```php
use Illuminate\Foundation\Auth\User as Authenticatable;
use Laravel\Cashier\Billable;
use Spatie\Sluggable\HasSlug;
use Spatie\Sluggable\SlugOptions;

class User extends Authenticatable
{

    use Billable, HasSlug;

    protected $fillable = [
        'name', 'email', 'password',
    ];

    protected $hidden = [
        'password', 'remember_token',
    ];

    /**
     * Get the options for generating the slug.
     */
    public function getSlugOptions(){
        return SlugOptions::create()
            ->generateSlugsFrom('name')
            ->saveSlugsTo('url');
    }
}
```

6. Let's watch it work:

```
>php artisan make:test SlugTest
```

```php
use ...

class SlugTest extends TestCase
{
    use DatabaseTransactions;

    /**
     * @test
     */
    public function see_if_slug_works()
    {
        $user = factory(\App\User::class)->create();

        $this->assertNotNull($user->url);

        var_dump($user->url);

    }
}
```

7. Okay, now we need to make this work on the route called `resources/views/nav_layout.blade.php` and update the `nav`:

```
@if(!Auth::guest())
    <li class="dropdown ">
        <a href="/wish_lists">
            Wish List
        </a>
    </li>
    <li class="dropdown ">
        <a href="/profile/{{ Auth::user()->url }}">
            Profile
        </a>
    </li>
```

Nav in Blade

8. The same is applicable for the `app/Http/routes.php` route:

```
Route::get('profile/{slug}', 'ProfileShowController@getAuthenticatedUsersProfile')->name('profile');
```

9. I now reseed my app, so I know that my account has this new feature and a new user to the system.

10. Then, I click on the profile page to get this URL—`https://recipes.dev/profile/alfrednutile`.

11. See it working just like before!

How it works...

So, we saw how easy it is to sluggify a URL. The magic is that this library makes use of the Eloquent Model events called `vendor/spatie/laravel-sluggable/src/HasSlug.php`:

```php
/**
 * Boot the trait.
 */
protected static function bootHasSlug()
{
    static::creating(function (Model $model) {
        $model->addSlug();
    });

    static::updating(function (Model $model) {
        $model->addSlug();
    });
}
```

This will take over during the creation and updating of the model to apply the URL logic. We added the URL field in our migrations to the database. Notice that I set it to `nullable` because I do not want the site crashing if this is null. But more importantly, for me, I'd rather have the logic to manage this field in the code.

I also set `\App\User` to not allow the name to be in blank `app/Providers/AppServiceProvider.php`:

```php
class AppServiceProvider extends ServiceProvider
{
    /**
     * Bootstrap any application services.
     *
     * @return void
     */
    public function boot()
    {
        \App\User::saving(function ($user) {
            if ( ! $user->name) {
                $user->name = substr($user->email, 0, strrpos($user->email, '@'));
            }
        });
    }
}
```

Also, note that I am putting this in another place where I can alter the model via the events of the `AppSericeProvider` class. Now, if the name is empty, then I copy the e-mail into this field using the part of the e-mail before `@` `symbol`. I have two tests for this `tests/SlugTest.php`:

```php
class SlugTest extends TestCase
{
    use DatabaseTransactions;

    /**
     * @test
     */
    public function see_if_slug_works()
    {
        $user = factory(\App\User::class)->create();

        $this->assertNotNull($user->url);

        var_dump($user->url);
    }

    /**
     * @test
     */
    public function see_if_slog_null_name()
    {
        $user = \App\User::create(
            [
                'email' => 'foo@foo.com'
            ]
        );

        $this->assertNotNull($user->url);

        $this->assertEquals('foo', $user->name);

        $this->assertEquals('foo', $user->url);
    }
}
```

Note that this library requires PHP 7, but just use this version of it `https://github.com/spatie/laravel-sluggable/releases/tag/1.2.0`; you can also use a version lower than 7 but Homestead 2 does come with PHP 7.

See also

- **Laravel docs and model events:** `https://laravel.com/docs/5.2/eloquent#events`
- **Laracasts (handling unique slugs in Laravel):** `https://laracasts.com/lessons/unique-slugs-in-laravel`

Using pusher for live notifications

Pusher is a great service and is a super simple way to start sending messages to the UI from the backend of your application. In this example, I will notify persons in the UI that they have a Favorite series that came out. I will cover setting up a pusher account, setting up Laravel to talk to pusher, and finally setting up Angular to show this message.

Getting ready

I have been building up a site throughout this book and will now plug this into the already built command to trigger the event that I will use to broadcast to pusher and Angular. Make sure you have Laravel freshly installed if you have not made it down to this part of the book.

How to do it...

1. Get pusher info, go to `https://pusher.com`, and sign up.
2. Then, create a new app, I will call it `recipes`; you will get a page like this:

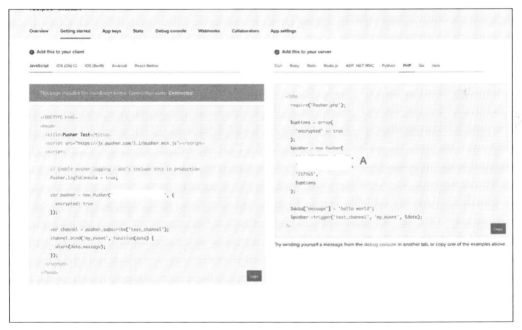

Pusher creating a new app

3. Plug this info into Laravel in the `config/broadcasting.php` file where we see all of our `env` settings just waiting for the settings that we see in A in the screenshot. So, add these keys as needed in your `.env` file. The nice thing about the following screenshot is it shows all this info:

```
'pusher' => [
    'driver' => 'pusher',
    'key' => env('PUSHER_KEY'),
    'secret' => env('PUSHER_SECRET'),
    'app_id' => env('PUSHER_APP_ID'),
    'options' => [
        //
    ],
]
```

4. Now, I want to make an event that will broadcast my message to pusher:

```
>php artisan make:event NewFavoriteSeriesEvent
```

5. Then, I'll update `app/Events/NewFavoriteSeriesEvent.php` to look like this:

```php
class NewFavoriteSeriesEvent extends Event implements ShouldBroadcast
{
    use SerializesModels;

    public $favorite;

    public function __construct(Favorite $favorite)
    {
        $this->favorite = $favorite;
    }

    public function broadcastAs()
    {
        return 'favorites.series';
    }

    public function broadcastOn()
    {
        return ['user-' . $this->favorite->user_id];
    }
}
```

6. I added this event to my previous console work class called `app/Console/Commands/GetUsersLatestsFavoritesConsole.php`, so it is triggered during the creation of Favorites:

```
/**
 * @TODO move this into NewSeriesFavorites Event
 * one Event 2 listeners
 */
$this->dispatch(new SendFavoritesEmail($favorite));
Event::fire(new NewFavoriteSeriesEvent($favorite));
}
```

I will explain this further, but `Event::fire` is added to trigger this event after the Favorite record is made.

7. Remember to install pusher for PHP:

```
>composer require "pusher/pusher-php-server":"~2.0"
```

8. Now, to see it working, I'll run my console command where I placed the event in step 6:

```
>php artisan comics:getlatestfavs
```

9. Then, if we go to pusher's debug console, we see it reaching pusher!

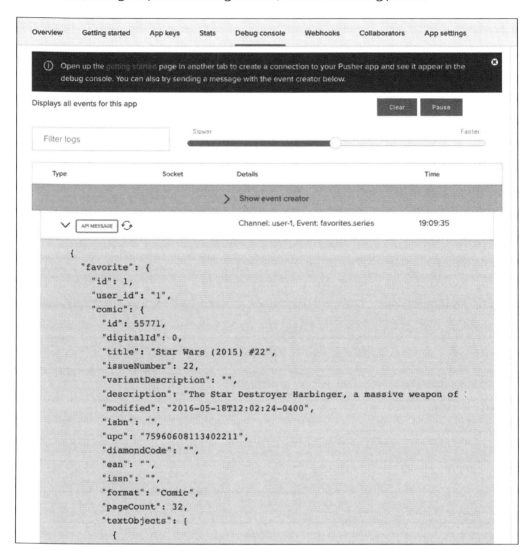

10. Now for Angular, first put this `https://js.pusher.com/3.1/pusher.min.js` file into your `resources/assets/js/vendor` folder, just like I talked about in *Chapter 6, Adding Angular to Your App*; do the same for this file `https://cdn.jsdelivr.net/angular.pusher/latest/pusher-angular.min.js` as well. Then, I will run Gulp to move this over as needed, or I will just run `gulp watch` to keep an eye on things. Or you can, for now, do what these sites say and just refer to the remote scripts right from your main blade file.

11. Set up the key to be in "window" just like I did in *Chapter 6, Adding Angular to Your App*. I now add this pusher key to the output. This keeps the pusher key from being hard coded in my code:

```php
public function index(Request $request)
{
    $name = $request->input('name');

    $results = $this->searchComicsRepository->getComicsByName($
    
    \JavaScript::put([
        'api_results' => $results,
        'user' => $this->getUserInfo(),
        'pusher_key' => env('PUSHER_KEY')
    ]);

    return Response::view('home.index', compact('results'));
}
```

Sending JavaScript to Window

12. Now, to get coding in Angular, get back to the file that I have been using this entire time—`resources/assets/js/custom/app.js`; I can load pusher the Angular wrapper:

```javascript
angular.module('app', ['ui.bootstrap', 'ngAnimate', 'toastr', 'googlechart', 'pusher-angular']);
```

13. Then, instantiate pusher the main library later on in this file. Notice `activate` it loaded every time this file is loaded I then call to set up pusher:

```
function activate()
{
    console.log("Here is angular");
    vm.api_results = $window.api_results;

    vm.smallnumPages = vm.api_results.total / vm.api_results.limit;
    vm.favorites = $window.user.favorites;
    console.log($window.user);

    setupPusher();

}

function setupPusher() {
    var client = new Pusher(window.pusher_key);
    var pusher = $pusher(client);
    var user_channel = pusher.subscribe('user-' + $window.user.id);

    user_channel.bind('favorites.series',
        function(data) {
            var title = data.favorite.comic.title;
            var url = data.favorite.comic.arts[0]['url'];
            var link = "<a href=" + url + " style=\"text-decoration: underline\">" + title + "</a>";
            var options = {};
            options.timeOut = 30000;

            toastr.success("just came out that is one of your favorites " + link, 'Yay! New comic ',
                { allowHtml: true, options: options });
        }
    );
```

I will cover this in detail in the *How it works...* section.

14. Alright, at this point, I can run the same command:

```
>php artisan comics:getlatestfavs
```

This forces the event to trigger and then broadcast to pusher that the previous JavaScript code is listening for. So, we end up seeing the nice notice here!

How it works...

Not too bad; with a bit of work, we can get this amazing feature of the backend, or we can get external systems talking to the frontend of our system! Pusher, as a service, removes the complications of having a service running.

Let's go through the steps. Of course, we have to create an account and then an app. With this, we get three keys that we need: PUSHER_KEY, PUSHER_SECRET, and then PUSHER_APP_ID (public key) that we can put into JavaScript and not worry about users seeing this. And Laravel comes with config/broadcasting.php, which is ready for us to set. Notice how we are not putting this info into our code.

A really good read to see how essential it is to use .env as Laravel and other frameworks do http://12factor.net/.

In the modern era, software is commonly delivered as a service called web apps or software-as-a-service. The twelve-factor app is a methodology for building software-as-a-service apps.

Note the part about queues in the docs *Queue Prerequisites* at https://laravel.com/docs/5.2/events. In my case, I already have QUEUE_DRIVER=sync in my .env file; so keep in mind that if this gets changed, you need to then have a default listener running to clear your queue. In my case, I have already set up the database queue and can change the setting to QUEUE_DRIVER=database, and then I will see this hit the database:

id	queue	payload	a
2	default	{"job":"Illuminate\\Broadcasting\\BroadcastEvent","data":{"event":"O:33:\"Ap...	

But if I run php artisan queue:listen, it is gone and we are back to things working again.

Now, for the event app/Events/NewFavoriteSeriesEvent.php file, just as the docs I talked about, I set up a public field on it named $favorite. So, I can access all the class info coming in JavaScript later on. It will not do this on non-public fields—those do not get serialized and placed into the queue. Then, I set broadcastAs to force a name for this event that is a bit cleaner than the default naming of the classpath. For the last setting, I want the listener to be related to the user. Remember the app we are making is recipes. The event is favorites.series and the channel I care about in this case is user-1.

Finally, for the backend, I fire the event. Pretty simple there, we just new up the class and add the data we care about. Notice that the constructor of the event was looking for the `Favorite` object, and we see this in pusher debug area. This area can be used to send events to your UI. In this case, I just send it via my console command.

Now, for the Angular side of things, we load the libraries into our system. I did not use Bower or NPM because they are handy tools; but for this, I just want to keep it simple. Gulp just puts all these files into the system for me using `all.js`. Then, I use my `activate` method, which is called on all page loads to `setupPusher`.

Now, I am ready to make the client from the pusher library, loading into it the `pusher_key` that I set up earlier in the controller. Then, I take this client and load it into the Angular `$pusher` module and with this, I subscribe to the `user-1` user channel. Then, I bind to the `favorites.series` event and do what I want to do with the data coming in. One thing to note here is I should go back to PHP and simplify this data. Let the class that broadcasts out make this data easier for Angular to parse. For example, `app/Events/NewFavoriteSeriesEvent.php` uses `app/ComicModel.php` that I made in PHP:

```php
class NewFavoriteSeriesEvent extends Event implements ShouldBroadcast
{
    use SerializesModels;

    public $favorite;

    public function __construct(Favorite $favorite)
    {
        $this->favorite = (new ComicModel())->setComic($favorite);
    }

    public function broadcastAs()
```

Using the Model

This model simplifies or centralizes how I handle this data:

```php
class ComicModel
{

    public $url;
    public $description;
    public $title;

    public function setComic($comic)
    {
        $this->title       = $comic['title'];
        $this->description = $comic['description'];
        $this->url         = $comic['urls'][0]['url'];
        return $this;
    }

    public function getDescriptionSafe()
    {
        return htmlspecialchars($this->description, HTML_ENTITIES);
    }
}
```

Now I can simplify how Angular accesses this data. Better yet, it will not care if it is a DC comic, Marvel Comic, or any other type.

```javascript
user_channel.bind('favorites.series',
    function(data) {
        var title = data.favorite.title;
        var url = data.favorite.url;
        var link = "<a href=" + url + " style=\"text-decoration: underline\">" + title + "</a>";
        var options = {};
        options.timeOut = 30000;

        toastr.success("just came out that is one of your favorites " + link, 'Yay! New comic ',
            { allowHtml: true, options: options });
    }
);
```

Notice that it is not digging into array 0 for the URL as this was way too specific. I also had to update the event class called `app/Events/NewFavoriteSeriesEvent.php` to this:

```php
class NewFavoriteSeriesEvent extends Event implements ShouldBroadcast
{
    use SerializesModels;

    /**
     * @var LatestFavorite
     */
    public $favorite;

    public function __construct(LatestFavorite $favorite)
    {
        $this->favorite = $favorite;
        $this->favorite->comic = (new ComicModel())->setComic($favorite->comic);
    }

    public function broadcastAs()
    {
        return 'favorites.series';
    }

    public function broadcastOn()
    {
        return ['user-' . $this->favorite->user_id];
    }
}
```

Pass `app/LatestFavorite.php` into `app/Console/Commands/GetUsersLatestsFavoritesConsole.php` instead:

```php
if(!$repeat)
{
    $latest = LatestFavorite::create([
        'comic' => $comic,
        'user_id' => $favorite->user_id,
        'favorite_id' => $favorite->id]);

    $count++;

    /**
     * @TODO move this into NewSeriesFavorites Event
     * one Event 2 listeners
     */
    $this->dispatch(new SendFavoritesEmail($favorite))

    Event::fire(new NewFavoriteSeriesEvent($latest));
}
```

I would like to come back and move out the dispatch into a listener of `NewFavoritesSeriesEvent` as well. This way, with this one event, I can have numerous listeners too as I update the features of this application; e-mails, UI notices, Facebook message, and so on, whatever it takes to keep people up to date.

This example of using pusher is just one of many things I could have done. I could have notified the user of other users who are friends of theirs, choosing Favorites, for example. But overall, we see how that however complex looking using pusher is at first, when done, it is really just a simple process of setting up an event and broadcasting the information to pusher.

See also

▸ **The Twelve Factor app:** `http://12factor.net/`

▸ **Laravel doc (esting and mocking events):** `https://laravel.com/docs/5.1/testing#mocking-events`

▸ **Echo**: a newer take on this: `https://laracasts.com/lessons/introducing-laravel-echo`

Adding a blog area to update users on new features

Laravel is not a CMS, but still, it is really nice to create a simple, markdown-based blog to quickly post updates about latest features and news for the comic site. In this section, I will show how we can use Slugs from the earlier recipe called *Adding clean URLs for the users profile page* in this chapter, and a markdown library, so we can make a blog area that is paginated and ready to show off our latest info written in markdown and converted into HTML.

Getting ready

A fresh install of Laravel is fine. I will continue on with the comic book site I have been making all along.

How to do it...

1. Use a scaffolding library that I talked about in *Chapter 5, Working with Data*:

```
>php artisan make:scaffold Blog --schema="title:string, mark_
down:text, html:text, active:boolean:default(0), url:string"
```

2. Make sure your migration ends up looking like this:

```
class CreateBlogsTable extends Migration {

    /**
     * Run the migrations.
     *
     * @return void
     */
    public function up()
    {
        Schema::create('blogs', function(Blueprint $table) {
            $table->increments('id');
            $table->string('title');
            $table->text('mark_down');
            $table->text('html');
            $table->boolean('active')->default(0);
            $table->string('url');
            $table->text('intro')->nullable();
            $table->string('image')->nullable();
            $table->timestamps();
        });
    }

    /**
     * Reverse the migrations.
     *
     * @return void
     */
    public function down()
    {
        Schema::drop('blogs');
    }
}
```

3. Then, I add the controller to my `app/Http/routes.php` file:

```php
Route::group(['middleware' => ['web']], function () {
    Route::auth();
    Route::resource("blogs","BlogController");
```

4. Then, I fix up the views the way I need them (visit GitHub at `https://github.com/alnutile/recipes` because the code screenshots are just for context).

    `resources/views/blogs/_form.blade.php`, I place all shared form elements here:

```blade
<div class="form-group @if($errors->has('title')) has-error @endif">
    <label for="title">Title</label>
    <input type="text" id="title" name="title" class="form-control" value="{{ $blog->title }}"/>
    @if($errors->has("title"))
        <span class="help-block">{{ $errors->first("title") }}</span>
    @endif
</div>

<div class="form-group @if($errors->has('intro')) has-error @endif">
    <label for="intro">Intro Plain Text</label>
    <textarea class="form-control" id="intro" rows="3" name="intro">{{ $blog->intro }}</textarea>
    @if($errors->has("intro"))
        <span class="help-block">{{ $errors->first("intro") }}</span>
    @endif
</div>

<div class="form-group @if($errors->has('mark_down')) has-error @endif">
    <label for="mark_down">Markdown Body</label>
    <textarea class="form-control" id="mark_down" rows="20" name="mark_down">{{ $blog->mark_down }}</textarea>
    @if($errors->has("mark_down"))
        <span class="help-block">{{ $errors->first("mark_down") }}</span>
    @endif
</div>

<div class="form-group">
    <label for="image">Attach Image</label>
    <input type="file" id="image" name="image">
    <p class="help-block">
        Upload Banner Image
        @if($blog->image)
            <img src="{{ asset('/blog') }}/{{$blog->image}}" class="post-img img-responsive" alt="" style="...">
        @endif
    </p>
</div>

<div class="form-group">
    <label for="active">Active</label>
    @if($blog->active == 1)
        <input type="checkbox" name="active" checked="checked" value="on">
    @else
        <input type="checkbox" name="active" value="on">
    @endif
</div>

<div class="well well-sm">
    <button type="submit" class="btn btn-primary" name="submit" id="submit">Save</button>
    <a class="btn btn-link pull-right" href="{{ route('blogs.index') }}"><i class="fa fa-backward"></i> Back</a>
</div>
```

```php
@extends('layout')

@section('header')
    <div class="page-header clearfix">
        <h1>ICDB Latest News and Features</h1>
    </div>
@endsection

@section('content')
    <div class="content" >
        <div class="container">
            <div class="col-lg-12">
                <div class="posts">
                    <div class="post">
                        <div class="post-aside">
                            <div class="post-date">
                                <span class="post-date-day">{{ $blog->created_at->day }}</span>
                                <span class="post-date-month">{{ $blog->created_at->month }}</span>
                                <span class="post-date-year">{{ $blog->created_at->year }}</span>
                            </div>
                        </div> <!-- /.post-aside -->

                        <div class="post-main">
                            <h3 class="post-title"><a href="/blogs/{{ $blog->url }}">{{ $blog->title }}</a></h3>

                            <div class="col-lg-3">
                                @if($blog->image)
                                    <img src="{{ asset('/blog') }}/{{$blog->image}}" class="post-img img-responsive" alt="">
                                @else
                                    <img src="/place_holder.png" class="post-img img-responsive" alt="">
                                @endif
                            </div>

                            <div class="post-content">
                                <p>{!! $blog->html !!}</p>
                            </div> <!-- /.post-content -->

                            @if(!Auth::guest() && Auth::user()->id == 1)
                                <br>
                                <div class="form-group">
                                    <a class="btn btn-primary" href="{{ route('blogs.show', $blog->url) }}">View</a>
                                    <a class="btn btn-warning " href="{{ route('blogs.edit', $blog->id) }}">Edit</a>
                                    <form action="{{ route('blogs.destroy', $blog->id) }}" method="POST" style="..."
                                        onsubmit="if(confirm('Delete! Are you sure!')) { return true } else {return false }">
                                </div>
                            @endif
                        </div> <!-- /.post-main -->
                    </div> <!-- /.post -->
                    <hr>
                </div>
            </div>
        </div>
    </div>
```

resources/views/blogs/show.blade.php

```
@extends('layout')

@section('header')
    <div class="page-header">
        <h1><i class="fa fa-plus"></i> Blogs / Create </h1>
    </div>
@endsection

@section('content')
    @include('error')

    <div class="row">
        <div class="col-md-12">

            <form action="{{ route('blogs.store') }}" method="POST" enctype="multipart/form-data">
                <input type="hidden" name="_token" value="{{ csrf_token() }}">

                @include('blogs._form')
            </form>

        </div>
    </div>
@endsection
```

resources/views/blogs/create.blade.php

```
@extends('layout')
@section('header')
    <div class="page-header">
        <h1><i class="fa fa-edit"></i> Blogs / Edit #{{$blog->id}}</h1>
    </div>
@endsection

@section('content')
    @include('error')

    <div class="row">
        <div class="col-md-12">

            <form action="{{ route('blogs.update', $blog->id) }}" method="POST" enctype="multipart/form-
                <input type="hidden" name="_method" value="PUT">
                <input type="hidden" name="_token" value="{{ csrf_token() }}">
                @include('blogs._form')
            </form>

        </div>
    </div>
@endsection
```

resources/views/blogs/edit.blade.php

```
@section('content')
    <div class="content" >
        <div class="container">
            <div class="col-lg-12">
                <div class="posts">
                    @foreach($blogs as $blog)
                        <div class="post">
                            <div class="post-aside">
                                <div class="post-date">
                                    <span class="post-date-day">{{ $blog->created_at->day }}</span>
                                    <span class="post-date-month">{{ $blog->created_at->month }}</span>
                                    <span class="post-date-year">{{ $blog->created_at->year }}</span>
                                </div>
                            </div> <!-- /.post-aside -->
                            <div class="post-main">
                                <h3 class="post-title"><a href="/blogs/{{ $blog->url }}">{{ $blog->title }}</a></h3>

                                <div class="col-lg-3">
                                    @if($blog->image)
                                        <img src="{{ asset('/blog') }}/{{$blog->image}}" class="post-img img-responsive
                                    @else
                                        <img src="/place_holder.png" class="post-img img-responsive" alt="">
                                    @endif
                                </div>
                                <div class="post-content">
                                    <p>{{ $blog->intro }}</p>
                                    <a href="/blogs/{{ $blog->url }}" class="btn btn-default">Read More...</a>

                                </div> <!-- /.post-content -->

                                @if(!Auth::guest() && Auth::user()->id == 1)
                                    <br>
                                    <div class="form-group">
                                        <a class="btn btn-primary" href="{{ route('blogs.show', $blog->url) }}">View</
                                        <a class="btn btn-warning " href="{{ route('blogs.edit', $blog->id) }}">Edit</
                                        <form action="{{ route('blogs.destroy', $blog->id) }}" method="POST" style="
                                    </div>
                                @endif
                            </div> <!-- /.post-main -->
                        </div> <!-- /.post -->
                    @endforeach

                    {!! $blogs->render() !!}

                    <hr>
                    @if(!Auth::guest() && Auth::user()->id == 1)
                        <a class="btn btn-success" href="{{ route('blogs.create') }}">Create</a>
                    @endif

                </div>
            </div>
        </div>
    </div>
```

Index Blade File

5. Just like the *Adding clean URLs for the user's profile page* recipe in this chapter, we add this to our `app/Blog.php` model file:

```php
namespace App;

use Illuminate\Database\Eloquent\Model;
use Spatie\Sluggable\HasSlug;
use Spatie\Sluggable\SlugOptions;

class Blog extends Model
{
    use HasSlug;

    protected $fillable = [
        'url',
        'active',
        'title',
        'mark_down',
        'html',
    ];

    public function getSlugOptions(){
        return SlugOptions::create()
            ->generateSlugsFrom('title')
            ->saveSlugsTo('url');
    }

}
```

6. While I am at it, I update my factory file called `database/factories/ModelFactory.php`:

```php
$factory->define(App\Blog::class, function (Faker\Generator $faker)
    return [
        'title' => "Blog Post " . rand(1, 1000),
        'mark_down' => $faker->sentence,
        'intro' => $faker->sentences($nb = 5, $asText = true),
        'html' => $faker->sentence,
        'active' => 1
    ];
});
```

7. Now, install the markdown library, and let's start plugging this into `BlogController` to begin with:

```
>composer require "michelf/php-markdown":"^1.6"
```

8. Then, I made a helper file for `app/MarkDownHelper.php`:

```php
<?php
/** Created by PhpStorm. ..,*/

namespace App;


trait MarkDownHelper
{

    protected $markdown_tool = null;

    /**
     * @return \App\MarkdownExtraParser();
     */
    public function getMarkdownTool()
    {
        if($this->markdown_tool == null)
            $this->setMarkdownTool();

        return $this->markdown_tool;
    }

    /**
     * @param null $markdown_tool
     */
    public function setMarkdownTool($markdown_tool = null)
    {
        if($markdown_tool == null)
            $markdown_tool = new \App\MarkdownExtraParser();

        $this->markdown_tool = $markdown_tool;
    }

}
```

9. I also made an override to their existing library by extending it to `app/MarkdownExtraParser.php`:

```php
<?php

namespace App;

use Michelf\MarkdownExtra;

class MarkdownExtraParser extends MarkdownExtra {

    public $code_attr_on_pre = true;

    function _doFencedCodeBlocks_callback($matches) {
        $classname =& $matches[2];
        $attrs     =& $matches[3];
        $codeblock = $matches[4];

        if ($this->code_block_content_func) {
            $codeblock = call_user_func($this->code_block_content_func, $codeblock, $classname);
        } else {
            $codeblock = htmlspecialchars($codeblock, ENT_NOQUOTES);
        }

        $codeblock = preg_replace_callback('/^\n+/',
            array($this, '_doFencedCodeBlocks_newlines'), $codeblock);

        $classes = array();
        if ($classname != "") {
            if ($classname[0] == '.')
                $classname = substr($classname, 1);
            $classes[] = $this->code_class_prefix.$classname;
        }
        $attr_str = $this->doExtraAttributes($this->code_attr_on_pre ? "pre" : "code", $attrs, null, ['prettyprint', 'linenums']);
        $pre_attr_str  = $this->code_attr_on_pre ? $attr_str : '';
        $code_attr_str = $this->code_attr_on_pre ? '' : $attr_str;
        $codeblock  = "<pre$pre_attr_str><code$code_attr_str>$codeblock</code></pre>";

        return "\n\n".$this->hashBlock($codeblock)."\n\n";
    }

}
```

10. Now is the time for `app/Http/Controllers/BlogController.php` that I used my `Markdown` class in; by the way, I would not typically have this much logic in a controller, but for this example, it's fine. Here are all of the methods:

❑ index: To show all the blog posts depending on who is looking at them:

```php
<?php namespace App\Http\Controllers;

use App\Http\Requests;

use App\Blog;
use Illuminate\Http\Request;
use Illuminate\Support\Facades\Auth;
use App\MarkDownHelper;

class BlogController extends Controller {

    use MarkDownHelper;

    public function __construct()
    {
        $this->middleware('is_admin', ['except' => ['index', 'show']]);
    }

    public function index(Request $request)
    {
        $blogs = Blog::where('active', '1')->orderBy('created_at', 'desc')->paginate(5);

        if( !Auth::guest() && Auth::user()->id == 1 )
        {
            $blogs = Blog::orderBy('created_at', 'desc')->paginate(100);
        }

        $title = "News and Blog";

        return view('blogs.index', compact('blogs', 'title'));
    }

    public function create()
    {
        $blog = new Blog();
        return view('blogs.create', compact("blog"));
    }
```

❑ `create` and `store`: To take care of new blog posts:

```php
public function create()
{
    $blog = new Blog();
    return view('blogs.create', compact("blog"));
}

public function store(Request $request)
{
    $blog = new Blog();

    $image_name = $this->setFileFromRequest($request);

    $blog->title        = $request->input("title");
    $blog->mark_down    = $request->input("mark_down");
    $blog->intro        = $request->input("intro");
    $blog->html         = $this->getMarkdownTool()->defaultTransform($request->input("mark_down"));
    $blog->intro        = $request->input("intro");
    $blog->image        = ($image_name) ? $image_name : null;
    $blog->active       = ($request->input("active") && $request->input("active") == 'on') ? 1 : 0;

    $blog->save();

    return redirect()->route('blogs.index')->with('message', 'Item created successfully.');
}
```

❑ `show`, `edit`, and `update`: To modify blog posts:

```php
public function show($id)
{
    if(is_numeric($id)) {
        $blog = Blog::findOrFail($id);
    } else {
        $blog = Blog::where('url', $id)->firstOrFail();
    }

    $blogs = Blog::where('active', 1)->orderBy('created_at', 'desc')->paginate(5);
    $title = $blog->title;
    return view('blogs.show', compact('blog', 'blogs', 'title'));
}

public function edit($id)
{
    $blog = Blog::findOrFail($id);
    return view('blogs.edit', compact('blog'));
}

public function update(Request $request, $id)
{
    $blog = Blog::findOrFail($id);

    $image_name = $this->setFileFromRequest($request);

    $blog->title        = $request->input("title");
    $blog->mark_down    = $request->input("mark_down");
    $blog->html         = $this->getMarkdownTool()->defaultTransform($request->input("mark_down"));
    $blog->intro        = $request->input("intro");
    $blog->image        = ($image_name) ? $blog->image : $image_name;
    $blog->active       = ($request->input("active") && $request->input("active") == 'on') ? 1 : 0;

    $blog->save();

    return redirect()->route('blogs.index')->with('message', 'Item updated successfully.');
}
```

Finally, I will use a `file` method and `delete`, though I am not dealing with delete right now, and I suggest you to take into consideration this—`https://laravel.com/docs/5.2/eloquent#soft-deleting`:

```php
private function setFileFromRequest($request)
{
    $image_name = false;

    if($request->file())
    {
        $image = $request->file('image');

        $image->move(storage_path('public/images'), $image->getClientOriginalName());

        return $image->getClientOriginalName();

    }

    return $image_name;
}

public function destroy($id)
{
    return redirect()->route('blogs.index')->with('message', 'Oops no delete just yet');
}
```

11. To get to this point, I used this unit test called `tests/BlogTest.php` to hash out all of the details outside what the scaffold offered. Now, to look at the test—here I test by updating the blog:

```php
<?php

use Illuminate\Foundation\Testing\WithoutMiddleware;
use Illuminate\Foundation\Testing\DatabaseMigrations;
use Illuminate\Foundation\Testing\DatabaseTransactions;
use Illuminate\Support\Facades\File;

class BlogTest extends TestCase
{
    use DatabaseTransactions, DatabaseMigrations, WithoutMiddleware;

    /**
     * @test
     */
    public function should_update_blog()
    {

        //Make the blog
        $blog = factory(\App\Blog::class)->create();

        $this->call('PUT', "/blogs/" . $blog->id,
            [
                "title" => "foo bar",
                "intro" => "intro here",
                "mark_down" => "#bar",
                "html" => "",
                "active" => 0
            ]);

        $blog = \App\Blog::find($blog->id);

        $this->assertEquals("foo bar", $blog->title);
        $this->assertEquals("#bar", $blog->mark_down);
        $this->assertContains("<h1>bar</h1>", $blog->html);
        $this->assertEquals(0, $blog->active);
        $this->assertEquals("foo-bar", $blog->url);
    }
}
```

And I test setting active and URL:

```
/**
 * @test
 */
public function should_update_to_active()
{
    $blog = factory(\App\Blog::class)->create();

    $this->call('PUT', "/blogs/" . $blog->id,
        [
            "title" => "foo",
            "intro" => "intro here",
            "mark_down" => "#bar",
            "html" => "",
            "active" => "on"
        ]);

    $blog = \App\Blog::find($blog->id);

    $this->assertEquals(1, $blog->active);
}

/**
 * @test
 */
public function should_set_url()
{
    $blog = factory(\App\Blog::class)->create();

    $this->call('PUT', "/blogs/" . $blog->id,
        [
            "title" => "foo",
            "intro" => "intro here",
            "mark_down" => "#bar",
            "html" => "",
            "active" => "on"
        ]);

    $blog = \App\Blog::find($blog->id);

    $this->assertEquals(1, $blog->active);
}
```

12. So, at this point, I can deal with the UI more easily because I worked out all the backend items in PHPUnit. I also wrote in about how to deal with image uploads.

13. Now make a folder named `images` with a `.gitignore` file `storage/public/images/.gitignore`:

Nothing much in there, I just want to keep the folder around.

14. Then run this command to symlink this to `public/blog`:

    ```
    >cd public && ln -s ../storage/public/images blog
    ```

15. Update your seed data, so you start off with some posts in `database/seeds/BlogTableSeeder.php`:

    ```php
    <?php

    use ...

    class BlogTableSeeder extends Seeder {

        public function run()
        {
            factory(\App\Blog::class, 20)->create();
        }

    }
    ```

16. Then your `database/seeds/DatabaseSeeder.php` would be:

    ```php
    <?php

    use Illuminate\Database\Seeder;

    class DatabaseSeeder extends Seeder
    {
        /**
         * Run the database seeds.
         *
         * @return void
         */
        public function run()
        {
            $this->call(UserTableSeeder::class);
            $this->call(WishListTableSeeder::class);
            $this->call(FavoritesSeeder::class);
            $this->call(BlogTableSeeder::class);
        }
    }
    ```

17. This is it. You now have a blog that you can write in markdown. Here is the index page as a non admin. Make sure to run your migrations:

```
>php artisan migrate:refresh --seed
```

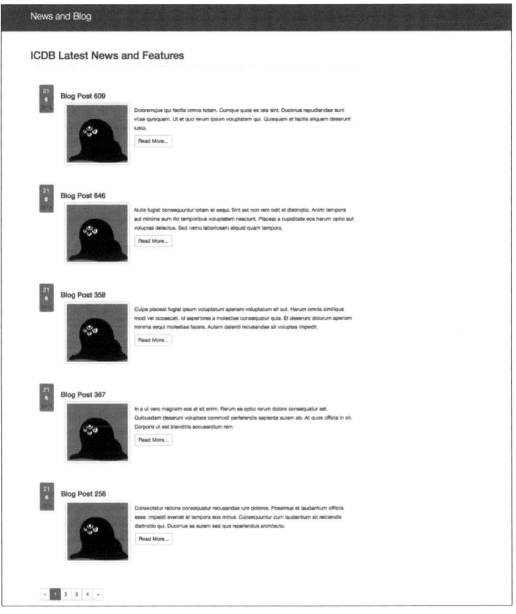

Index page with seed data

Here is the edit page:

Edit page

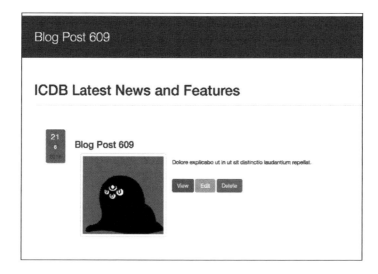

Here is the admin page for index:

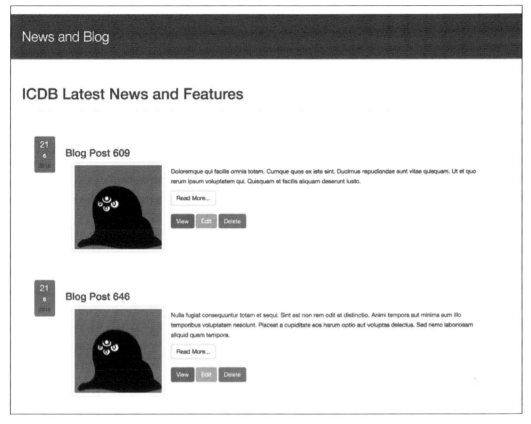

News and Blog

ICDB Latest News and Features

21
6

Blog Post 609

Doloremque qui facilis omnis totam. Cumque quos ex iste sint. Ducimus repudiandae sunt vitae quisquam. Ut et quo rerum ipsum voluptatem qui. Quisquam et facilis aliquam deserunt iusto.

Read More...

View   Edit   Delete

21
6

Blog Post 646

Nulla fugiat consequuntur totam et sequi. Sint est non rem odit et distinctio. Animi tempora aut minima eum illo temporibus voluptatem nesciunt. Placeat a cupiditate eos harum optio aut voluptas delectus. Sed nemo laboriosam aliquid quam tempora.

Read More...

View   Edit   Delete

Edit page

How it works...

This was a lot of steps to do something that is quite simple: save some content. But we have some nice features, such as markdown to HTML and image uploads. Now, let's take a look at all the steps.

First, I use the scaffold library, and with this, I get a solid base to build on. It has all the views, migrations, models, controllers, and more that I need. Then, I take a bit of time to alter the views just the way I like them; alter the controller to consider admin and the file upload.

You will notice that the views have a `_form` Blade file. I like to have one form shared by `create` and `update`. I can separate the part of the form that each one needs. This would include the route I am submitting the form to and the method `PUT` or `POST`. I can also deal with CSRF and hidden methods as needed. But then, each form shares the details found in fields, so I can update it in one place. It might seem like overkill, but it is just something I like to do when possible. Either way, the process is about the same, and thanks to Blade, it is really easy to work with.

Then, in `index.blade.php` call to `{!! $blogs->render() !!}` and this takes care of the pagination since my controller uses it in the query:

```
$blogs = Blog::where('active', '1')->orderBy('created_at', 'desc')->paginate(5);
```

Again, Laravel will make this stuff super easy.

You will also notice I have no validation in my controller. For now, this blog is just for me, but if I want others to work with it, then I will use Laravel's great validation features to take it up a level, especially form request validation at `https://laravel.com/docs/5.2/validation#form-request-validation`.

Then, there is the file storage location, which Laravel docs suggest to be placed into `storage/public`, then symlinked over `https://laravel.com/docs/5.2/filesystem#configuration`. The process is rather simple; just make sure your workflow allows this to take place without you having to touch the servers that the code is going to live on. Ideally, it should be part of your build process.

Another key feature to all this are slugs or sane URLs that you can share with people. Instead of `blogs/1`, we are able to share `blogs/nicer-title`. Using the library, we will just make sure to set the `app/Blog.php` model where the `title` is the field we want to use for the slug and the `URL` field is where we save it.

As far as my little class goes, to override the markdown library, I am sure that I could have set a setting as needed, but I found this to be an easier way to add `css` classes around the moments where I outline code in my markdown. Okay, so a comic site will not do this, but you can see here an option to extend and alter a library but still use the library to do the bulk of the work.

Finally, as a note to save you tons of time pulling your hair out, when you tear down a test, make sure to not do `parent::teardown()` until you are done using any Facades, since after you run this, all classes registered with dependency injection have been deregistered, leaving "file" no longer related to any concrete class:

```
public function tearDown()
{

    if(File::exists(base_path('tests/fixtures/file_upload_blog.jpg')))
        File::delete(base_path('tests/fixtures/file_upload_blog.jpg'));

    parent::tearDown();
}
```

See also

▸ **Form validation:** `https://laravel.com/docs/5.2/validation`

▸ **Form request validation:** `https://laravel.com/docs/5.2/validation#form-request-validation`

▸ **PyroCMS:** `https://www.pyrocms.com/`

10
Deploying Your App

In this chapter, we'll cover the following topics:

- ▸ Setting up Forge, AWS, and `CodeDeploy`
- ▸ Setting up Travis to auto deploy when all is passing
- ▸ Working with your `.env` file
- ▸ Testing your application on production with Behat
- ▸ Making a `composer` package out of our client

Introduction

All of these recipes around building have left out one key step—deploying. This is something I would have done from the start, typically. Ideally, as you show progress to a product owner or work with a team, your work is not truly done until it is merged with other work and seen on a `staging` area. Having something work on your machine is really half the battle.

This chapter will go over some key steps to getting you application to deploy. I will look at the easy-to-use workflow with Forge, but then I will also add a bit extra to it. Also, I will then cover testing your production app with Behat and managing your `.env` file.

Finally, I will pull out the client that I have been using all along to make a library, that out of it shrinking down the code I am testing and deploying.

Setting up Forge, AWS, and CodeDeploy

Forge has changed the game. Taylor Otwell did an amazing job of making it super easy to put an app online. I want to show you how to use this with AWS and `CodeDeploy`. Digital Ocean is an amazing service, but sometimes, you need to use AWS as per the customer requirement, or more importantly, you want to benefit from a lot of the features that it provides.

Second, I want to show `CodeDeploy` since it can deploy Artifacts. The killer feature I know is that what is working on Travis CI will work on the server, since I do not need to do another Git pull, composer install, Gulp, and so on. But I am just copying over a zipped artifact of the application in a passing state.

In the steps that follow, we are going to perform the following:

1. Setting up Forge
2. Setting up the EC2 with a role that will allow it to work with `CodeDeploy`
3. Setting up the EC2 to work with Forge
4. Setting up the EC2 to listen for `CodeDeploy` pushes
5. Setting up an S3 to store the Artifacts
6. Setting up an `IAM User` to use for pushing this Artifact from Travis CI to S3 and then to `CodeDeploy`

Some simple AWS terms to come to terms with are as follows:

- **VPC (Virtual Private Cloud)**: The default AWS one is all that you need right now and is all done for you.
- **Security Group**: Just imagine that this as the router your cloud sits behind.
- **EC2**: This is a Linux box of some sort that is, in this example, 2 CPU and 2-4 Gigs of memory.
- **EBS**: The default storage we use will be 20 gigs to help with the `CodeDeploy` images. And basically, there is not much more for you to worry about as far as this setting goes.
- **Public IP**: This is how people are going to reach our server.
- **IAM**: In this area of AWS, we manage Users, Policies, and Roles that we can attach to Users or EC2 Instances.

- **Roles**: These are just some ways to attach Policies to Services and Users.

- **CodeDeploy**: This is the service that we will use to move our code from S3 to the server:

    - **Application**: This is the application, for example, `recipes`

    - **Groups**: These are the environments for the application, for example, production, staging, and QA

- **S3**: This is a really amazing remote filesystem. Imagine a secure, object-oriented version of FTP.

Getting ready

You will need to have a Forge account, and in this example, we will use AWS.

How to do it...

1. Set up Forge as normal. But it is the moment we go to *make server* in Forge that I will point it to a *Custom VPS*. You could let Forge set up the entire server, but I will not, because I need the server to have some settings or a role that Forge does not do.

2. Now, go over to **AWS** and make a Role for EC2 as follows:

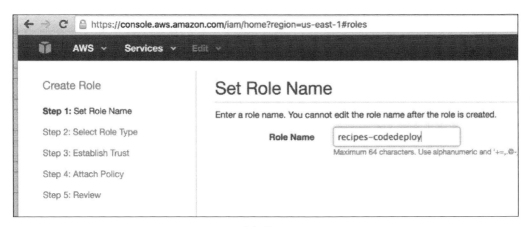

Role Name

3. Select the **Role Type**:

4. Attach this policy to this role:

Attach Policy

5. Then, create a custom policy for the S3 access that we will need later for `CodeDeploy`:

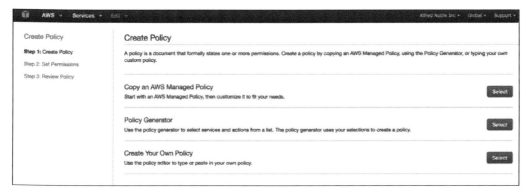

Create Policy

6. Set it to look like the following:

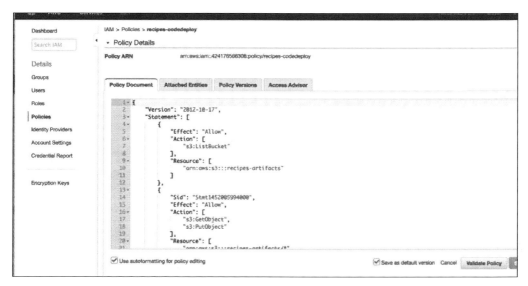

Policy Editor

You can see `server_config/s3_policy.json` here as well.

And we will attach this to the Role to the EC2 when we set it up:

Remember that, later on, you can add more policies to this role to update the EC2 as needed, but you can never add a new role to an EC2 after it is built, which is why doing a role now, even an empty one, is best practice. Visit `http://docs.aws.amazon.com/AWSEC2/latest/UserGuide/iam-roles-for-amazon-ec2.html` for more information.

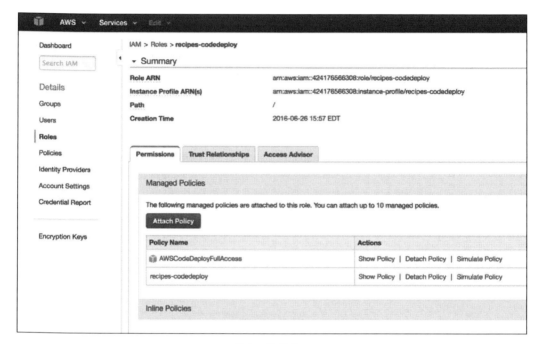

Role with Policy

7. Now we can build EC2 for Forge to later do its setup work on. Go to the EC2 area of AWS, and create a new instance, choosing Ubuntu 16.04 as Forge requires `ami-0188b76b`:

Select Ubuntu

8. From there, just start with `m1.medium` so that `CodeDeploy` has enough room to work:

Choose Storage

> I am using `N.Virginia` or `us-east-1`; your region may have different options.

9. Then, in step 3 of the installation, I assign the role that we made above to the EC2:

Instance Details

> In the **User data** area, I can add more setup details if needed, but in this case, Forge is doing a lot of work for me. I will note some ideas later in the *How it works...* section.
>
> Also, you will see in a number of steps next that I have to add SSH into the server to set up Ruby 2.0, but I could have just done this here.

Some key points are here:

- ❑ Use the default VPC that comes with AWS and **Enable** the public IP
- ❑ Use the default **Subnet** preferences that come with AWS
- ❑ **Enable Auto-assign Public IP**

10. Step 4 adding storage just go with the defaults:

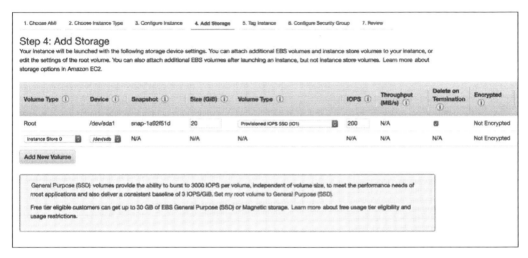

Storage

11. Step 5 is important as well since these tags are what will connect it to `CodeDeploy` later on:

Tagging

12. Then in step 6, I made a very simple Security Group for it so I can have SSH into the box, and connect over ports 80 and 443:

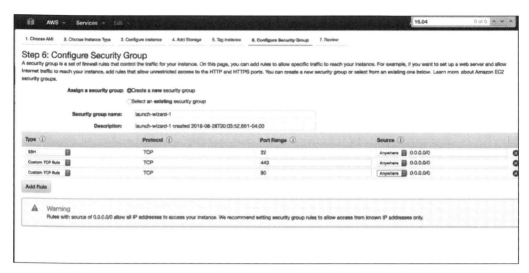

Security Group

 I do not open up MySQL to the public network. You can connect over SSH if you need to manage it, through any decent MySQL tool.

---

13. Finally, in Step 7, I made sure to download the key that I will later use to SSH into:

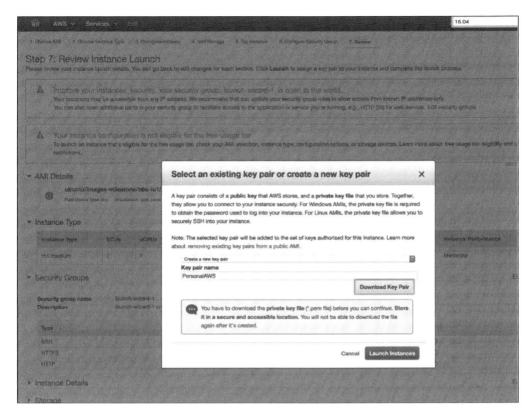

Download Key

14. When it is done building, I can start to work on the Forge side of things.

15. Going to Forge, I choose the **Custom VPS** tab:

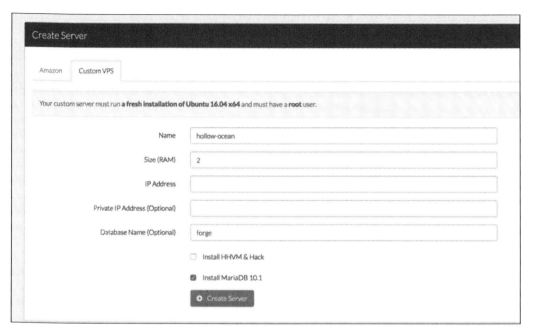

Forge Settings

16. In here, I plug in the information needed to get started—the IP that I was given on the AWS instance page. In this case, I will let Forge set up the database and not use Amazon's RDS alternative:

```
ssh -i ~/.ssh/PersonalAWS.pem ubuntu@54.84.51.50
```

This is the PEM file you downloaded when you made AWS IAM User.

17. From here, I run the command as per Forge's instructions, which is available at `https://forge.laravel.com/servers/86149/vps?forge_token=oUcaWrJ rkfg7i7mjfwjHru1P1G4xOoSNKVn8P7Tn`:

> **wget -O forge.sh**

 If I did this step first, I could have entered it into `User Data` for the EC2 and been done with it during the setup!

18. This will take some time to run, but after this, you will get an e-mail with the connection information that you need. And going back to Forge, you will see the AWS connected:

Name	Provider	IP Address	H8-IVM	Status	Connection	Manage
deep-atoll	Custom VPS	54.84.51.50	● No	✔ Active	● Successful ⟳	⊘

Forge Success

19. So now, click on the *pencil* icon to manage the server.

20. Then, follow the instructions here to install the `CodeDeploy` agent as seen at `http://docs.aws.amazon.com/codedeploy/latest/userguide/how-to-run-agent-install.html`.

    If you have trouble with the version of Ruby, choose 2.0 `https://gorails.com/setup/ubuntu/16.04` and follow this as well.

21. To finalize AWS security settings, we need to make a `CodeDeploy` service policy as the documents note at `http://docs.aws.amazon.com/codedeploy/latest/userguide/how-to-create-service-role.html`:

    ❑ As noted, we provision `IAM User` and attach a custom policy to it:

CodeDeploy Policy Review

Attach Policy

Select one or more policies to attach. Each user can have up to 10 policies attached.

Filter:	Policy Type ▼	code		

		Policy Name ⇕	Attached Entities ⇕	Creation Tim
☐	📦	AWSCodeDeployFullAccess	1	2015-05-19
☐		recipes-codedeploy	1	2016-06-26
☐	📦	AmazonEC2RoleforAWSCodeDeploy	0	2015-05-19
☐	📦	AmazonElasticTranscoderFullAccess	0	2015-02-06
☐	📦	AmazonElasticTranscoderJobsSubmitter	0	2015-02-06
☐	📦	AmazonElasticTranscoderReadOnlyAcc...	0	2015-02-06
☐	📦	AmazonElasticTranscoderRole	0	2015-02-06
☐	📦	AWSCodeCommitFullAccess	0	2015-07-09
☐	📦	AWSCodeCommitPowerUser	0	2015-07-09
☐	📦	AWSCodeCommitReadOnly	0	2015-07-09
☐	📦	AWSCodeDeployDeployerAccess	0	2015-05-19
☐	📦	AWSCodeDeployReadOnlyAccess	0	2015-05-19
☐	📦	AWSCodeDeployRole	0	2015-05-04
☐	📦	AWSCodePipelineCustomActionAccess	0	2015-07-09
☐	📦	AWSCodePipelineFullAccess	0	2015-07-09
☐	📦	AWSCodePipelineReadOnlyAccess	0	2015-07-09
☑		code-deploy-user	0	2016-07-09

Attach Policy

22. Make sure to save `API KEY` and `SECRET` for the user; we will need it shortly, but in the meantime, if this is your first **AWS** user, type `aws configure` and add `KEY` and `SECRET`. Otherwise, type `vim ~/.aws/config` and make it look like this:

```
[default]
output = json
region = us-east-1
[profile code-deploy]
output = json
region = us-east-1
```

23. Then, make the profile called `vim ~/.aws/credentials`:

```
[default]
aws_access_key_id = AKIAJS6QZJPOXA
aws_secret_access_key = H8lnYawidc
[code-deploy]
aws_access_key_id = AKIAIINMCESDJH
aws_secret_access_key = L3dp+B9b2
```

AWS Credentials File

In my case, I have a default user that I do not use for all my apps, and then one user per app. Note too that `code-deploy` is the same name of the profile from the previous one:

 You had to have installed the `AWS CLI` in Homestead. Just go here and set it up, it takes only a couple of minutes: `http://docs.aws.amazon.com/cli/latest/userguide/installing.html`.

24. Then, as these docs note, we add a Service Role called `AWS CodeDeploy`:

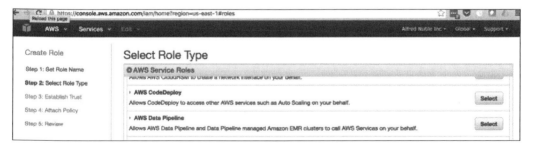

Role Type

And attach the default `AWSCodeDeployRole` to that:

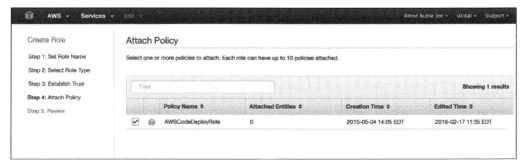

Attach Policy

So, we end with this Role:

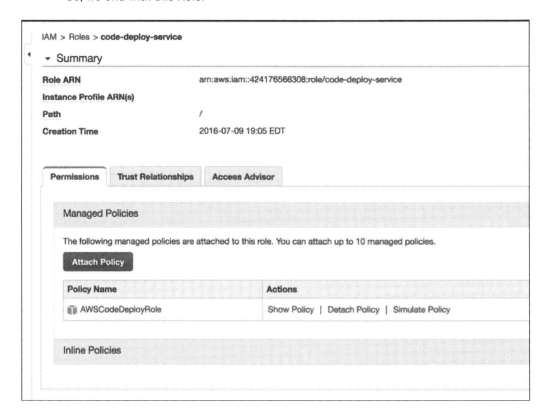

Now, let's go to `CodeDeploy` to make an Application and a deployable group that will use this Role:

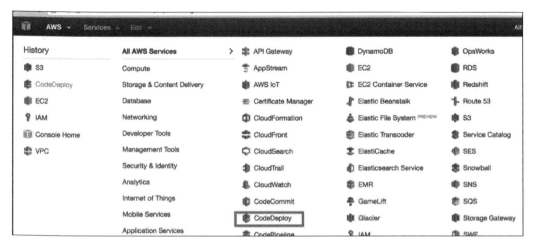

Busy AWS Menu

25. Notice here that we used the key and tag value we made during the EC2 creation to connect `CodeDeploy` to know what EC2 instance or instances to deploy to:

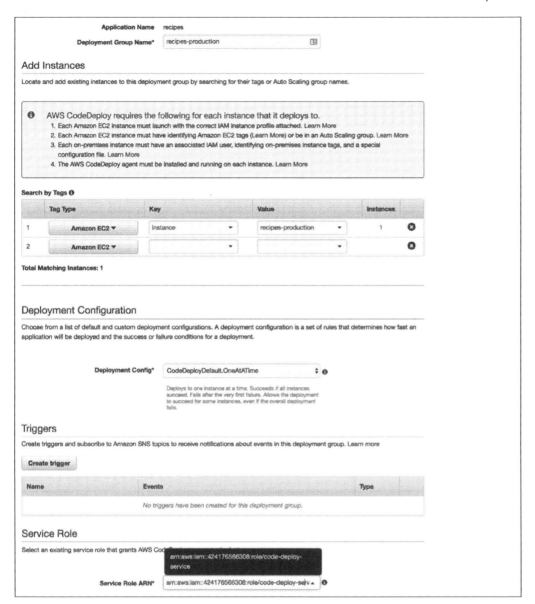

Adding Instance

And, finally, at the bottom is the Service Role we made.

26. Now, are we ready? Well, they tell me I can run the command in the following screenshot:

But, we never made the S3 bucket! So, let's do this and give the proper permission to it for the User, EC2, and `CodeDeploy`.

27. The typical way to deploy from Forge is GitHub or BitBucket, but since we are going to go with `CodeDeploy` for this recipe, we need to set up an S3 bucket for it called recipe-artifacts:

Creating an S3 Bucket

Wait! You cannot do this because I just did. Buckets are similar to domain names. So maybe stick to prefixing your buckets with your business domain, such as `alfred-nutile-inc-recipes`.

28. Now, add `appspec.yml` to the root of your Laravel application and have it look like this for now:

```yaml
version: 0.0
os: linux
files:
  - source: /
    destination: /home/forge/app
permissions:
  - object: /home/forge/app
    owner: forge
    group: www-data
    mode: 775
    type:
      - file

  - object: /home/forge/app
    owner: forge
    group: www-data
    mode: 755
    type:
      - directory

hooks:
#  ApplicationStop:
#    - location: deployment/scripts/application_stop.sh
#      timeout: 300
#      runas: forge
#  BeforeInstall:
#    - location: deployment/scripts/before_install.sh
#      timeout: 300
#      runas: forge
#  DownloadBundle:
#    - location: deployment/scripts/download_bundle.sh
#      timeout: 1200
#      runas: forge
#  AfterInstall:
#    - location: deployment/scripts/after_install.sh
#      timeout: 300
#      runas: forge
#  ApplicationStart:
#    - location: deployment/scripts/application_start.sh
#      timeout: 300
#      runas: forge
#  ValidateService:
#    - location: deployment/scripts/validate_service.sh
#      timeout: 300
#      runas: forge
```

Forge makes folders as per website, so there would be /home/
forge/universalscomicshub.io and /home/forge/
staging.univeralscomicshub.io, but I run one site as
per the server, and to keep my scripts simple, I make a symbolic
link from /home/forge/universalscomicshub.io to /
home/forge/app so that Forge can keep working the way it
likes to and all my scripts can keep working as well.

29. In your Vagrant box that you do your work in, add the `config` and `crendential`
files. I can type at the command line as the user in my Vagrant box where I installed
the AWS CLI tools into:

```
>aws --profile=code-deploy deploy push --application-name recipes
--description "First Push" --ignore-hidden-files --s3-location
s3://recipe-artifacts/latest.zip --source .
```

Now, if you look, when this is done, you have an Artifact on S3:

S3 has versioning, so you can write the same name many times, but
you will have numerous options later on in the `CodeDeploy` UI.

30. Later, we will have Travis do this work for us, but for now, let's go to AWS and the `CodeDeploy` group using this Artefact:

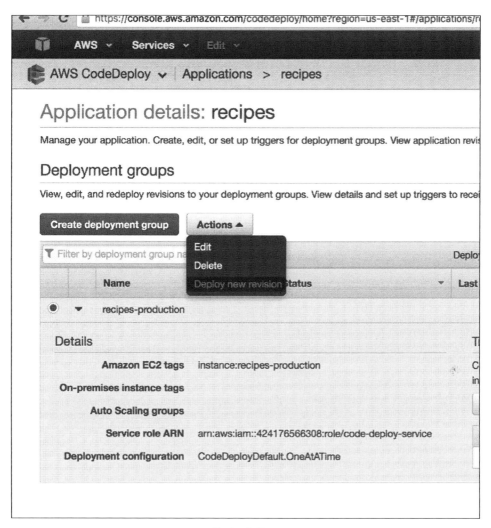

Deploy Options

31. Now it will ask a couple of questions, then you will be set to go:

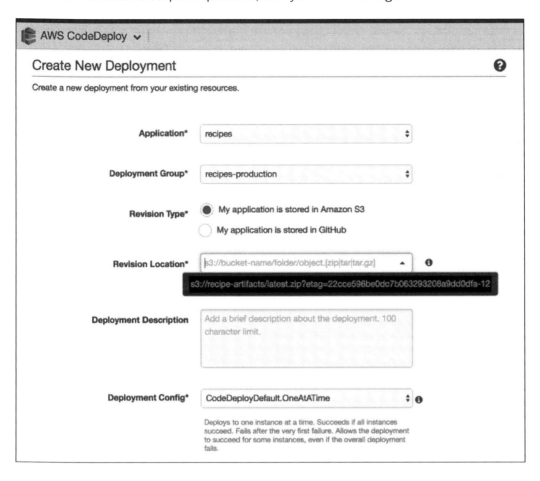

32. Go to the dashboard, and keep an eye on it:

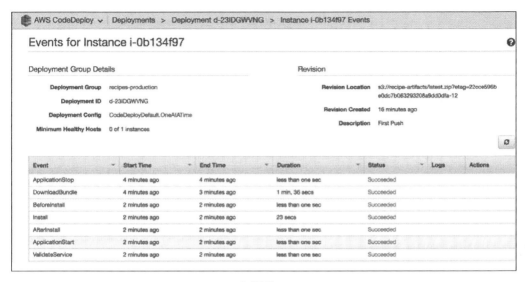

Build Steps

33. Great! The code is now there on `/home/foge/universalcomicshub.io`, but we have not done any migration and do not have a `.env` file yet. As I covered in the *Managing your ENV file* section, we can push our local `.env` file up to the server with just one command. To start, I will add SSH in and make the database:

```
ubuntu@deep-atoll:~$ mysql -uforge -p
Enter password:
Welcome to the MariaDB monitor.  Commands end with ; or \g.
Your MariaDB connection id is 4
Server version: 10.1.15-MariaDB-1~xenial mariadb.org binary distribution

Copyright (c) 2000, 2016, Oracle, MariaDB Corporation Ab and others.

Type 'help;' or '\h' for help. Type '\c' to clear the current input statement.

MariaDB [(none)]> create database recipes_prod;
```

34. Then from my Vagrant box, I will upload my updated `.env` file, so my website is ready to connect to the database:

```
vagrant@homestead:~/Code/recipes$ php artisan envdeploy:push production
start scp on host 52.22.30.227 in directory /home/forge/universalcomicshub.io/
100/100 [████████████████████████] 100%


Done copying file to target host 52.22.30.227
vagrant@homestead:~/Code/recipes$
```

35. We will automate this later, but let's run `php artisan migrate --force` since we are here already, and I seeded it as well to get it going:

```
ubuntu@deep-atoll:~/app$ php artisan migrate:refresh --seed --force
Rolled back: 2016_06_18_140240_create_blogs_table
Rolled back: 2016_06_13_234030_alter_user_table_add_url
Rolled back: 2016_06_09_233516_create_jobs_table
Rolled back: 2016_06_05_122239_create_latest_favorites_table
Rolled back: 2016_05_21_153145_create_cashier_migrations
Rolled back: 2016_05_21_132909_alter_user_table_add_is_admin
Rolled back: 2016_05_19_233915_add_favorites_feature_flag
Rolled back: 2016_05_16_220136_create_favorites_table
Rolled back: 2016_04_22_235405_create_wish_lists_table
Rolled back: 2016_04_22_140602_create_profile_table
Rolled back: 2016_04_19_232922_alter_users_table_add_twitter_name_field
Rolled back: 2016_01_24_154346_feature_flags
Rolled back: 2014_10_12_100000_create_password_resets_table
Rolled back: 2014_10_12_000000_create_users_table
Migrated: 2014_10_12_000000_create_users_table
Migrated: 2014_10_12_100000_create_password_resets_table
Migrated: 2016_01_24_154346_feature_flags
Migrated: 2016_04_19_232922_alter_users_table_add_twitter_name_field
Migrated: 2016_04_22_140602_create_profile_table
Migrated: 2016_04_22_235405_create_wish_lists_table
Migrated: 2016_05_16_220136_create_favorites_table
Migrated: 2016_05_19_233915_add_favorites_feature_flag
Migrated: 2016_05_21_132909_alter_user_table_add_is_admin
Migrated: 2016_05_21_153145_create_cashier_migrations
Migrated: 2016_06_05_122239_create_latest_favorites_table
Migrated: 2016_06_09_233516_create_jobs_table
Migrated: 2016_06_13_234030_alter_user_table_add_url
Migrated: 2016_06_18_140240_create_blogs_table
Seeded: UserTableSeeder
Seeded: WishListTableSeeder
Seeded: FavoritesSeeder
Seeded: BlogTableSeeder
```

36. So now, in order to now run migrations manually every time, we take advantage of the file called `appspec.yml` that we made earlier, which now looks like this:

```
version: 0.0
os: linux
files:
  - source: /
    destination: /home/forge/app
permissions:
  - object: /home/forge/app
    owner: forge
    group: www-data
    mode: 775
    type:
      - file

  - object: /home/forge/app
    owner: forge
    group: www-data
    mode: 755
    type:
      - directory

hooks:
#  ApplicationStop:
#      - location: deployment/scripts/application_stop.sh
#        timeout: 300
#        runas: forge
#  BeforeInstall:
#      - location: deployment/scripts/before_install.sh
#        timeout: 300
#        runas: forge
#  DownloadBundle:
#      - location: deployment/scripts/download_bundle.sh
#        timeout: 1200
#        runas: forge
  AfterInstall:
     - location: deployment/scripts/after_install.sh
       timeout: 300
       runas: forge
#  ApplicationStart:
#      - location: deployment/scripts/application_start.sh
#        timeout: 300
#        runas: forge
#  ValidateService:
#      - location: deployment/scripts/validate_service.sh
#        timeout: 300
#        runas: forge
```

37. Then, I make this `deployment/scripts/after_install.sh` file and have it look like this:

```sh
#!/bin/sh
cd ~/app
php artisan migrate --force
```

38. Now, run the command again to send it to `CodeDeploy`, and then deploy it from the `CodeDeploy` UI; and you now have migrations running!

How it works...

Wow! This was a lot of work for deploying code if you compare it to the more common way to deploy code; for example, take a look at the following:

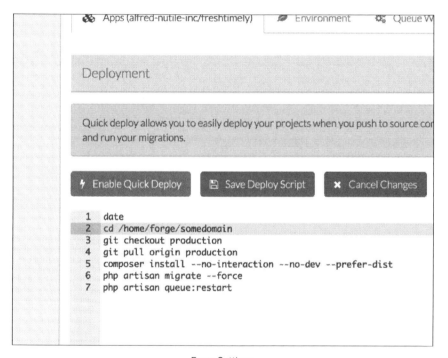

Forge Settings

You might wonder why you should bother with this? As I mentioned previously, in my case, it is key to have Artifacts to deploy, as this prevents issues that can happen when deploying from, say, *Staging* to *Production*; but something, this goes wrong with GitHub, NPM, and what not. Or a version of a library changes when the time Staging is in review.

Also, since all our servers are the same, QA can be confident that if xyz Artifact is passing, then it can be deployed to Production with confidence.

In the future, my workflow will just go to Production from every passing push, and this gives me one layer of confidence in the workflow.

Lastly, we get one extra feature—a very simple way to roll back once the deployment is done.

But enough trying to sell the idea. Let me follow up here with some details about the previous part. I start by going over some of the terms that AWS tends to use for things that are different than what we have experienced outside of AWS. Once you get comfortable with these and some of the ways that AWS has abstracted DevOps and Linux behind its services, it will begin to make more sense.

Then, I go into making the EC2, showing how you can attach a Role to it that can later be modified. And the Role that we make allows it to talk to `CodeDeploy` and later S3. Keep in mind that EC2s can have permissions granted to them outside of the `KEY` and `SECRET`, which we made for `IAM User`, to communicate to other services. This has nothing to do with Linux, but just how AWS manages interresource communications. So, when dealing with AWS, there is a point where Linux or the OS is the OS, and then there is a wrapper around it, which is the AWS API.

We then take a moment to easily build this EC2 in the UI! This is really easy and only gets easier as you graduate to OpsWorks or CloudFormations. We take advantage of the default VPC and Subnet that comes with AWS. The same is applicable with storage, just setting some defaults. After this, we tag our resource for `CodeDeploy`; keep in mind that tagging all resources for your project pays off later for billing and reporting.

When this is done, we save `KEY` and `SECRET` that it gave us. Do not lose this. And do not use this for all your apps. Use a service such as LastPass or Passpack to store this and make one per server. Just in case one leaks out, not all your applications are compromised.

Then, we get into Forge. Running the command it gives us, the server will be about 100% ready for our Laravel site.

 This is a bash script that it downloads and runs; open it up and explore it! This is not magic, but just lots of pain and time to get this stuff to work right by Taylor and many other people on the Internet. I saved a copy at `https://gist.github.com/alnutile/f8efe2793f7fafa25e373612cc3caa8b`.

Then, there is the `CodeDeploy` setup. We make a user that we or Travis CI can run the commands as. We make an S3 bucket to store the artifacts, and finally, we set up the daemon on the server to listen for the `CodeDeploy` service to talk to it. Once it gets a request, it will get the ZIP file from S3 and get it into place. This is when the file called `appspec.yml` comes into play. With this, we let it know what to do during the many hooks it offers during the process. Many of my projects use Ansible for this, and it has a built-in module for Slack, so we are even notified during the process.

Then, there is the `CodeDeploy` UI to see progress. Keep in mind the server has logs as well and you can

```
>tail -f /var/log/aws/codedeploy-agent/codedeploy-agent.log
```

to keep an eye on them. By the way, `CodeDeploy` and your Artifacts live in the `/opt` folder.

For now, I am manually running `CodeDeploy` via the command line and the UI. For the command line, I had to install the AWS command-line tools. And in doing so, I had to configure my profile for this user and application. You could actually never go to the AWS UI for any of this. Logging, pushing the app to S3, and deploying the Artifact can all be done at the command line. But, heck, the UI is not that bad really once you get used to it.

Oh, and I also give a bit of attention to my package at `https://packagist.org/ packages/alfred-nutile-inc/env-deployer`; when I really need to push a `.env` file around, this package makes it quite easy.

At this point, you have a server that can easily increase in storage size and computing size, which can be put behind an AWS load balancer. It can communicate with AWS Queues (SQS), RDS, free AWS SSL management, and more because it is part of the AWS services ecosystem. And it will be deployed to each passing CI build. You can even deploy to numerous servers at once behind the load balancer!

See also

AWS docs are really not that bad; check out:

- `http://docs.aws.amazon.com/codedeploy/latest/userguide/getting- started-setup.html`
- `http://docs.aws.amazon.com/codedeploy/latest/userguide/how-to- create-service-role.html`
- `http://docs.aws.amazon.com/codedeploy/latest/userguide/app- spec-ref.html`

- ▸ Take an AWS course as it's well worth the money ($10 to $20) and time: `https://linuxacademy.com/amazon-web-services/training/course/name/aws-certified-solutions-architect-associate`

- ▸ Jez Humble—Continuous Delivery: `https://continuousdelivery.com/wp-content/uploads/2011/04/deployment_production_line.pdf`

Setting up Travis to auto deploy when all is passing

Level 0 of any work should be getting a deployment workflow set up. What this means in this case is that a push to GitHub will trigger our CI. And then from the CI, if the tests are passing, we trigger the deployment. In this example, I am not going to hit the URL that Forge gives you, but I am going to send an Artifact to S3, and then have `CodeDeploy` to deploy this Artifact.

As you will see in *Chapter 4, Building Views and Adding Style* under the *Using Travis to run tests on every push* section, I have covered setting up this app in Travis CI (`https://travis-ci.org/`); in this section, I will cover adding `CodeDeploy` as a part of this step.

Getting ready

You really need to see the section before this, otherwise continuing to know this will make no sense.

How to do it...

The following are the steps:

1. Install the `travis` command-line tool in Homestead as noted in their docs at `https://github.com/travis-ci/travis.rb#installation`. Make sure to use Ruby 2.x:

   ```
   sudo apt-get install ruby2.0-dev
   sudo gem install travis -v 1.8.2 --no-rdoc --no-ri
   ```

2. Then in the `recipe` folder, I run the command:

   ```
   > travis setup codedeploy
   ```

3. Answer all the questions, keeping in mind the following:

   ❏ KEY and SECRET are the ones we got for IAM User in the section before this.

   ❏ The S3 KEY is the filename and not KEY we used for *a* previously. So, in my case, I just use the name again of the latest.zip file, since it sits inside the recipe-artifact bucket.

4. Finally, I open the .travis.yml file, which the previous one modifies, and I update the before-deploy area, so the zip command ignores my .env file; otherwise, it would overwrite the file on the server:

```
language: php
dist: trusty
group: edge
php:
- '7.0'
services:
- mysql
before_script:
- cp .env.travis .env
- mysql -e 'create database recipes_test;'
- travis_retry composer self-update
- travis_retry composer install --prefer-source --no-interaction --dev
- php artisan migrate:refresh --seed
- sleep 3
script:
- phpunit
deploy:
- provider: s3
  access_key_id: 
  secret_access_key: &1
    secure: 
  local_dir: dpl_cd_upload
  skip_cleanup: true
  on: &2
    repo: alnutile/recipes
  bucket: recipe-artifacts
- provider: codedeploy
  access_key_id: 
  secret_access_key: *1
  bucket: recipe-artifacts
  key: latest.zip
  bundle_type: zip
  application: recipes
  deployment_group: recipes-production
  on: *2
before_deploy:
- zip -r --exclude=*.env* --exclude="storage/logs/laravel.log" latest.zip *
- mkdir -p dpl_cd_upload
- mv latest.zip dpl_cd_upload/latest.zip
```

How it works...

Well, if you did the `CodeDeploy` section before this one, you will know this is not as easy as it looks. After all the previous work we were able to do with the one command `travis setup codedeploy`; punch in securely all the needed info to get this *passing build* to deploy. So, after `phpunit` reports things are passing, we are ready.

With that said, we had to have a lot of things in place: an S3 bucket to put the artifact, permission with `KEY` and `SECRET` to access the Artifact along with `CodeDeploy`, and a `CodeDeploy` group and an application to deploy to. All of this was covered in the previous section.

After this, it is just the magic of Travis and `CodeDeploy` working together to make this look so easy.

See also

Travis docs available at the following sites:

- `https://docs.travis-ci.com/user/deployment/codedeploy`
- `https://github.com/travis-ci/travis.rb`
- `https://github.com/travis-ci/travis.rb#installation`

Working with your .env file

The workflow around this can be tricky. Going from Local, to Travis CI, to `CodeDeploy`, and then to AWS without storing your information in `.env` on GitHub can be a challenge. What I will show here are some tools and techniques to do this well.

Getting ready

A base installation is fine; I will use the existing installation to show some tricks around this.

How to do it...

1. Minimize the `.env` variable using *Conventions* as much as possible:

   1. `config/queue.php` I can do this to have one or more Queues:

```php
'sqs' => [
    'driver' => 'sqs',
    'key'    => env('AWS_ACCESS_KEY_ID'),
    'secret' => env('AWS_SECRET_ACCESS_KEY'),
    'prefix' => 'https://sqs.us-east-1.amazonaws.com/12345678',
    'queue'  => env('APP_NAME') . '-default-' . env('APP_ENV') . env('SHADOW_SUFFIX'),
    'region' => 'us-east-1',
],

'sqs-2' => [
    'driver' => 'sqs',
    'key'    => env('AWS_ACCESS_KEY_ID'),
    'secret' => env('AWS_SECRET_ACCESS_KEY'),
    'prefix' => 'https://sqs.us-east-1.amazonaws.com/12345678',
    'queue'  => env('APP_NAME') . '-other-' . env('APP_ENV'),
    'region' => 'us-east-1',
],
```

   2. `config/filesystems.php`:

```php
's3' => [
    'driver' => 's3',
    'key'    => env('AWS_ACCESS_KEY_ID'),
    'secret' => env('AWS_SECRET_ACCESS_KEY'),
    'region' => 'us-east-1',
    'bucket' => 'subname-' . env('APP_NAME') . '-' . env('APP_ENV'),
],
```

2. Use the `Config` file as much as possible. For example, this is in my `.env`:

```
MARVEL_API_KEY=eeaef8ccb27b7aa1e20c80bd2f0d78a6
MARVEL_API_SECRET=7ba1bfda7586b8392174ae93471383ff549a6be2
MARVEL_API_BASE_URL=https://gateway.marvel.com
MARVEL_API_VERSION=/v1/public
```

But I can also add `config/marvel.php`, and then make it look like this:

```php
<?php

return [

    'MARVEL_API_KEY'        => env('MARVEL_API_KEY'),
    'MARVEL_API_SECRET'     => env('MARVEL_API_SECRET'),
    'MARVEL_API_BASE_URL'   => env('MARVEL_API_BASE_URL', 'https://gateway.marvel.com'),
    'MARVEL_API_VERSION'    => env('MARVEL_API_VERSION', '/v1/public'),

];
```

My `.env` file can be trimmed down by `KEY=VALUES` later on I can call to those:

- `Config::get('marvel.MARVEL_API_VERSION)`
- `Config::get('marvel.MARVEL_API_BASE_URL')`

```
MARVEL_API_KEY=eeaef8ccb27b7aa1e20c80bd2f0d78a6
MARVEL_API_SECRET=7ba1bfda7586b8392174ae93471383ff549a6be2
```

3. Now, to easily send to Staging or Production using the `EnvDeployer` library, run the following:

    `>composer require alfred-nutile-inc/env-deployer:dev-master`

    Follow `readme.md` for this library. Then, as mentioned in the docs, set up your config file so that it matches the destination IP/URL, the username, and the path for those services.

I ended up with this `config` file and `config/envdeployer.php`:

```php
<?php

return [

    'connections' => [

        /*
         * The environment name.
         */
        'production' => [

            /*
             * The hostname to send the env file to
             */
            'host'  => 'icdb.io',

            /*
             * The username to be used when connecting to the server where the logs are located
             */
            'user' => 'ubuntu',

            /*
             * The full path to the directory where the .env is located MUST end in /
             */
            'rootEnvDirectory' => '/home/ubuntu/app/',

            'port' => 22
        ],
    ],
];
```

Now, the trick to this library is you start to enter `KEY=VALUES` into your .env file stacked on top of each other. For example, my database settings look like this:

```
#@production=recipes-production.12345.us-east-1.rds.amazonaws.com
DB_HOST=localhost
DB_PORT=3306
#@production=recipes_prod
DB_DATABASE=recipes
#@production=recipes_user
DB_USERNAME=homestead
#@production=iedaeKaechoo8ave
DB_PASSWORD=secret
```

So now I can type the following:

```
>php artisan envdeployer:push production
```

Then, this will push over SSH your `.env` file to production and swap out the related @ `production` values for each `KEY` they are placed before.

How it works...

The first mindset to follow is *conventions* before you put a new `KEY=VALUE` into the `.env` file is step back, and figure out defaults and conventions around what you already must have in this file. For example, you must have `APP_ENV`, and then I always have `APP_NAME` so that these two together do a lot to make databases, queues, buckets, and so on all around the existing keys.

It really does add up; whether you are working alone or on a team, focus on these conventions. Then use the `config/some.php` file workflow to set up defaults.

Then the libraries that I used previously can push this information around with ease. Similar to Heroku, you can command-line these settings up to the servers as needed.

See also

▸ Laravel Validator for the `.env` file: `https://packagist.org/packages/mathiasgrimm/laravel-env-validator`

▸ Laravel 5 Fundamentals: Environments and Configuration: `https://laracasts.com/series/laravel-5-fundamentals/episodes/6`

Testing your app on Production with Behat

So, your application is now on Production! Start clicking away at hundreds of little and big features, so you can make sure everything went okay; or, better yet, run Behat! Behat on Production? Sounds crazy, but I will cover some tips on how to do this, including how to set up some remote conditions and clean up when you are done.

Getting ready

Any application will do. In my case, I am going to hit production with some tests I made earlier.

How to do it...

The following are the steps to be followed:

1. Tag a Behat test called `@smoke` or just a scenario that you know is safe to run on Production, for example, `features/home/search.feature`:

```
home/search.feature - recipes - [~/Code/recipes]
Feature: Search using Angular from the Home page
  Searching Marvel using Angular
  As a user on the sight
  So the results are fast

  @javascript @smoke
  Scenario: Search for Wolverine
    Given I go to the search page
    And I search for "Wolverine"
    Then I should see a ton of results about him
    And if I click the Next in the Pagination I can see even more "Wolverines (2015) #5"
```

2. Update `behat.yml` by adding a profile to it called `production`:

```
            contexts: [ MainContext ]
        extensions:
            Laracasts\Behat:
                env_path: .env.behat
            Behat\MinkExtension:
                default_session: laravel
                base_url: https://recipes.dev
                laravel: ~
                selenium2:
                    wd_host: "http://selenium.dev:4444/wd/hub"
                browser_name: chrome

    production:
      extensions:
        Behat\MinkExtension:
          base_url: http://universalcomicshub.io
```

3. Then run the following:

```
> vendor/bin/behat -shome_ui --tags=@smoke --profile=production
```

 I run an Artisan command to run all of these.

Then, you will see it hit the production URL and only the scenarios you feel are safe for Behat.

4. Another method is to log in as a demo user. And after logging in as the user, you can see data that is related to the user only, so you can test the authenticated level of data and interactions. For example, `database/seeds/UserTableSeeder.php` adds the demo user to the `run` method:

```php
factory(\App\User::class)->create(
    [
        'email' => 'demo@foo.com',
        'password' => bcrypt(env('DEMO_PASSWORD'))
    ]
);
```

5. Then, update your `.env` file:

```
#@production=rujiebae3aiVesha
DEMO_PASSWORD=Ahle6Vee4di3aiga
```

6. Now, push the `.env` setting up to Production:

```
>php artisan envdeploy:push production
```

7. Then, we update our `behat.yml` file to run this test even on Production `features/auth/login.feature`:

```
Feature: Login Page
  Login page to do authenticated tasks
  As an anonymous user
  So we can protect some personal and administrative parts of the site

  @happy_path @smoke
  Scenario: A user can login and see their profile
    Given I am on the login page
    And I fill in the login form with my proper username and password
    Then I should be able to see my profile page
    Then when I logout and revisit that profile page I will be redirected to the lo

  @smoke
  Scenario: A non logged in user can not get a profile
    Given I am an anonymous user
    And I go to the profile page
    Then I should get redirected with an error message to let me know the problem
```

Login Test

8. Now, we need to commit our work and push to GitHub, so Travis CI can deploy the changes:

```
>php artisan migrate:refresh --seed
```

 Since this is a seed and not a migration, I need to rerun seeds on production. Since this is a new site, and no one has used it, this is fine, but of course, this would have been a migration if I had to do this later in the application's life.

9. Now, let's run this test from our Vagrant box:

```
> vendor/bin/behat -slogin_ui --profile=production
```

10. But it fails because I am setting up the state of this test for my local database, not the remote database called `features/bootstrap/LoginPageUIContext.php`:

```
/**
 * @Then I should be able to see my profile page
 */
public function iShouldBeAbleToSeeMyProfilePage()
{
    //Make a profile to see
    factory(\App\Profile::class)->create([
        'favorite_comic_character' => 'Spider-Man', 'user_id' => $this->user->id]);
    //Now visit profile
    $this->visit($this->baseUrl . '/profile/' . $this->user->url);
    //see my profile
    $this->assertPageContainsText('Favorite Comic Character: Spider-Man');
    $this->assertPageNotContainsText('Error getting profile :(');
}
```

11. So, I can basically begin to create a way to setup the state of the world on the remote server:

```
> php artisan make:controller SetupBehatController
```

12. Update the controller to do the setup:

```php
<?php

namespace App\Http\Controllers;

use App\User;
use Illuminate\Http\Request;

use App\Http\Requests;
use Illuminate\Support\Facades\Auth;

class SetupBehatController extends Controller
{

    public function __construct()
    {
        $this->middleware('auth');
    }

    public function setupProfile() {
        if(Auth::user()->email != 'demo@foo.com') {
            redirect()->route('home');
        }

        $user = User::where('email', 'demo@foo.com')->firstOrFail();
        $user->favorite_comic_character = "Spider-Man";
        $user->save();

        redirect()->route('profile', [$user->url]);
    }
}
```

Remote Behat Controller

13. Make the route called `app/Http/routes.php`:

```php
Route::group(['middleware' => ['web']], function () {

    Route::auth();

    Route::resource("blogs","BlogController");

    Route::get("/setup/profile", "SetupBehatController@setupProfile");
```

14. Then, update the Behat test called `features/bootstrap/LoginPageUIContext.php`:

```
/**
 * @Then I should be able to see my profile page
 */
public function iShouldBeAbleToSeeMyProfilePage()
{
    $this->visit('/setup/profile');
    $this->visit($this->baseUrl . '/profile/' . $this->user->url);
    $this->assertPageContainsText('Favorite Comic Character: Spider-Man');
    $this->assertPageNotContainsText('Error getting profile :(');
}
```

15. We should do some cleanup! First, add a new method to `features/bootstrap/LoginPageUIContext.php`:

```
/**
 * @AfterScenario @profile
 */
public function cleanupProfile() {
    $this->visit('/cleanup/profile');
}
```

16. Then, add this tag to the scenarios this is related to `features/auth/login.feature`:

```
Feature: Login Page
  Login page to do authenticated tasks
  As an anonymous user
  So we can protect some personal and administrative parts of the site

  @happy_path @smoke @javascript @profile
  Scenario: A user can login and see their profile
    Given I am on the login page
    And I fill in the login form with my proper username and password
    Then I should be able to see my profile page
    Then when I logout and revisit that profile page I will be redirected to the login

  @smoke @profile
  Scenario: A non logged in user can not get a profile
    Given I am an anonymous user
    And I go to the profile page
    Then I should get redirected with an error message to let me know the problem
```

17. Then, add the controller just as before, and route `app/Http/Controllers/CleanupBehatController.php`:

```php
<?php

namespace App\Http\Controllers;

use App\User;
use Illuminate\Http\Request;

use App\Http\Requests;
use Illuminate\Support\Facades\Auth;

class CleanupBehatController extends Controller
{
    public function __construct()
    {
        $this->middleware('auth');
    }

    public function cleanupProfile() {
        if(Auth::user()->email != 'demo@foo.com') {
            redirect()->route('home');
        }

        $user = User::where('email', 'demo@foo.com')->firstOrFail();
        $user->favorite_comic_character = "CleanUp";
        $user->save();

        redirect()->route('profile', [$user->url]);
    }
}
```

18. Then, push it, and we are ready to test this user with fresh state, and then clean up when they are done! In this case, I could test editing the profile from one state to another.

How it works...

Not too hard! Now we have a workflow that can save us a ton of clicking around Production after every deployment.

To begin with, I added the tag called `@smoke` to the tests that I considered *safe* for Production. What does safe mean? Basically, I read only the tests that I knew would not affect the site's data. Using the `@smoke` tag, I had a consistent way to make Suites or Scenarios safe to run on Production.

But then I took it a step further and created a way to test the authentication-related state, similar to making a Favorite or update a Profile! By using some simple routes and a user, I can begin to test many other things on my long list of features that I need to consider after every deploy.

All of this happens with the configurability of Behat and how it allows me to manage different Profiles and Suites in the `behat.yml` file!

Lastly, I tied into the fact that Behat has hooks. In this case, I tie in to the `@AfterScenario` hook by adding it to my Annotation. And I added another hook called `@profile` so that it only runs if the scenario has the tag.

This is it; thanks to Behat, Hooks and how easy it is to make Routes in Laravel, I can easily take care of a large percentage of what otherwise would be a tedious process after every deployment.

See also

- ▸ Behat Docs on Hooks—`http://docs.behat.org/en/v3.0/guides/3.hooks.html`
- ▸ Saucelabs—on `behat.yml` setting later and you can test your site on numerous devices—`https://saucelabs.com/`

Making a composer package out of our client

One practice you will start to do a lot is making packages you can use in other projects. In this example, I will start to move the Marvel client into its own namespace and rename it `UniversalComicClient`. Then, once this is working, I will pull it completely out and put it onto `Packagist`.

Getting ready

A fresh installation of Laravel is fine. The code for the client can just be moved around in there.

How to do it...

1. Make a new folder called `app\UniversalComicsClient\src` as we are going to make this a universal client.

 Later, I will rename all of this Comic singular.

2. Then move the files here:
   - `app/UniversalComicsClient/src/MarvelApiClient.php`
   - `app/UniversalComicsClient/src/ComicClientInterface.php`
   - `app/UniversalComicsClient/src/MarvelApi.php`

3. Update all these namespaces to be `YourGithubName\Package`, so in my case `Alnutile\UniversalComicsClient` example:

```php
<?php

namespace Alnutile\UniversalComicsClient;

use Alnutile\UniversalComicsClient\MarvelApi;
use Illuminate\Support\Facades\Config;
use Illuminate\Support\ServiceProvider;
use GuzzleHttp\Client;

class MarvelApiClient extends ServiceProvider
{
    /**
     * Bootstrap the application services.
     *
     * @return void
     */
    public function boot()
    {
        $this->app->bind(\Alnutile\UniversalComicsClient\Comic
```

Provider Boot

 Alnutile is my GitHub name, and in this case, it is my vendor name.

4. Now, set up the local `composer.json` that has this namespace:

```
},
"autoload": {
    "classmap": [
        "database"
    ],
    "psr-4": {
        "App\\": "app/",
        "Alnutile\\UniversalComicsClient\\": "app/UniversalComicsClient/src/"
    },
    "files": [
        "app/helpers.php"
    ]
}
```

5. Now, since this is part of my previous setup, I will update `config/app.php`:

```
Alnutile\UniversalComicsClient\MarvelApiClient::class,
```

6. Then, run the following to update the `autoloader`:

   >composer dump

7. Okay, before we move this out into its own package, let's see if it works by visiting the home page again. Great! It works after I did a search for `App\Interfaces\ComicClientInterface` and replaced it with `Alnutile\UniversalComicsClient\ComicClientInterface`, the website is working just like before.

8. Alright, now we will move it out of our app. First, install the composer require called `pingpong/workbench`.

9. As noted in the docs, add it to `config/app.php`, and then run the following:

   > php artisan vendor:publish --provider="Pingpong\Workbench\WorkbenchServiceProvider"

10. Now, edit the file called `config/workbench.php` so that it matches your e-mail and name on GitHub (ideally):

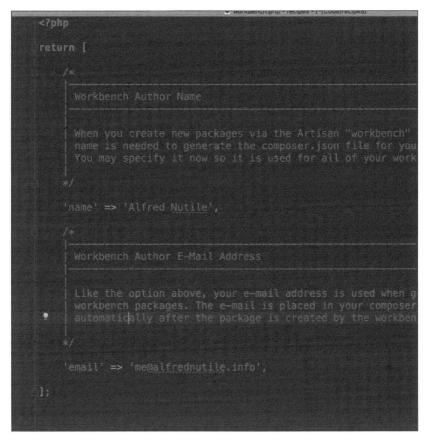

Workbench

11. Now, run the following:

```
> php artisan workbench alnutile/universal-comic-client
--resources
```

12. Lots of stuff will happen at this moment, and you will have this new structure in the root of your application:

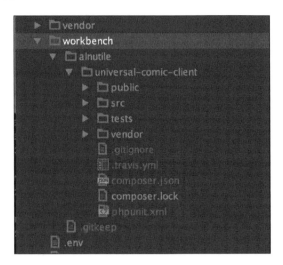

13. Now, let's add Guzzle to the `workbench/alnutile/universal-comic-client/` `composer.json` file, since I will need this as part of this library:

```json
{
    "name": "alnutile/universal-comic-client",
    "description": "",
    "authors": [
        {
            "name": "Alfred Nutile",
            "email": "me@alfrednutile.info"
        }
    ],
    "require": {
        "php": ">=5.5.9",
        "illuminate/support": "5.2.*",
        "guzzlehttp/guzzle": "^6.1"
    },
    "autoload": {
        "classmap": [
            "src/migrations"
        ],
        "psr-4": {
            "Alnutile\\UniversalComicClient\\": "src/Alnutile/UniversalComicClient"
        }
    },
    "minimum-stability": "stable"
}
```

14. Next, let's change what we added to the root called `composer.json` in the starting steps, leaving it like this:

```
{
    "type": "vcs",
    "url": "https://github.com/alnutile/l5scaffold.git"
}
],
"autoload": {
    "classmap": [
        "database"
    ],
    "psr-4": {
        "App\\": "app/",
        "Alnutile\\UniversalComicClient\\": "workbench/alnutile/universal-comic-client/src/Alnutile/UniversalComicClient"
    },
    "files": [
        "app/helpers.php"
    ]
},
"autoload-dev": {
    "classmap": [
        "tests/TestCase.php"
    ]
},
```

15. I update `config/app.php`, as I took advantage of the better name of the provider that this package made for me; since I am making this universal, I should not name things Marvel:

```
Alnutile\UniversalComicClient\UniversalComicClientServiceProvider::class,
```

16. Make sure to run `composer dump` again.

17. So at this point, all my files live in here:

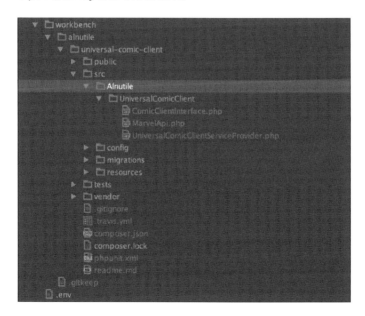

18. Then, the next step is to make `config/marvel.php` part of the install `app/UniversalComicsClient/config/marvel.php` this file now looks like `workbench/alnutile/universal-comic-client/src/Alnutile/UniversalComicClient/UniversalComicClientServiceProvider.php`:

```php
public function boot()
{

    $this->app->bind(\Alnutile\UniversalComicClient\ComicClientInterface::class, function () {
        $config = [
            'base_uri'          => Config::get('marvel.MARVEL_API_BASE_URL'),
            'timeout'           => 0,
            'allow_redirects'   => false,
            'verify'            => false,
            'headers'           => [
                'Content-Type'  => 'application/json'
            ]
        ];

        $client = new Client($config);
        $key = env('MARVEL_API_KEY');
        $secret = env('MARVEL_API_SECRET');
        $client = new MarvelApi($key, $secret, $client);
        $client->setApiVersion(Config::get('marvel.MARVEL_API_VERSION'));
        return $client;
    });

    $this->loadTranslationsFrom(__DIR__ . '/../../resources/lang', 'universal-comic-client');

    $this->loadViewsFrom(__DIR__ . '/../../resources/views', 'universal-comic-client');

    $this->publishes([
        __DIR__ .'/../../../src/config/marvel.php' => config_path('marvel.php'),
    ], 'config');
}
```

19. Then, when we run this command, we can see that the file moved back into the root of our application at the `config/marvel.php` file:

```
vagrant@homestead:~/Code/recipes$ php artisan vendor:publish --provider="Alnutile\UniversalComicClient\UniversalComicClientServiceProvider" --tag="config"
Copied File [/workbench/alnutile/universal-comic-client/src/config/marvel.php] To [/config/marvel.php]
Publishing complete for tag [config]!
vagrant@homestead:~/Code/recipes$
```

Running the Command Above

20. Then, let's see our test working inside our package called `workbench/alnutile/universal-comic-client/tests/MarvelApiClientTest.php`:

```php
<?php

use Alnutile\UniversalComicClient\ComicClientInterface;
use Illuminate\Support\Facades\App;

class MarvelApiClientTest extends TestCase
{
    /**
     * @test
     * @vcr stub_comics_request
     */
    public function test_first_setup()
    {
        $client = App::make(ComicClientInterface::class);

        $ts = '1459629709';

        $results = $client->setTimeStamp($ts)->comics();

        $this->assertEquals(200, $results['code']);
    }
}
```

21. Also, to make my package testable outside Laravel, install the update called `workbench/alnutile/universal-comic-client/composer.json`:

```json
        "guzzlehttp/guzzle": "6.1"
    },
    "require-dev": {
        "fzaninotto/faker": "~1.4",
        "mockery/mockery": "0.9.*",
        "phpunit/phpunit": "~4.0",
        "symfony/css-selector": "2.8.*|3.0.*",
        "symfony/dom-crawler": "2.8.*|3.0.*",
        "php-vcr/phpunit-testlistener-vcr": "*",
        "laravel/laravel": "dev-master"
    },
    "autoload": {
        "classmap": [
            "src/migrations",
```

Composer.json with our Client

22. Then, in `workbench/alnutile/universal-comic-client`, run the following:

```
>rm -rf vendor composr.lock && composer install
```

23. Once this is done, copy `tests/TestCase.php` into `workbench/alnutile/universal-comic-client/tests/TestCase.php` and make it look like the following:

```php
<?php

class TestCase extends Illuminate\Foundation\Testing\TestCase
{

    /**
     * The base URL to use while testing the application.
     *
     * @var string
     */
    protected $baseUrl = 'http://localhost';

    /**
     * Creates the application.
     *
     * @return \Illuminate\Foundation\Application
     */
    public function createApplication()
    {

        $dot = new \Dotenv\Dotenv(__DIR__ .'/../');
        $dot->load();

        $app = require __DIR__.'/../vendor/laravel/laravel/bootstrap/app.php';

        $app->make(Illuminate\Contracts\Console\Kernel::class)->bootstrap();

        return $app;
    }

}
```

24. Make sure to add it to the *autoload* section in the `workbench/alnutile/universal-comic-client/composer.json` under files:

```json
    "laravel/laravel": "dev-master"
    },
    "autoload": {
        "files": [
            "tests/TestCase.php"
        ],
        "classmap": [
            "src/migrations"
        ],
        "psr-4": {
            "Alnutile\\UniversalComicClient\\": "src/Alnutile/UniversalComicClient"
        }
```

Adding our Path

25. Then comes my very bad example of a test, but it is good enough to show you some of Laravel's features that come together; `workbench/alnutile/universal-comic-client/tests/MarvelApiClientTest.php` looks like this now:

```php
<?php

use Alnutile\UniversalComicClient\MarvelApi;
use Illuminate\Support\Facades\App;

class MarvelApiClientTest extends TestCase
{
    /**
     * @test
     * @vcr stub_comics_request
     */
    public function test_first_setup()
    {
        $config = [
            'base_uri'          => env('MARVEL_API_BASE_URL'),
            'timeout'           => 0,
            'allow_redirects'   => false,
            'verify'            => false,
            'headers'           => [
                'Content-Type'  => 'application/json'
            ]
        ];

        $guzzle = new \GuzzleHttp\Client($config);
        $key = env('MARVEL_API_KEY');
        $secret = env('MARVEL_API_SECRET');
        $client =  new MarvelApi($key, $secret, $guzzle);
        $client->setApiVersion(env('MARVEL_API_VERSION'));

        $ts = '1459629709';

        $results = $client->setTimeStamp($ts)->comics();

        $this->assertEquals(200, $results['code']);
    }
}
```

Provider

26. Now, we can test our app as needed:

```
vagrant@homestead:~/Code/recipes/workbench/alnutile/universal-comic-client$ phpunit --filter=test_first_setup
PHPUnit 4.8.26 by Sebastian Bergmann and contributors.

.

Time: 6.09 seconds, Memory: 10.00MB

OK (1 test, 1 assertion)
vagrant@homestead:~/Code/recipes/workbench/alnutile/universal-comic-client$
```

27. Then, let's wrap it up and push it as a package to GitHub that we can pull down later on as needed in other applications. First, make a GitHub repo as I did in here:

28. Then, set up the folder called `~/Code/recipes/workbench/alnutile/universal-comic-client` for Git:

   ```
   >git init
   ```

   ```
   >git remote add origin git@github.com:alnutile/universal-comic-client.git
   ```

   ```
   >git add --all
   ```

   ```
   >git commit -m "Getting started"
   ```

   ```
   >git push origin master
   ```

29. After you push your code to GitHub, go to Packagist at `https://packagist.org/` and make an account to log in.

30. Once logged in, `submit` a package:

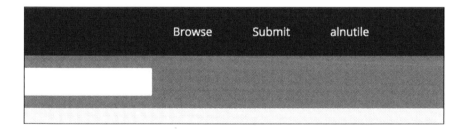

31. Then, add the GtiHub URL:

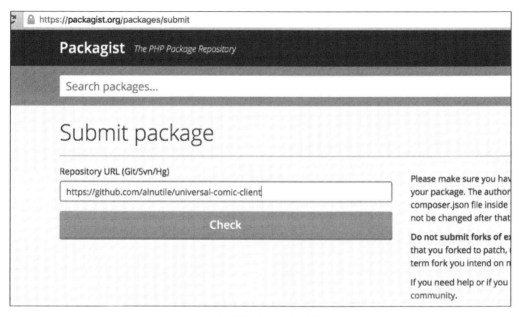

Adding Client to Packagist

32. Then, you will see your package!

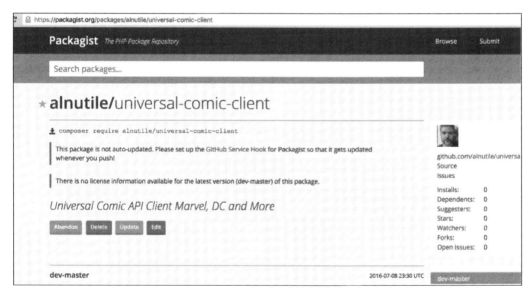

Final Results

A good `readme.md` is really key to a good package. Take time to make this, and write it as if you have no clue how to use this package.

33. Now, to just see how `phpunit` works in our standalone package, let's download and composer install this package in its folder outside of Laravel, and see how our tests work:

    ```
    >git clone git@github.com:alnutile/universal-comic-client.git
    ```

34. Change into this folder:

    ```
    >cd universal-comic-client/
    ```

35. Now, we need a `.env` file to help our very forced and lacking test. More on this is available in the *How it works...* section:

    ```
    MARVEL_API_KEY=foo
    MARVEL_API_SECRET=bar
    MARVEL_API_BASE_URL=https://gateway.marvel.com
    MARVEL_API_VERSION=/v1/public
    ```

36. Then, run `composer install`, and it defaults to installing the `require-dev` packages from `composer.json` as well.

37. Now, run `vendor/bin/phpunit`, and you will see your tests working outside of a Laravel application:

    ```
    vagrant@homestead:~/Code/universal-comic-client$ phpunit
    PHPUnit 4.8.26 by Sebastian Bergmann and contributors.

    .

    Time: 4.88 seconds, Memory: 10.00MB

    OK (1 test, 1 assertion)
    vagrant@homestead:~/Code/universal-comic-client$
    ```

38. This is it; you now have a testable package; now go add a Travis CI workflow to it for every push.

How it works...

Alright, so now is the time to take it from the top again with some details. We will start with the folder I made called `app\UniverisalComicsClient\src`. This gave me a place to namespace a set of files that I am later on planning to move out to their own library. This is really amazing, since I can work inside my core app, build this library, and basically, as you saw, copy the folder to its own area and make a library. I only do this when I really think I am making something into a standalone external library. Otherwise, I just keep it simple and default the `App` namespace.

The previous only works because I set `composer.json` to look in this path for a `psr-4` formatted namespace. From here, I just need to load the provider I made to truly pull it into Laravel. The Composer dump command will then simply update Composer to make this all ready to use.

When I am really ready to move this out, I begin to move it into "workbench". This is when it will become its own Git repository, and eventually, its own `Packagist`. The docs for `Pingpong\Workbench` got me going, and after I set up `config/workbench.php`, I was ready to make a library with the proper `composer.json`, its own `vendor` folder, and more.

Then, I also show that it can even run its own `phpunit` tests, which just shows how you have to start thinking about this package as being something testable outside of Laravel.

The last step is to really make this its own `Packagist` package, something that I or others can install using composer! If you follow these steps, then as you have seen previously, you are ready to pull this down into any project that is compatible with it. And more importantly, when you are cloning it to its own folder, you can run tests and continue to work on it with Laravel pulled into its `vendor` folder for you to reference, if needed. In this case, I load some of Laravel in my `tests/TestCase.php` file, so I can have some access to features in Laravel that I know I will have when I later use this in a real Laravel installation. Yes, this tightly couples this library to Laravel. This is a good example of a library that could be made to work in any framework that is `psr-4` compatible, but in this case, I am just using it for an example.

Ideally, I would take time at this point to set up Travis CI to run my tests on every push. But also note that I would never leave the `MarvelApiClientTest.php` test in there, hitting a real API. Maybe I would use it weekly to notify it about the API changes; but for the most part, this is not a great example of a test. I just wanted to show how I can plug in some of the different features of Laravel even from a standalone package.

Index

Symbols

12 Factor App
reference 11
$inject
reference 137
.env
using, for local build 9-11
working with 355-359

A

admin interface
creating, for subscriptions 225-232
Ajax request
handling 138-149
Angular
favorites Ajax widget, building in 164-173
setting up, Elixir used 183-189
setting up, Gulp used 183-189
Angular page
testing, with Behat 157-161
Angular request
handling 138-149
Angular results
paginating 149-156
Angular search
adding, to search page 130-137
Ansible
reference 280
API / JSON route
building, for searching 33-36
API, Laracasts
reference 149
API testing
VCR, using 247-251

application

setting up, in Homestead 6-9
troubleshooting 268-270
Artisan command
creating 272-277
Artisan signatures, Laravel docs
reference 277
authentication pages
making 61-65
authorization, Laravel Docs
reference 195
AWS
setting up 324-352
AWS Docs
references 352
AWS, terms
EBS 324
EC2 324
IAM 324
public IP 324
roles 325
Security Group 324
VPC (Virtual Private Cloud) 324

B

Behat
Angular page, testing with 157-161
app, testing on production 359-365
reference 161
Behat Docs, on Hooks
reference 366
behat.yml file
reference 98
Blade files
organizing 49-55

G

generator
used, for scaffolding user wishlist area 90-94
Git
reference 247
GitHub
code, getting onto 244-247
reference 234
guard
using 192-195
Gulp
reference 15
setting up 14, 15
used, for setting up Angular 183-189
Gulp watch
launching, into workflow 259-261
Guzzle
reference 21

H

Homebrew
reference 4
Homestead
application, setting up in 6-9
reference 3
setting up 1-3
HTTP middleware, Laravel docs
reference 210

I

IAM 324
incoming input
validating 173-176
interface
creating, for managing subscriptions 222-224
iTerm
reference 2

J

JSON API Spec
reference 37

L

l5scaffolding package
reference 90
Laracast
reference 69
Laracast migrations
reference 84
Laracasts Gulp TDD
reference 261
Laracasts-Incremental APIs
reference 40
Laracasts-Series on API
reference 37
Laracasts-TDD Acceptance
reference 45
Laravel
reference 4
used, for setting up subscription site 211-221
Laravel 5
reference 161
Laravel 5.2 Socialite Facebook login
reference 206
Laravel Docs for Homestead
reference 9
Laravel Docs-Routing
reference 47
Laravel Docs-Testing
reference 45
Laravel Documentation
reference 55
Laravel Testing Decoded
reference 27
Laravel validation
reference 112
Laravel Validator, for .env file
reference 359
layout.blade.php file
reference 60
live notifications
pusher, using for 293-302
local build
.env, using for 9-11
local machine
composer, setting on 4, 5
PHP, setting on 4, 5

Printed in Poland
by Amazon Fulfillment
Poland Sp. z o.o., Wrocław

22294795R00226